ETHNOGRAPHIES OF POWER

CRITICAL THINKERS

The Wits University Press Critical Thinkers series explores field-defining concepts developed by African intellectuals whose ideas have had a far-reaching impact on scholarship and society. Through critical engagement, and treating their work as an object of study, the series demonstrates the reverberation of their intellectual labour across global arenas and to the broader public. A fundamental objective of the series is to integrate praxis and pedagogy, and to offer working concepts, theories and methodologies that enable other scholars to develop expertise in their own research fields and teaching.

ETHNOGRAPHIES OF POWER

Working radical concepts with Gillian Hart

EDITED BY Sharad Chari, Mark Hunter and Melanie Samson

WITS UNIVERSITY PRESS

Published in South Africa by:
Wits University Press
1 Jan Smuts Avenue
Johannesburg 2001

www.witspress.co.za

First published 2022

http://dx.doi.org.10.18772/22022076666

978-1-77614-666-6 (Paperback)
978-1-77614-775-5 (Hardback)
978-1-77614-771-7 (Web PDF)
978-1-77614-677-2 (EPUB)
978-1-77614-683-3 (Open Access PDF)

This publication is peer reviewed following international best practice standards for
academic and scholarly books.

The financial assistance of the National Institute for the Humanities and Social Sciences
(NIHSS) towards this publication is hereby acknowledged. Opinions expressed and those
arrived at are those of the authors and cannot necessarily be attributed to the NIHSS.

NATIONAL INSTITUTE
FOR THE HUMANITIES
AND SOCIAL SCIENCES

Project manager: Lisa Compton
Copyeditor: Alison Lockhart
Proofreader: Lee Smith
Indexer: Christopher Merrett
Cover design: Hothouse
Typeset in 11.5 point Crimson

For Gillian Hart: comrade, mentor, friend

Contents

    Engagements with Antonio Gramsci   163
    Michael Ekers, Stefan Kipfer and Alex Loftus
8   Make 'Articulation' Gramscian Again   187
    Zachary Levenson
9   Grappling with 'Nationalism': Thinking alongside Gillian
    Hart at a South African Landfill   217
    Melanie Samson

    Contributors   239
    Index   243

List of Illustrations

Acknowledgements

We are grateful to all the authors in this book for their commitment, care and patience. Several papers were first presented at sessions in honour of Gillian Hart at the 2016 Annual Meeting of the American Association of Geographers in San Francisco. We are grateful to all participants at these sessions. Roshan Cader saw promise in this project early on, and we are grateful for her work at every stage. Warm gratitude to the Wits University Press production and marketing crew, including Kirsten Perkins, Lisa Compton, Corina van der Spoel, Veronica Klipp and, not least, Alison Lockhart for eagle-eyed line editing. Many thanks to the National Institute for the Humanities and Social Sciences for subsidising production to make this an open access title. Finally, on behalf of all the contributors, warm thanks to Gillian Hart for living the reason to write this book and for the open invitation to walk alongside her.

Sharad Chari (Berkeley)
Mark Hunter (Durban)
Melanie Samson (Johannesburg)

Introduction | Working Radical Concepts with Gillian Hart

Sharad Chari, Mark Hunter and Melanie Samson

What does it mean to work with radical concepts?

We live in a time in which the forces of capital, imperialism, nationalism, racism and populism continue to connect people and places, yet also profoundly differentiate them. For successive generations of scholars engaging with these processes, extant concepts often seem too abstract or blunt to illuminate lived struggles and the ways they are bound up with race, gender, class, sexuality and other social relations. When a concept outlives its purpose in actual struggles, should it be archived for use when similar struggles might re-emerge? Alternatively, ought concepts to be reviewed and renewed with the regularity of doing the weekly laundry – and would this offer fresh insights into what might appear obvious or staid in both radical analysis and politics?

The idea of collating concepts for radical critique owes a debt to Raymond Williams' classic, *Keywords: A Vocabulary of Culture and Society* ([1975] 2015). Williams begins the book with a story about his return to Oxford University, after serving in the army during the Second World War, when he encountered another veteran. He recounts their shared sense of disconnection with the society they had returned to, as they both felt that people around them did not 'speak the same language' as they did. Williams reflects on this turn of phrase, often used between generations, classes, genders and societies. He introduces *Keywords* not so much as a glossary or dictionary, but rather as an exploration of 'the problem of vocabulary' (Williams [1975] 2015, xxvii). Several books have followed this cue, including those that examine South African social life, with its particular preoccupations with segregation and desegregation, among other things (Boonzaier and Sharp 1988; Shepherd and Robins 2008). These texts provide a useful exploration of the social life of words and the profound power of the state in shaping everyday vocabularies.

Another kind of approach considers the multiplicity of theoretical traditions eclipsed by scholars' single-minded focus on the legacies of the European Enlightenment and its imperial effects. Barbara Cassin et al.'s *Dictionary of Untranslatables: A Philosophical Lexicon* (2014), for instance, begins with the engaging premise that there is considerable loss in the meanings of philosophical, literary and political concepts across languages and cultures. The Portuguese notion of *saudade*, for instance, is better expressed in the dulcet tones of Cesária Évora than in translation as 'sadness' or 'sorrow', which hold nothing of the bitter-sweet history of surviving slavery and colonialism in Cape Verde. Many things remain untranslatable, caught between the many differences that persist.

Ethnographies of Power takes a different journey to concepts than the above two approaches; it is directed at how scholars use radical concepts in social research in mutual relation to real-world struggles with a view towards expanding social justice. We begin this book with the suggestion that scholars, like all people, engage with the world with their bodies and minds, and attempt to work with concepts that might illuminate how they encounter seemingly unalterable forces that shape their condition. Rather than developing concepts through abstract thought processes, scholars' labour to create radical concepts must be understood in light of Italian militant Antonio Gramsci's attention to 'praxis', the inseparability of theory and practice. This focus on praxis is central to the critical ethnographic approach that the scholars in this book exemplify. In linked ways, we propose ethnographies of power as a way to learn from and advance movements for a radically different world.

As is evident in our subtitle, 'Working Radical Concepts with Gillian Hart', this book is also inspired by the work of Gillian Hart, who has honed a geographical approach to critical ethnography as a way to generate concepts emerging from intensive and comparative engagement with the experienced world, in solidarity with a range of radical movements. Professor emerita at the University of California, Berkeley, in the United States and distinguished professor at the University of the Witwatersrand, South Africa, Hart is an internationally recognised key thinker across the fields of human geography, African studies, political economy and development studies. She has also been a powerful and passionate teacher who has shaped several generations of radical scholars and activists from Berkeley to Johannesburg, as well as the world over. This book honours Hart by continuing the praxis of critical ethnography as pedagogy for social change. As you read this book, you will read about how Hart produced and refined concepts through social science research. But you will also see all the contributors to this book demonstrating how they have used particular concepts, transporting them elsewhere and transforming them while putting them to work in new contexts. We intend this to be a living text and invite you to work with these concepts yourself to see how they might be used in the contexts that are important to you.

Ethnographies of Power is not a complete lexicon of radical concepts; it does not tell the reader what to think in order to be radical, nor is it a dictionary of fixed categories – such a thing cannot exist in a changing world. The important thing about all the concepts in this text is that they are inspired by political work in the world, or might be put to work in the service of social change. We ask readers to consider how they might work with these and other concepts in relation to real-world struggles, while considering their uses in other places in our interrelated world. Indeed, we ask you to be open to surprises as you experiment with radical concepts to explain the forces that structure the problems and situations vital to your own lives. We hope this experimental quality will be useful for students at any level, in formal institutions or in the school of life and struggle, whether in designing and conducting social science research or in trying to explain and transform the reality around them.

Working concepts for critical ethnography

This book is organised around a series of working concepts emerging from Hart's published work. Most, though not all, chapters diagnose and rethink these concepts in three moves, as follows. First, the author takes a concept from Hart's writings, keeping in mind how she uses this concept in the task of explanation. Second, the author works backwards through the genealogy of this concept in Hart's work. This operation of 'working backwards' helps provide a sense of the praxis that lies behind what appears to be an inert concept to show how theory and practice are intertwined in scholarship more generally. Third, the author looks forward in relation to their own research concerns and contexts. We offer this as one approach to epistemic decolonisation, but readers will find others in the chapters that follow, all of which focus in different ways on the conceptual productivity of critical ethnography.

In other words, we find in Hart's work a powerful argument that ethnography, when informed by social theory, is also able to generate and revise concepts. Underlying this argument is Karl Marx's understanding that rather than being composed of elements that are isolatable or independent 'factors', the social world is always relational and its elements always exist in dialectical relation to each other (Ollman 1976, 14–16). As David Harvey clarifies, 'elements, things, structures, and systems do not exist outside of or prior to the processes, flows, and relations that create, sustain, or undermine them' (1996, 49). Or, to turn to a text important to Hart's thought, Stuart Hall (2003) argues in a careful reading of Marx's method that 'the concrete' ought never be considered as empirically given, which is the common-sense view of ethnography as thick description of all that is obvious. Rather, Hall argues, when the world is seen as composed by dialectical forces beyond our perception, our task as critics is to represent any concrete situation by understanding it 'as the "unity of many determinations"' (2003, 115). In other words, ethnography without concepts to grasp these determinative forces is left grasping for the complexity of the world without the ability to explain it, let alone propose to change how or for whom it works. Indeed, explanation, in this Marxist tradition, is necessary for coming to terms with the contradictions through which we might discern even minor possibilities for meaningful social change. By refining concepts, in other words, ethnography can become 'radical' – by which we do not mean judgemental, but rather that it can explain how reality got to be this way and what might be done to change it.

There is another element that we draw on in this critical ethnographic approach to concepts: all the writers in this book, in one way or another, have been shaped by contemporary human geography and its concern to understand space as not simply an inert backdrop or an empty box in which the world unfolds. Rather, geographers seek to understand social space as a historian understands time, as made, fought for, destroyed, rebuilt and pulled apart in different ways. Key to this active, productive and dialectical understanding of space is the thought of Henri Lefebvre (see, for instance, Lefebvre [1974] 1991).

Drawing on Lefebvre's theory of the production of space, Hart argues that critical ethnography has to think of space and time in active terms. In this, she was fundamentally influenced by Doreen Massey's argument that places are always intersections of far-flung spatial processes. Importantly, Massey (1994, 154) adds that the social and spatial relations that make places distinct are not limited to the period being studied, nor are they contained within any particular place, whether the place is a room, a city or an empire. Places always 'include relations which stretch beyond' them, linking what appears to be inside the place to that which appears external to it (5). The key point is that the here-and-now always exists in relation to the elsewhere-and-then, as well as, in our time of anticipation of further pandemics and climate emergencies, in relation to fragile futures. To put it simply, no place is an island. The implication of thinking geographically about both space and time, about spatio-temporal relations, is that critical ethnography can never be mired in localism. Massey's intervention was a clarion call to avoid this kind of intellectual enclavism; it forces us to be our most internationalist selves. As Hart says regarding the power of critical ethnography attentive to such a relational conception of place: '[The] conception of places as nodal points of connection in socially pro-duced space moves us beyond "case studies" to make broader claims: it enables, in other words, a non-positivist understanding of generality. In this conception, particularities or specificities arise through *interrelations* between objects, events, places, and identities; and it is through clarifying how these relations are produced and changed in practice that close study of a particular part can generate broader claims and understandings' (Hart 2006a, 995–996; emphasis in original).

With this active understanding of place, Hart refuses the assumption that the 'concrete studies deal with what is local and particular, and that abstract theory encompasses general (or global) processes that transcend particular places' (Hart 2006a, 995–996). Practising this is no easy task. Thankfully, we do have examples to think with. Hart's journey has in many ways been an attempt to respond to this challenge.

Gillian Hart's intellectual journey

Hart's intellectual work reflects an interdisciplinary and interna-tionalist journey through which she has honed a distinctively radical ethnographic approach to political economy. Along the way, she has picked up concepts, worked with them, put some of them aside, revis-ited classic texts in light of new concerns, shifted disciplinary gears, refused various orthodoxies, and refined her political commitments in relation to the societies in which she has lived and worked. In this overview, we journey with this key thinker, following her trail of interconnected insights. Important to Hart's journey is her dogged determination to demonstrate the analytical and political power of an ethnographic approach to the critique of capitalism in the post-colonial world, grounded in social theory and engaged with broader geographical processes that have sought to scaffold regional hegemonies in apartheid South Africa, Suharto's New Order Indonesia, Bangladesh under martial law, Malaysia under Mahathir's tightening second term, post-apartheid South Africa under multiple regimes, and resurgent populist nationalisms across the world today, not least in the spectacularly cynical forms of Trumpism-Bannonism in the United States and Hindutva (Hindu ethno-racial supremacy) in India. Hart's main concern across these places is how we might understand complex forces that constitute a historical conjuncture, in order to call their stability into question.

In 1971, Hart journeyed from South Africa to Ithaca, New York, to begin postgraduate studies in economics at Cornell University. Intending to work on Nigeria, she was drawn to Bangladesh through the outpouring of Western support for the liberation movement and began studying Bangla. However, rising authoritarianism in Bangladesh forced Hart to think of another potential region and she would not return to Bangladesh until another conjuncture, another political opening at the decade's end. Through fortuitous events, Hart's dissertation research turned to Java, to a study of agrarian change in the wake of Green Revolution technologies in rice-growing regions. This was a hot research topic at the time, as scholars sought to understand the effects of capital and technology in the countryside; a polemical way of putting the question was whether the Green Revolution might turn red, advanced by the making of a class-conscious rural proletariat. The concept of agrarian revolution, after all, implied both the technological transformation of agriculture through capitalism and the making of agrarian revolutionary movements across the developing world, with China, Cuba and Vietnam as archetypes. The Marxist interrogation of 'the agrarian question' was in many ways reinvigorated in this intellectual conjuncture, as scholars explored the effects of agrarian capitalism on peasantries, households, labour, poverty, class, gender, food security and agrarian mobilisation.

Hart's doctoral dissertation sought to respond to large-scale survey research on the impact of Green Revolution technology through intensive 'village studies'. She sought to work on multiple villages and finally settled on one. She arrived for 19 months of dissertation research in Java in 1975 and worked with the Indonesian Agro-Economic Survey at Bogor Agricultural University, where she engaged with key figures in Indonesian rural sociology and agrarian change, Professor Sajogyo, Sediono Tjondronegoro, Gunawan Wiradi and expatriate Marxist anthropologist Ben White. White's library was a crucial space for Hart to hone her analytical tools and one where they, like many other agrarian scholars of this time, returned with fresh eyes to the classical agrarian question and to Vladimir Lenin and Alexander Chayanov. Lenin's late-nineteenth-century argument about the polarisation of agrarian classes had been read as the antinomy of Chayanov's on the endurance of peasant households, while both arguments had been made on the basis of the same *zemstvo* (local, self-government bodies in Russia) statistics and with different theoretical frameworks. These agrarian scholars of the 1970s saw class polarisation and household persistence held in tense dialectical relation, a perspective that would be vital to Hart's study of a village in coastal north-east Java she called Sukodono.

In brief, Hart's dissertation research shows extreme concentration of land, high rates of waged labour and important differences between smallholder and landless households; the landless earned significantly less and worked long hours in poorly remunerated non-farm work, while smallholders were increasingly indebted to large landholders. In relation to broader debates about rural employment in Java in the 1970s, Hart showed that rather than 'surplus labour' being drawn out of agriculture by the benign forces of competitive labour markets, landless labour was being compelled to leave a class-differentiated agrarian structure in which they, unlike smallholders, were not the beneficiaries of seasonal labour relations (Hart 1978, 1980, 1981). A key insight was that relations of debt and labour were tightly intertwined.

In important articles from this period, Hart reflects on scholarship across South and South East Asia, particularly rice-farming regions subject to technological change, where land, labour and credit relations appeared to 'interlock' in ways that concentrated power in some hands while subjecting most people to place-based structures of preference and inequality. Responding to both neoclassical and Marxist political economists, Hart deftly explains 'exclusionary labour arrangements' as neither feudal hangovers nor archaisms bound to dissolve with the spread of markets, but rather as institutional reconfigurations within agrarian capitalism (Hart 1986a, 1986b). While economists politely acknowledge the importance of 'extra-economic' relations, Hart shows that they do not come to terms with the exercise of power.

On completing her dissertation, Hart decided to leave the tightening authoritarianism of Suharto's Indonesia to return to Bangladesh in a period of reform, with vibrant space for critique. Returning over multiple research trips between 1979 and 1981, Hart began to see her Indonesian research in comparative terms, to later publish on densely populated rice-growing regions supposedly defined by surplus labour, contending with periodic labour shortages under parallel conditions of landholding inequality, demography, agricultural commercial-isation and Green Revolution technology, but under substantially different power relations linking the state to landed elites as well as operating across agrarian classes (Hart 1983, 1984 and particularly 1988). This insight, still percolating in her writing, was key to her first book-length monograph. This multi-scalar attentiveness to compari-son would mark Hart's method for decades to come.

Hart's first monograph, *Power, Labor, and Livelihood: Processes of Change in Rural Java* (1986c), builds on her critique of the interlock-ing transactions debate, as well as implicitly on her experience of the very different political conjuncture in Bangladesh, to show how specific relations of power, mediated differently by the colonial state and by Suharto's New Order state, have been central to the fate of the peasantry. Hart pushed well beyond Clifford Geertz's classic thesis on 'agricultural involution' in rice-growing Java, which posited that the agrarian system bequeathed by Dutch colonialism was unproductive and that it created a landscape of generalised poverty. Rather, Hart shows that the New Order state had intensified the role of the state in village life by offering patronage to the dominant landholding class, which in turn strengthened its power vis-à-vis a middle group of small-holders through sharecropping and exclusionary labour arrangements while dominating the landless poor. The state reinforced this social domination over the landless through minimal public works proj-ects. However, Hart notes that the New Order state of the mid-1980s was also reliant on oil wealth that had become increasingly precari-ous, calling into question the stability of the entire class structure of agrarian inequality.

Questions of the state and of agrarian classes continued in Hart's work of the subsequent decade, as she shifted, given her language skills in Bahasa, to work in Malaysia in 1987–1988, in the rapidly transform-ing rice-farming Muda region of northern Malaysia (Hart 1987, 1989a, 1989b, 1991, 1992a, 1992b). The 1980s are an important conjuncture in Hart's work in many respects. She had quickly gained substantial com-parative expertise across rice-farming areas in South and South East Asia and co-edited, with Andrew Turton, Ben White, Brian Fegan and Lim Teck Ghee, *Agrarian Transformations: Local Processes and the State in Southeast Asia* (Hart et al. 1989), an important collection that linked localised and longitudinal studies of agrarian change in rice-growing regions in Thailand, the Philippines, Malaysia and Indonesia to larger political economic forces. Hart's own chapter in this book deepened her analysis of state patronage in the countryside.

In this period, Hart also found that her analysis of the political medi-ation of interlocked transactions in land, labour and credit mirrored the insights of fieldwork-based agrarian studies across Asia and Africa.

While she had been engaging with the Marxist critique of the household since her time at Bogor in Java, Hart encountered a different milieu while a professor at Boston University. She was drawn into an important network of Africanist scholars of gender, households and agrarian change, including Sara Berry, Pauline Peters, Jane Guyer and, further afield, geographers Michael Watts and Judith Carney. Parallel inspiration came from innovations in feminist social science from Joan Scott, Dorothy Smith, Henrietta Moore, Diane Wolf and others. Hart's writing emerging from this moment shows a determination to critique the economics of households on its own terms, with this feminist work in mind (Hart 1992b, 1995c, 1997a), but her writings from Malaysia activate the politics of gender in her research in new ways, as she attends to rural women's labour, migration and militancy in the wake of the gendered politics of the patronage relations she had long studied (Hart 1991, 2007).

In the late 1980s, Hart credits her graduate students in a seminar at the Massachusetts Institute of Technology for leading her to Massey's critiques of the 'localities debate' in British economic geography, through which Massey had arrived at an understanding of the politics of place that paralleled the work that scholars of agrarian Asia, Africa and Latin America had been engaged in. Hart also began looking critically at a phenomenon that would sweep across specific parts of agrarian Asia, and which was being seen quite differently from varied theoretical and political perspectives, and this was the process of agrarian diversification and rural industrialisation, which had taken surprising paths in Taiwan and post-Maoist China. This led her to a critical perspective with respect to the rural–urban interface and back to the agrarian question for its broader implications for regional change. But by this time, her research focus was shifting again, this time back to her native South Africa (Hart 1995a, 1995b, 1996a, 1996b, 1997b; Hart and Todes 1997).

Something else was happening in the late 1980s following clandestine interactions between elements of South African capital and state with some from the African National Congress (ANC) at a time of political and economic stalemate brought on by economic sanctions pressured by the global Anti-Apartheid Movement (AAM), unstoppable labour and community struggles in the country, and the dissolution of the Soviet Union as imagined patron of a socialist South Africa. Multiple forces came together in the unbanning of liberation movement organisations in early 1990. Hart had been engaged in political work aligned with the AAM in Boston. At this conjuncture, she returned to South Africa, rebuilding connections with activists and scholars in Johannesburg, Durban, Grahamstown and Cape Town, including her childhood friend, Sheila Weinberg. In 1991, she moved to the University of California, Berkeley, where she hosted South African scholars and activists including Vishnu Padayachee, Ari Sitas and Astrid von Kotze. She developed close relationships with many South Africans and began to focus her intellectual and political life in Durban in the early 1990s.

There is much to say about Hart's subsequent three decades of work in South Africa, on which we will be succinct. From the early 1990s through the early 2000s, Durban and specific pockets at the University of Durban-Westville and the University of Natal, Durban (later amalgamated with the Pietermaritzburg campus into the University of KwaZulu-Natal), had forged connections between social science and movements for social justice in post-apartheid times. Hart built relationships with activists, ranging from lifelong members of the ANC to members of the social movements emerging outside of the Tripartite Alliance of the ANC, the South African Communist Party (SACP) and the Congress of South African Trade Unions (COSATU). Hart became involved with Padayachee and other Durban-based colleagues in setting up an important coursework master's programme at what was then the University of Durban-Westville, and subsequently with David Szanton in training doctoral students in linking social theory and social research in writing a dissertation proposal or prospectus. Hart had also begun long-term research in rural KwaZulu-Natal in a complex project that drew significantly on her Asian expertise and on the ways in which the lessons of agrarian transition and industrialisation were being misconstrued in the confluence of neo-liberalism and democratic transition in South Africa in the late 1990s (Hart 1998a, 1998b, 2002c).

Hart's *Disabling Globalization: Places of Power in Post-Apartheid South Africa* (2002a), with its powerful cover image by Trevor Makhoba depicting apartheid forced removals, pulls together a complex set of comparisons in a powerful argument about the dilemmas of post-apartheid capitalism. At the heart of the book is a comparison of two formerly white towns with their black township hinterlands, a comparison that allows Hart to explore divergent trajectories of agrarian change, racialised dispossession, industrialisation and political mobilisation during and after apartheid. The decades of Hart's departure had seen a deepening of the controversial apartheid policy of industrial decentralisation to attract capital to the borderlands between white areas and the dense quasi-rural black townships. The state had offered subsidies to Taiwanese capital to locate here; in the 1990s, these subsidies ended, some labour-intensive industries went into precipitous decline and work politics became increasingly despotic, citing the influx of cheap Chinese commodities and putatively high local wages. The Ladysmith–Newcastle comparison is one aspect of this study, but the other is shaped by Chinese connections and comparisons. A chapter on the history of industrialisation in East Asia shows that it was premised on land reform and supports to the social wage, which had been fundamentally dismantled through the long history of dispossession in South Africa.

Hart extended this argument in multiple papers (Hart 2002c, 2004c, 2006a, 2006b; Hart and Sitas 2004), while also writing a series of pieces on development theory and practice, neo-liberalism, critical ethnography and pedagogy (Hart 2001, 2002b, 2004a, 2006a, 2008a, 2008b, 2009, 2010). She also returned to Indonesia and wrote important pieces with Nancy Peluso and others (Afiff et al. 2005; Hart 2004b; Hart and Peluso 2005). An important paper returns to Hart's preoccupation since her Boston years: the way in which Stuart Hall had effectively reshaped the race–class debate on apartheid capitalism (Hart 2007). Another piece reflects on Massey's influence on her thought (Hart 2018a). An important collaboration with Michael Ekers, Stefan Kipfer and Alex Loftus (Ekers et al. 2013) on the geographical significance of Gramsci's thought led to the edited *Gramsci: Space, Nature, Politics*, with chapters by Hart on translation and populism, in which Hart also uses Gramsci's notion of passive revolution to think comparatively about South Africa and India.

Hart's book *Rethinking the South African Crisis: Nationalism, Populism, Hegemony* (2013) picks up on some of the threads of *Disabling Globalization*, notably the comparative lens of Ladysmith and Newcastle and their township peripheries, at a moment after the political effervescence in post-apartheid Durban that she had been a part of. The cover image by Blessing Ngobeni, in contrast to the 2002 book, shows artistically the distance that two decades from the democratic transition has meant. Makhoba's realist portrayal of apartheid-era forced removals represents certainties about politics in *Disabling Globalization* that have entirely evaporated in Ngobeni's rich and troubled mosaic on the cover of *Rethinking the South African Crisis*. After the end of a rising tide of civic activism, Hart argues that we ought to consider formations of popular anger that persist, often directed at local government and in relation to the commodification of municipal service provision of water, electricity and housing. Carefully working from within her ethnographic context, Hart shows that popular politics ought to be understood as part of the crisis provoked by the unravelling of the hegemonic project of the ruling Alliance. Fundamental to understanding how this crisis plays out is a complex political-economic analysis of nationalism as simultaneously a process of 'de-nationalisation' that has produced capital flight, currency volatility, a narrowing industrial base and deepening inequality, as well as 're-nationalisation' in various rounds of remaking populist government. Hart shows why we must take these dialectics of nationalism seriously, as they refract through local government struggles over a racialised landscape of inequality.

As Hart's interlocutors in Durban had begun to disperse, she began to spend increasing amounts of time in the 2010s in Johannesburg, eventually moving her South African home to the city of her birth. A number of her key interventions in this period were in dynamic public seminars at the University of the Witwatersrand and through debate and discussion with her rich network of friends and comrades across academia and popular movements.

An abiding concern that has in effect been foisted on Hart's trajectory at every turn in her journey is that she has consistently followed in the tracks of authoritarian power. Sometimes she has evaded moments of repression and at other times she has been witness to moments of political awakening. This realisation has perhaps brought her to a comparative study of nationalism and populism, looking outward from her work on South Africa in the 2010s to the Bharatiya Janata Party under Modi in India and to Trumpism-Bannonism in the United States (Hart 2015, 2019, 2020a, 2020b), as well to rethinking what she calls 'relational comparison' or 'conjunctural comparison', as her work has in a sense always involved comparative insights (Hart 2015, 2018b, 2020a, 2020b, 2021). We look forward to Hart's current book project on these themes as it will undoubtedly inspire other people to walk alongside her to engage with the turbulent 2020s, as the Covid-19 pandemic further exacerbates crises of racial capitalism across the world in different ways.

Hart's journeys are instructive in many ways: for a dogged commitment to engaging with political-economic and intellectual conjunctures, for a fearless will to take on orthodoxies based on faulty analysis, for engagement with militants spanning a wide section of the left, for a curiosity about what constitutes the detail of popular struggle in particular places and a desire to contribute to these, for an attentiveness to comparative lessons with a similar openness and rigour, and, not least, for a commitment to working with concepts as powerful weapons with which we might yet expose the contradictions sown by authoritarian power everywhere.

The structure of this book

As noted above, Hart's ongoing refinement of concepts has occurred in conjunction with some significant moves: from economics to geography, South East Asia to South Africa and Boston to Berkeley. In organising the chapters in this volume, we follow a broadly chronological timeline to reflect the progression of Hart's thought, beginning with concepts forged while she worked in South East Asia and moving to those developed when her research moved to South Africa. Inseparable from Hart's scholarship is her commitment to undergraduate teaching, including a large course on what she calls Big-D theories of Development and little-d processes of capitalist development, and her passionate engagement in her teaching and writing with the work of Gramsci.

In chapter 1, Bridget Kenny elucidates the concept of gendered labour, returning the reader to Hart's early work on South East Asia. In the 1980s, Hart and other feminist scholars offered a groundbreaking critique of 'malestream' social science by insisting that the household is a contested gendered domain. Hart also revealed how gender and class relations were formed through a relational understanding of space through reading Lefebvre and Massey. Kenny uses these approaches to critique labour politics in South Africa and how it has downplayed the multiply determined reasons for why and when people act politically and collectively in specific sites. Kenny's research, which traces gendered meanings and practices in retail worker politics in Johannesburg over nearly a century, develops a rich spatial analysis to explore shifts in the political subject 'workers'.

In chapter 2, Sharad Chari brings into relation two apparently unrelated concepts: interlocking transactions and racial capitalism. With deep roots in the South African left, the concept of racial capitalism has attained something of a revival in recent years, buoyed by the passing of Cedric Robinson and unrelenting evidence of brutal and systemic anti-black racism. Chari returns to Hart's agrarian studies research in South and South

East Asia, where she intervened in debates about interlocking or inter-linked land, labour and credit relations by arguing that situated forms of social power and exclusion were at the heart of uneven geographies of agrarian capitalism. Chari argues that Hart's response mirrors what is now called racial capitalism and that while Robinson focuses on the endur-ing power of racial consciousness, there is a reason he did not engage with the agrarian studies debates. Divergent theoretical routes took Robinson to an argument about racial consciousness, while Hart, like Hall, focuses on the micro-foundations of political economic relations. By reading Hart in relation to racial capitalism debates, Chari argues that Hart's response to the interlinkage debate might contribute to a more granular and mate-rialist analysis of geographies of racial capitalism.

In chapter 3, Mark Hunter also returns to Hart's work in South East Asia to illuminate key roots of the concept of relational compar-ison. This term, which has animated debates on method within and beyond geography, is most fully developed in Hart's book *Disabling Globalization* (2002a), which centres on two distinct locations in South Africa, Newcastle and Ladysmith. Hunter's chapter describes Hart's situated practices of method-making in a context where the discipline of geography has an ambivalent relationship to discussions on method. His own study of three areas of Durban, connected by children's movement for schooling, uses an approach with broad affinities to the relational comparison method to show how race and class have been remade during and after apartheid.

In chapter 4, Jennifer A. Devine explores multiple trajectories of glo-balisation. Hart developed this concept in part to challenge what she called the impact model of globalisation, which sees globalisation as an inexo-rable force from the global to the local. By showing multiple socio-spatial trajectories at work in South Africa, Hart developed an important cri-tique of the post-apartheid government's embrace of neo-liberal thought. In the second part of her chapter, Devine charts multiple trajectories in northern Guatemala to challenge popular policy and media discourses that define the Maya Biosphere Reserve as an 'ungovernable' place.

In chapter 5, Ahmed Veriava brings to life Hart's critique of linear models of political and economic change by focusing on discussions in the 2000s by President Thabo Mbeki on the 'second economy'. Instead of choosing a concept that Hart uses, Veriava shows how her intellectual engagement allowed her to adopt a critical relationship to the second economy. Veriava argues that the development and deployment of the concept – used by Mbeki to explain the persistence of poverty in South Africa – tells us a lot about how neo-liberal governmentality articulates with nationalism.

In chapter 6, Jennifer Greenburg shows how the concept of D/development simultaneously foregrounds the Development project of interventions in the so-called Third World while refusing teleological accounts of economic development. The chapter reveals the theoretical influence of Gramsci, Polanyi and Lefebvre on the concept and demonstrates how Greenburg's use of D/development enabled her to illuminate key aspects of the rise of for-profit D/development military contracting in the period leading up to and following 9/11.

In chapter 7, Michael Ekers, Stefan Kipfer and Alex Loftus give attention to – and show connections between – Hart's use of the concepts of articulation, translation and populism. Co-editors and co-authors with Hart of *Gramsci: Space, Nature, Politics* (Ekers et al. 2013), they show how the Italian Marxist influenced Hart's political analysis of distinct historical and geographical conjunctures. They argue that her Gramscian perspective innovatively bridges political economy and cultural studies, refusing the position that these two are irreconcilable.

In chapter 8, Zachary Levenson advances a particular focus on articulation to bring attention to how political subjectivity is forged in capitalist societies. In South Africa, land dispossession by white settlers fuelled the fire of anti-apartheid activities, but after 1994, when the country became a democracy, contestations over land did not diminish. Levenson demonstrates the political salience of Hart's Gramscian understanding of articulation through analysis of how even though people involved in two land occupations in Cape Town encountered

similar material conditions, the divergent ways in which they articulated their demands were of profound importance to the outcome
of their struggles. The discerning reader will note that the concept
of articulation recurs in multiple chapters. One reason is that Hart
appears to have settled on this concept as key to her method. However,
our deeper argument is that each use – or articulation – of the concept
is borne through struggles in which the concept is mobilised to enable
different kinds of political work.

In chapter 9, Melanie Samson engages with the concept of nationalism, which became central to Hart's work in the 2010s, greatly
shaping her book *Rethinking the South African Crisis* (2013). Samson
traces how Hart's attention to nationalism developed in relation to
not only the populism of Jacob Zuma, who succeeded Mbeki as president of South Africa, but also to Trumpism in the United States and
the Hindu nationalism of Modi in India. In her ethnographic work,
Samson shows how everyday nationalism plays out among reclaimers
of reusable and recyclable materials at a Soweto landfill. In grounding
nationalism, Samson is able to understand the struggles over value at
the landfill and to illuminate broader processes at work. As with all
the chapters in this book, Samson's careful study demonstrates the
power of critical ethnography to generate non-positivist generalisa-
tions and to develop concepts valuable for understanding and transforming current realities.

REFERENCES

Afiff, Suraya, Noer Fauzi, Gillian Hart, Lungisile Ntsebeza and Nancy Peluso.
2005. 'Redefining Agrarian Power: Resurgent Agrarian Movements in
West Java, Indonesia'. University of California, Center for Southeast Asian
Studies, September. https://escholarship.org/content/qt7rf2p49g/qt7rf2p49
g_noSplash_7f6356670ed31af2856b368bbb8dab6b.pdf?t=krn8hu (accessed
7 February 2022).

Boonzaier, Emile and John Sharp, eds. 1988. *South African Keywords: The Uses &*
Abuses of Political Concepts. Cape Town: David Philip.

Cassin, Barbara, Emily Apter, Jacques Lezra and Michael Wood, eds. 2014. *Dictionary of Untranslatables: A Philosophical Lexicon.* Princeton: Princeton University Press.

Ekers, Michael, Gillian Hart, Stefan Kipfer and Alex Loftus, eds. 2013. *Gramsci: Space, Nature, Politics.* Oxford: Wiley-Blackwell.

Hall, Stuart. 2003. 'Marx's Notes on Method: A "Reading" of the "1857 Introduction"'. *Cultural Studies* 17, no. 2: 113–149.

Hart, Gillian. 1978. 'Aspects of Rural Labor Market Operation: A Javanese Case Study'. *American Journal of Agricultural Economics* 60, no. 5: 821–826.

Hart, Gillian. 1980. 'Peasant Decision-Making: The Limitations of Household Level Analysis'. In *Agriculture and Home Economics in the Third World*, edited by M. Seltzer, 86–95. Minneapolis: University of Minnesota Press.

Hart, Gillian. 1981. 'Patterns of Household Labor Allocation in a Javanese Village'. In *Household Studies in Asia*, edited by R. Evenson and H. Binswanger, 188–217. Singapore: Singapore University Press, for the Agricultural Development Council.

Hart, Gillian. 1983. 'Productivity, Poverty and Population Pressure: Female Labor Deployment in Rice Production in Java and Bangladesh'. *American Journal of Agricultural Economics* 65, no. 5: 1037–1042.

Hart, Gillian. 1984. 'Agrarian Labor Arrangements and Structural Change: Lessons from Java and Bangladesh'. World Employment Research Papers No. 10-6/WP65.

Hart, Gillian. 1986a. 'Exclusionary Labour Arrangements: Interpreting Evidence on Employment Trends in Rural Java'. *Journal of Development Studies* 22, no. 4: 681–696.

Hart, Gillian. 1986b. 'Interlocking Transactions: Obstacles, Precursors or Instruments of Agrarian Capitalism?' *Journal of Development Economics* 23, no. 1: 177–203.

Hart, Gillian. 1986c. *Power, Labor, and Livelihood: Processes of Change in Rural Java.* Berkeley: University of California Press.

Hart, Gillian. 1987. 'The Mechanization of Malaysian Rice Production: Will Petty Producers Survive?' World Employment Research Papers No. 10-6/WP82, March. https://EconPapers.repec.org/RePEc:ilo:ilowps:992523483402676 (accessed 7 February 2022).

Hart, Gillian. 1988. 'Agrarian Structure and the State in Java and Bangladesh'. *Journal of Asian Studies* 47, no. 4: 249–267.

Hart, Gillian. 1989a. 'Changing Mechanisms of Persistence: Reconfiguration of Petty Production in a Malaysian Rice Region'. *International Labour Review* 128, no. 6: 815–831.

Hart, Gillian. 1989b. 'The Growth Linkages Controversy: Some Lessons from the Muda Case'. *Journal of Development Studies* 25, no. 4: 571–574.

Hart, Gillian. 1991. 'Engendering Everyday Resistance: Gender, Patronage, and Production Politics in Rural Malaysia'. *Journal of Peasant Studies* 19, no. 1: 93–121. Reprinted in *Development: Critical Essays in Human Geography*, edited by Stuart Corbridge, 153–181. Aldershot: Ashgate Publishing, 2008.

Hart, Gillian. 1992a. 'Household Production Reconsidered: Gender, Labor Conflict, and Technological Change in Malaysia's Muda Region'. *World Development* 20, no. 6: 809–823.

Hart, Gillian. 1992b. 'Imagined Unities: Constructions of the Household in Economic Theory'. In *Understanding Economic Process*, edited by Sutti Ortiz and Susan Lees, 111–129. Lanham: University Press of America.

Hart, Gillian. 1995a. 'Beyond the Rural-Urban Dichotomy: Rethinking Agrarian Reform in South Africa'. In *Proceedings International Congress Agrarian Questions: The Politics of Farming*, edited by M. Endeveld and The Agrarian Questions Organising Committee. Wageningen: Wageningen Agricultural University.

Hart, Gillian. 1995b. 'Clothes for Next to Nothing: Organised Labour, Global Competition, and the Land Question'. *South African Labour Bulletin* 19, no. 6: 41–47.

Hart, Gillian. 1995c. 'Gender and Household Dynamics: Recent Theories and Their Implications'. In *Critical Issues in Asian Development: Theories and Policies*, edited by M.G. Quibria, 39–74. Oxford: Oxford University Press.

Hart, Gillian. 1996a. 'The Agrarian Question and Industrial Dispersal in South Africa: Agro-Industrial Linkages through Asian Lenses'. In *The Agrarian Question in South Africa*, edited by Henry Bernstein, 245–275. London: Frank Cass.

Hart, Gillian. 1996b. 'The Agrarian Question and Industrial Dispersal in South Africa: Agro-Industrial Linkages through Asian Lenses'. *Journal of Peasant Studies* 23, no. 2–3: 245–277.

Hart, Gillian. 1997a. 'From "Rotten Wives" to "Good Mothers": Household Models and the Limits of Economism'. *IDS Bulletin* 28, no. 3: 14–25.

Hart, Gillian. 1997b. 'Multiple Trajectories of Rural Industrialization'. In *Globalising Food: Agrarian Questions and Global Restructuring*, edited by David Goodman and Michael Watts, 56–78. New York: Routledge.

Hart, Gillian. 1998a. 'Multiple Trajectories: A Critique of Industrial Restructuring and the New Institutionalism'. *Antipode* 30, no. 4: 333–356.

Hart, Gillian. 1998b. 'Regional Linkages in the Era of Liberalization: A Critique of the New Agrarian Optimism'. *Development and Change* 29, no. 1: 27–54.

Hart, Gillian. 2001. 'Development Critiques in the 1990s: *Culs de Sac* and Promising Paths'. *Progress in Human Geography* 25, no. 4: 649–658.

Hart, Gillian. 2002a. *Disabling Globalization: Places of Power in Post-Apartheid South Africa*. Berkeley: University of California Press.

Hart, Gillian. 2002b. 'Geography and Development: Development/s beyond Neoliberalism? Power, Culture, Political Economy'. *Progress in Human Geography* 26, no. 6: 812–822.

Hart, Gillian. 2002c. 'Linking Land, Labour, and Livelihood Struggles'. *South African Labour Bulletin* 23, no. 6: 31–38.

Hart, Gillian. 2004a. 'Development and Geography: Critical Ethnography'. *Progress in Human Geography* 28, no. 1: 91–100.

Hart, Gillian. 2004b. 'Power, Labor, and Livelihood: Processes of Change in Rural Java – Notes and Reflections on a Village Revisited'. University of California International and Area Studies Global Field Notes, Paper No. 2, 13 December. https://escholarship.org/uc/item/6fx315qt (accessed 7 February 2022).

Hart, Gillian. 2004c. 'Reworking Apartheid Legacies: Export Production, Gender, and Social Wages in South Africa, 1980–2000'. In *Globalization, Export-Oriented Employment and Social Policy: Gendered Connections*, edited by Ruth Pearson, Caroline Danlov and Shahrashoub Razavi, 193–228. Basingstoke: Palgrave Macmillan.

Hart, Gillian. 2006a. 'Denaturalizing Dispossession: Critical Ethnography in the Age of Resurgent Imperialism'. *Antipode* 38, no. 5: 977–1004.

Hart, Gillian. 2006b. 'Post-Apartheid Developments in Historical and Comparative Perspective'. In *The Development Decade? Economic and Social Change in South Africa, 1994–2004*, edited by Vishnu Padayachee, 13–32. Cape Town: HSRC Press.

Hart, Gillian. 2007. 'Changing Concepts of Articulation: Analytical and Political Stakes in South Africa Today'. *Review of African Political Economy* 34, no. 111: 85–104.

Hart, Gillian. 2008a. 'Pedagogy, Politics, and *Playing with Fire*'. *Social & Cultural Geography* 9, no. 2: 218–220.

Hart, Gillian. 2008b. 'The Provocations of Neoliberalism: Contesting the Nation and Liberation after Apartheid'. *Antipode* 40, no. 4: 678–705.

Hart, Gillian. 2009. 'Developments after the Meltdown'. *Antipode* 41, suppl. 1: 117–141.

Hart, Gillian. 2010. 'Redrawing the Map of the World? Reflections on the 2009 World Development Report'. *Economic Geography* 86, no. 4, October: 341–350.

Hart, Gillian. 2013. *Rethinking the South African Crisis: Nationalism, Populism, Hegemony*. Pietermaritzburg: University of KwaZulu-Natal Press.

Hart, Gillian. 2015. 'Political Society and Its Discontents: Translating Passive Revolution in India and South Africa Today'. *Economic & Political Weekly* 50, no. 43: 43–51.

Hart, Gillian. 2018a. 'Becoming a Geographer: Massey Moments in a Spatial Education'. In *Doreen Massey: Critical Dialogues*, edited by Jamie Peck, Marion Werner, Rebecca Lave and Brett Christophers, 75–89. New York: Columbia University Press.

Hart, Gillian. 2018b. 'Relational Comparison Revisited: Marxist Postcolonial Geographies in Practice'. *Progress in Human Geography* 42, no. 3: 371–394.

Hart, Gillian. 2019. 'From Authoritarian to Left Populism? Reframing Debates'. *South Atlantic Quarterly* 118 no. 2: 307–323.

Hart, Gillian. 2020a. 'Resurgent Nationalisms and Populist Politics in the Neoliberal Age'. *Geografiska Annaler* 102, no. 3: 233–238.

Hart, Gillian. 2020b. 'Why Did it Take so Long? Trump-Bannonism in a Global Conjunctural Frame'. *Geografiska Annaler* 102, no. 3: 239–266.

Hart, Gillian. 2021. 'Decoding "the Base": White Evangelicals or Christian Nationalists?' *Alternatives* 102, no. 1: 61–76.

Hart, Gillian and Nancy Peluso. 2005. 'Revisiting Rural Java: Agrarian Research in the Wake of *Reformasi*'. *Indonesia* 80: 177–195.

Hart, Gillian and Ari Sitas. 2004. 'Beyond the Urban–Rural Divide: Linking Land, Labour, and Livelihoods'. *Transformation* 56: 31–38.

Hart, Gillian and Alison Todes. 1997. 'Industrial Decentralisation Revisited'. *Transformation* 32: 31–53.

Hart, Gillian, Andrew Turton and Ben White, with Brian Fegan and Lim Teck Ghee, eds. 1989. *Agrarian Transformations: Local Processes and the State in Southeast Asia*. Berkeley: University of California Press.

Harvey, David. 1996. *Justice, Nature, and the Geography of Difference*. Oxford: Blackwell.

Lefebvre, Henri. (1974) 1991. *The Production of Space*. Oxford: Blackwell.

Massey, Doreen. 1994. *Space, Place and Gender*. Cambridge: Polity.

Ollman, Bertell. 1976. *Alienation: Marx's Conception of Man in Capitalist Society*. Cambridge: Cambridge University Press.

Shepherd, Nick and Steven Robins, eds. 2008. *New South African Keywords*. Johannesburg: Jacana.

Williams, Raymond. (1975) 2015. *Keywords: A Vocabulary of Culture and Society*. London: Fontana.

1 | The Politics of Gendered Labour

Bridget Kenny

It was May 2019, just after a high-stakes national election in South Africa, in which the power and popularity of the African National Congress (ANC) had been tested following nearly a year of public hearings on corruption related to Jacob Zuma's presidency. A smaller media moment in the year's elections was the rather embarrassing non-story of the newly launched Socialist Revolutionary Workers Party (SRWP) by its founding trade union, the National Union of Metalworkers of South Africa (NUMSA), which split from the historically powerful Congress of South African Trade Unions (COSATU) over ANC Alliance politics. This new party of the nominal left did not win a single seat in parliament and got many fewer votes than its NUMSA membership figures would have predicted. Not only did the ANC's hold on hegemony appear to endure with South Africa's new president Cyril Ramaphosa seated, but the seemingly erstwhile trade union movement had little effect on this historical moment. This is a conjuncture on which it is worth pausing, if only for what it distracts us from.

Much of labour sociology in South Africa would argue that the changing class composition of the workforce, the increasing precariousness of work, as well as a reliance on non-wage income for household livelihoods, combined with organisational and political inabilities (and we might include abilities) of the trade unions over the past 30 years, explain the starkness of the decline in organised labour's power.

Such assessments are commonplace. I cannot say that I know a single person working with the labour movement, except for the most disciplined of COSATU cadre, who would say that the labour movement is not in crisis. However, South African sociology would benefit from rereading Gillian Hart's long-time efforts to instantiate gendered labour within multiple sets of relations in time and space (for example, Hart 1986a, 1986b, 1988, 1989, 1991, 1992, 1997). I contend that this longer trajectory offers a demonstration of her moves toward a conjunctural analysis of capitalism. Hart (2018b, 388) uses 'conjunctural', quoting Antonio Gramsci, to refer to ' "the relations of force at various levels" ', which articulate specifically and thus offer an 'analytical tool' through their very unpacking. Here, 'articulation' combines the double meaning of the word – 'linking together' and 'giving expression to', which emphasises the material relations and forces (Hart 2007, 91; Hart 2002; and see Hall 1980). For Hart, such analysis, then, is also always spatially situated; it demands attention to the connections between places and the production of their distinctiveness, emphasising their co-constitution, which opens politics and possibilities (Hart 2018b, 373). Such efforts can help to track meaningful and everyday relations not limited to institutional or electoral politics.

Tracing Hart's work on gendered labour, specifically, from her fieldwork in the 1980s to her later work on South Africa, I play with three conjunctural moments of her expanding work. If 'thinking conjuncturally', as John Clarke says of Stuart Hall's work, involves an 'orientation to the particularity of the conjuncture', understanding the moment through 'the forces, tendencies, forms of power, relations of domination and subordination that were condensed' therein (Clarke 2014, 115), then situating Hart's conceptual development helps to track both her deepening practice and how her work has intertwined with my own engagement.

The first conjuncture is epistemological. As Hart argues in 'Relational Comparison Revisited', methods are theory and vice versa (Hart 2018b). Her work on divisions of labour of rural producers in the 1980s and early 1990s posed questions about how relations and meanings are articulated historically. Thus, while broader debates in the anthropology of work at the time examined multiple forms of resistance of newly proletarianised women workers, Hart documented both what enabled rural women to contest dramatically changing relations within the introduction of capitalist markets as well as where they faced limits and contradictions of their politics. Grounding her work (in particular, her work as an economist) in ethnography enabled her to demonstrate how to do an analysis of the important articulations (the identification of which was part of the process). Her early work, at least as I experienced it from the perspective of the anthropology of work, taught me that in fact, one has to enter that complexity and explain the concrete relations and meanings that track outward and back again, from households to world markets, from national political machinations to labour teams.

The second conjuncture is scalar. Relatedly, Hart's work in the late 1980s and early 1990s demonstrated how multiple interconnected conditions and relations explained not 'local responses' to global phenomena, but the very nature and dynamic of multiply connected relations across scales themselves, which she made more explicit in her work in the 1990s and early 2000s. The significance of these multiple connections came, particularly to me, through how she traced shifts in such configurations in *Disabling Globalization* (Hart 2002). Gendered labour was one of these dimensions, but here she expanded her view of labour market changes within a much more complex set of forces. It influenced my PhD research, beginning in about 1997, in which I wanted to understand workers' changing politics, not through a national institutional story of trade union power, but rather by placing workers (specifically women retail workers) within a generational history of local labour market changes on the East Rand (Ekurhuleni). Her argument in this book against an 'impact model' of political economy (Hart 2002) condensed what I had been attempting to defend through my in-depth ethnographic local labour market study.

Finally, I identify a third conjuncture important to my thinking in Hart's ongoing and more explicit development of 'relational comparison' (2018b; see also chapter 3 in this volume), which has deepened her non-teleological and dialectical method. This approach helped me to frame a historical comparative project on women's service labour in racially segregated cities and the temporality of these phenomena across space – in Johannesburg and Baltimore, Maryland, in the United States. Hart offers tools to understand the political logics of class, race and gender relations attuned to multidimensional political economies and thus brings much to South African sociology. Currently, the study of the discipline seems more and more compartmentalised, more inclined to isolate its sites of study from understanding how social relations and forces are reproduced and transformed beyond the immediate bargain in question.

Tracing gendered labour: Epistemologies, scales and relations

I read Hart's work in the 1980s and early 1990s as part of a milieu of what was then called the anthropology of work. Feminist ethnographers (and the occasional economist) examined structural changes to capitalist relations and critiqued approaches to resistance against the backdrop of global Southern (then 'Third World') women workers entering production in the so-called new international division of labour (Elson and Pearson 1981; Fuentes and Ehrenreich 1985; Lamphere 1987; Leacock and Safa 1986; Nash and Fernandez-Kelly 1983; Ong 1987; Stoler 1985; Ward 1990; Zavella 1987). This moment integrated critiques of a narrow focus on the workplace as a site of class politics with those of the household as a bounded and altruistic labour sharing unit. These thinkers insisted on examining the relationship of reproductive, unpaid labour with women's waged work and in wider histories (see, for instance, Collier and Yanagisako 1987; Collins and Gimenez 1990; Fox 1980; Murray 1987; Smith and Wallerstein 1992).

Authors writing about gendered forms of labour and resistance problematised voluntarist or celebratory stories of resistance. They located women's labour within structures of power and explained specifically the forms that resistance took, within local and historical colonial systems of meaning, and the effects that these had (Ong 1987; Stoler 1985). Because many of the studies engaged with newly proletarianised 'peasants', debates raised questions of changes to the organisation of agricultural production and intersected with larger discussions on the character of the development of capitalism (see Arizpe and Aranda 1988; Stolcke 1984). Hart's work cross-cut these debates, engaging with the nature of resistance (or what she more simply called politics), labour use and relations, and the agrarian question (or rural transformation) within theorisations of capitalism (Hart 1986a, 1986b, 1988, 1989, 1997).

Hart's early work was of its time in taking up these questions and yet it was particularly clear for explicating a fine-tuned sensitivity to the conjunctural importance of a host of historical relations explaining a range of 'market dynamics'. For instance, in her journal article 'Exclusionary Labour Arrangements: Interpreting Evidence on Employment Trends in Rural Java' (1986a), Hart examines changes in agricultural and non-agricultural labour arrangements in rural Java in the late 1960s and 1970s. Her concern is to explain rural labour demand and supply dynamics at a moment when relations were indeed changing through wider political and economic forces, including stratified access to land, labour control mechanisms, relative household indebtedness, national political power and macro-economic policy, and gender and age differences of workers. By doing so, Hart argues, on the one hand, for the importance of local-level studies to offer explanations, which often belie interpretations of national survey and census data. On the other hand, she shows how local labour-control practices alone cannot explain changes in labour market dynamics. Rather, understanding the connections between the 'local logics' and the wider national political economic contexts is critical to differentiating labour use systems and how those systems change over time (Hart 1986a, 681). In this early piece of work, there is already an analysis of the connection of local and wider relations that explain labour patterns in place.

Towards this effort Hart offered country comparisons as a mechanism to identify specific historical and situated dynamics of labour control (Hart 1986b), state patronage (Hart 1989) and post-colonial state power and its relation to rural elites (Hart 1988) to explain enduring and changing rural labour systems (of sharecropping specifically) and agricultural production in general. While this early work examined the specifics of different countries in comparison with one another, Hart emphasised in each context the complexity of inter-scalar dynamics through which rural labour systems were reproduced and changed. Changing labour markets could not be explained by market efficiency, nor could tied labour (a range of forms of bonded labour) be seen as a remainder of pre-capitalist arrangements. These were dynamic terrains, which required attentiveness to the embedded divisions tracking the logics of control, relative stability, reproduction and critique under changing national political economic contexts, which required in-depth, local-level study attentive to comparative difference.

I was a student of anthropology and sociology at the University of Wisconsin-Madison from 1989 to 1993. Hart's demonstration of this type of analysis was energising. As we debated the importance of contemporary changes to capitalist relations (that would later be called neo-liberalism), it was to these debates about the nature of capitalist change in post-colonial places that I was most drawn. If we were to explain, as I was interested in doing, the significance of the wage labour relationship and labour politics in a place like South Africa, not only did we have to understand the history of labour as embedded relationship of power, but we also had to see forms of taken-for-granted agency as specifically constituted in place and time, meaningfully as well as materially.

Indeed, as part of her critique of multi-scalar power relations explicating labour systems, in 'Engendering Everyday Resistance', an article published in the *Journal of Peasant Studies*, Hart (1991, 95) offered a complex rendering of politics. Rather than assuming resistance, she showed how specific people engaged in politics in specific (and changing) ways. A major contribution to my thinking from her work in this period was how these processes are always contradictory. We do not find pure subjects, nor do we arrive at predicted actions and outcomes.

Hart made important epistemological and methodological interventions. She raised questions that challenged neoclassical and neo-institutional economists and conclusions based on generalised (and predicable) 'household behaviour' (Hart 1992, 1997). She interrogated notions of uniform subaltern 'agency', such as in James Scott's (1985) *Weapons of the Weak* (see Hart 1991, 1997). Instead, the questions she asked pushed analysis to why differences existed among subalterns, in her case by ethnicity, class and gender. She asked what could explain why working-class women workers in rural Malaysia acted collectively as workers but the men did not. She did not toggle from class politics to peasant informal resistance, but showed how multiple responses occurred within the same locale among rural labourers, which demanded a more complex explanation of actions (indeed, of capitalist relations). She demonstrated how politics was co-constituted through national party politics, local patronage networks, religious and ethnic factions, regional and local elite networks of power, and intra-household gender relations and divisions of labour (Hart 1991).

Poor women workers' situated critique of employers and of husbands showed the intertwining of gender and class consciousness as well as the spaces of workplace, household and community (Hart 1991). Drawing on the work of Joan Wallach Scott (1988), Hart emphasised how gender was both imbricated with other social relations and meaningful – that is, the semiotics of gendered meanings served to give force and content to political struggles (Hart 1991, 95). Hart offered a gendered critique of James Scott (Hart 1997, 22), thereby re-examining the Malaysian context from her own research for how gender worked to explain 'everyday resistance' among rural producers (Hart 1991).

Furthermore, intra-household relations explained differences in labour deployment but also gendered meanings of collective identification (Hart 1992, 1997). The household was not an altruistic unit that could be assumed to be acting together, as economists argued, but another space of power and politics. Neither the market nor the household were 'natural' institutions predicting behaviour as neoclassical and neo-institutional models suggested (Hart 1992, 1997). Hart argued that intra-household contests and hierarchies of power explained differences in labour use and, in turn, of women's collective organisation. In 'From "Rotten Wives" to "Good Mothers"' she wrote: 'Taking gender seriously is not simply a matter of adding women, recognising their contribution, or being more generous towards them. Rather, it forces attention to the exercise of power within and beyond the household. It also disrupts claims of prediction' (Hart 1997, 14).

In short, gender relations and representations were 'an integral part of the politics of production and class processes' (Hart 1991, 115). As a result, then, gender 'can only be comprehended in terms of how larger configurations of political-economic forces – in turn the product of the history of race-class struggle – have defined the terrain of conflict at the local level' (110). For Hart, gender was not a vector to be intersected by other variables, but was always co-constitutive within this complex set of relations in time and space (see Hart 2002, 36–37). The stand she took to interrogate predictive modelling entailed a clear stake – for through such a focus, possibilities became open futures, not closed ones where prior abstractions were then demonstrated to confirm predictions.

Her analysis of intra-household tension and contestation produced a different analysis of rural villagers. Tracing gendered differences not only highlighted distinctive dynamics, but could also then offer a very different understanding of agency that did not locate it in a subject position defined a priori ('peasant'), but explained people's actions from their specific multiple and contradictory relations. Hart argued against a fixed identity from which people act and for an epistemology that opens to how identities and interests are 'forged through political struggle (in its extended sense)' (Hart 1997, 20).

By the 1990s, Hart had come to be influenced by Doreen Massey (see Hart 2018a), who helped her to argue more forcefully for the relevance of space and place (Hart 1997). It was Massey's 'extroverted sense of place' (1994, 155) to which she was drawn, in which place is 'not a bounded unit but nodal points of interconnection in socially produced space' (Hart 2018a, 80).

Hart had already noted this problem of scale clearly in relation to understanding changes to labour markets in her earlier work. In her article 'Agrarian Structure and the State in Java and Bangladesh' she wrote: 'Contemporary theories typically abstract from larger structures of political and economic power' (Hart 1988, 249) and she contended that 'the analytical tools for linking local-level agrarian processes with the wider political-economic system are poorly developed' (249–250). Her work, especially involving country comparison, sought to show differences in how state power, national accumulation, elite patronage networks, local labour use, histories of production systems, and gendered and class divisions of labour affected 'power at different levels of society' (250). This work showed definitively the need to 'look beyond the labor market in order to explain the different patterns of agrarian relations' (256) and the relevance of 'a historically specific analysis of the exercise of power at different levels' to rural relations (Hart 1989, 31). With Massey, Hart was able to move beyond country comparison to think about interconnections between spaces and how places themselves were constituted through these processes. As she says in her chapter in the edited collection *Doreen Massey: Critical Dialogues*, this is when she became a geographer (Hart 2018a).

Hart's *Disabling Globalization* (2002) was a culmination of this evolving perspective. In this multi-sited ethnography, she showed the centrality of local government in Ladysmith and Newcastle to defining post-apartheid national terrain (and specifically so in the post-apartheid period) and thus the differential lineaments constituting local places, as well as the significance of this for processes of national hegemony. In this story, gendered labour remains an important strand of relationship. The labour market, defined through low-wage, Taiwanese-owned textile factories in the 1990s in KwaZulu-Natal, was constituted through prior investment and state development agendas as well as through trade union organisation, itself gendered. In Hart's book, we see how Taiwanese employers' racist and sexist relationships to South African black women workers located power relations in the new factories, but also how they emerged out of longer historically determined social relations in Taiwan, imbricating masculinity, generation and class processes of reproduction there. Gendered and familial forms of factory discipline did not work in the same way in South Africa. Hart connected the deeper story of the precariousness of South African workers, in turn, to the forms of dispossession of the South African working class from the land with its gendered presumptions of wage work and reproductive wage-subsidising labour. She contrasts these articulations with Taiwanese industrialists' investments in Taiwan and China, who benefited from land redistribution, which subsidised labour reproduction, and from differently gendered divisions of labour, labour use practices and relations of obligation (see Hart 2006; Hart and Sitas 2004).

Hart's earlier focus on gendered labour becomes repositioned within this multi-scaled political and economic history in ways that de-emphasise labour as a site of political collective mobilisation. This also, it must be said, converges with a time when labour politics had become displaced by social movements in South Africa, including those demanding access to land. By linking women workers' interconnected lives within these other sets of relations, Hart also signalled that she was moving towards other questions – around hegemony and its reproduction and transformation.

The analysis she offered in *Disabling Globalization* spoke back to South African labour sociology at the time, which was refiguring strategic union interventions by reimaging, for instance, 'social movement unionism', as a way to remobilise trade union politics where South Africa was held up as an optimistic solution for modelling working-class politics (Webster, Lambert and Bezuidenhout 2008). Hart showed, rather, how the very moment of the South African 'transition' was, in fact, multiply and contradictorily constituted simultaneously (Hart 2002, 2006, 2008). As Hart so carefully documented, local state forms themselves became recrafted through these contradictions in ways that left little room to a labour politics configured to defend wage-earners as workers (Hart 2002).

The interconnections between labour and longer histories of racialised dispossession have been primary in Hart's work, precisely because of how an attentiveness to the often-forgotten third dimension of capitalist relations – nature/land (the other two being capital and labour) – spatialises and historicises post-colonial practices of exploitation and extraction in place. Thus, processes of ongoing dispossession explain the complexities of politics in South Africa (Hart 2002, 38; 2006; 2008, 694; Hart and Sitas 2004). This work marks a clear move away from labour politics per se, towards struggles and movements around reproduction and decommodification broadly.

Finally, working on analysing South Africa's contested hegemony in this period, particularly as anger with President Thabo Mbeki's class project ushered in Jacob Zuma's schizoid role as 'popular' leader (Hart 2008), Hart's energies shifted to forms of popular nationalisms. In this, her gendered lens remained, as, for instance, in understanding how Zuma's initial popularity drew on forms of masculinity to reinscribe state power and authority (Hart 2008, 692) – and indeed continues as one thread in her latest project, which tracks these forms across India, South Africa and the United States (Hart 2020).

With this latest demonstration of 'relational comparison', Hart gives clearer expression to her dialectical method, while moving away from grounded examination of gendered labour, in line with the trajectory that I trace above. In 'Relational Comparison Revisited' (2018b), Hart defines her method based on a non-teleological, open dialectics. By focusing on both what makes a method relational as well as what makes it comparative, Hart usefully elaborates a way of doing post-colonial research and writing. Following Harry Harootunian and Fernando Coronil, Hart begins from the premise that those having experienced colonisation or subjugation 'live comparatively' (Hart 2018b, 371, quoting Harootunian) – that is, they are held up within an already existing system defined through hierarchical classifying. She seeks, and indeed has practised in her work on gender throughout her career, a 'Marxist postcolonial' conjunctural analysis (372). For Hart, to be conjunctural means 'bringing key forces at play in South Africa and other regions of the world into the same frame of analysis, as connected yet distinctively different nodes in globally interconnected historical geographies – and as sites in the production of global processes in specific spatio-historical conjunctions, rather than as just recipients of them' (373). 'Gender' or 'gendered labour' is one of the many forces and relations that co-constitute these dynamics and places. The moments of Hart's work that I outline bring together the imbrication of epistemologies, scales and relations as her way of doing feminist analysis. I turn now to the development of my own work, which tracks with these three conjunctures of Hart's.

Labour politics and intimate publics

I began my scholarship analysing changes to the labour markets of contingent wage workers. This focus came out of my experience working for a workers' advice office in Johannesburg, the Industrial Aid Society, from 1994 to 1997. The IAS was a historic worker advice office founded in the 1970s to support emergent independent trade unions organising black workers, which had continued to offer assistance to precarious workers during this heady time of change in South Africa. In 1997, I moved to the Society, Work and Politics Institute (SWOP) at the University of the Witwatersrand. Specifically, my early work for SWOP produced some of the first studies documenting the ongoing and changing forms of casualisation and externalisation of employment in post-apartheid South Africa (Kenny and Bezuidenhout 1999; Kenny and Webster 1999). While this work was generally written for a South African sociological audience, which debated the character of labour market restructuring during South Africa's democratic transition, my orientation was to try to understand what these changes meant to workers within their situated histories. Part of this involved research for my PhD, which focused on the regional dynamics of the East Rand (Ekurhuleni), east of Johannesburg. My larger question was about how these changes related to changing worker politics in these years.

My PhD work was influenced by discovering Massey's *Spatial Divisions of Labour* (1984) in 1992 during my graduate studies. I initially planned a comparative project examining labour market shifts towards service work in the Eastern Cape and in Gauteng, two regions where manufacturing labour was key to constituting strong trade union politics. I wanted to think through changes to women's labour opportunities in relation to changing national policies, global shifts and local labour market dynamics, to understand how labour politics had changed, and thus how workers' politics might be understood in more nuanced, specifically located ways. The regional comparison was dropped in the final project, but I incorporated a historical examination of changes to the local labour market on the East Rand, a centre of manufacturing labour in Gauteng since the 1940s, the growth of service work in the 1970s, expansion in the 1990s, and the subsequent shifts to precarious service labour. These generational changes in place (following Massey) helped me to understand changes to worker politics and the production of new meaningful divisions of labour by workers themselves, specifically defined through gendered meanings and relations (Kenny 2004a).

Hart's work from the 1980s and the 1990s influenced these concerns. I wrote about how casual and contract retail jobs had to be understood within more general shifts in household precariousness and changing gendered relations there, connected to shifting legal terrain and local economies. I linked workers across a range of contracts of employment, including casual, outsourced ('contract') and permanent,

to their household situations. I argued that workers across these contracts each dealt with relations and responsibilities within complex
household arrangements (Kenny 2001). I engaged with the implications
of these shifts within households in the local labour market of the East
Rand, where workers' parents migrated to the area in the 1940s and
1950s to get jobs in new manufacturing industries. The retail workers
were the children of this earlier generation of migrants. They went to
high school and were politicised by the 1976 school movement, influenced by the Black Consciousness Movement, and from there entered
(white-collar) work of clerical and service jobs opening to black men
and women at the time. This was the generation that mobilised in a
trade union around militant race and class subjectivities defined by
these broader historical and situated relations. It was they who were
'full-time permanent' workers when I did my fieldwork in the late
1990s, while those who were casual and contract workers had entered
the labour market later, when full-time jobs were rarer. By the 1990s,
the shifting terrain of labour demand and supply was shot through
with changing gendered meaning, affecting ideas of masculinity, care,
parenthood and dependency (Kenny 2003). In an article titled 'Selling
Selves' in the *Journal of Southern African Studies* I detailed how gender,
class and racial meanings of work and labour conditions constituted
workers' politics in different periods, how broader shifting political
economic terrains helped to explain changing labour markets, and in
turn how these relations affected how workers understood their collective identities, with the re-imagining critically shaped through gendered materialities and meanings (Kenny 2004b, 2007).

I also examined the gendered and racialised social constitution
of employment law and sectoral legal categories historically from the
1930s onwards. Thus, 'casual' labour in the sector had a long history
of use, for filling 'extra time', and was associated with (white male) student labour initially and then, in the 1980s, with black young people
working extra jobs to assist families. 'Part-time' contracts emerged
as a mechanism to keep white women in employment in the 1950s.

In the late 1980s, when retailers extended trading hours, employers and unions alike agreed to staff later and weekend shifts with 'casual' labour (not 'part-time') because of its association with dependency and youth, while at the same time trying to stabilise 'adult' full-time jobs as retrenchments loomed. These already constituted and meaningful legal categories influenced how sector labour use shifted, explaining the expansion of 'casual' labour in the late 1980s, which then became more widespread by the 1990s, and in turn affected regulatory reform in the post-apartheid period, when legislation inscribed new categories of 'flexible' labour as essential to the sector (Kenny 2009). In 'Servicing Modernity', published in *African Studies*, I considered how historically white women's labour constituted the labour market and labour process of the jobs into which black women moved in the 1970s (Kenny 2008). Thus, my work detailed the changes to the local labour market of workers I spent time with and interviewed.

These changing relations were located within the specific time and place of greater Johannesburg. This work showed the meaning of service jobs in different periods, the gendered constitution of the work and labour market and legal categories, how changes within the townships, households and workplaces affected residents and workers as South Africa went through its democratic transition and how these in turn affected labour politics of newly segmented groups of workers. In my PhD, I argued that while it appeared from a distance that labour politics had been demobilised by the late 1990s, in fact, workers' collective politics abided, but now within new (deeply gendered) divisions of labour, which could only be explained by how workers themselves remade the site of work meaningful (Kenny 2004a).

These various situated analyses helped me to move towards my book, *Retail Worker Politics, Race and Consumption in South Africa* (Kenny 2018), in which I rely on Stuart Hall's concepts of articulation, conjuncture and 'subjects in struggle' (1980, 1985, 1986), Hart's work pushing against an 'impact model' of change, as well as her intermediation of Hall through her expanded work on relational comparison (2002, 2018b;

see also Hart 2007). In this book, by examining the long history of retail worker politics in greater Johannesburg, I argue that the enduring appeal of the political subject 'worker' (or, really, the collective form, *abasebenzi* – workers in isiZulu) is a question that requires a historical and spatial explanation (Kenny 2018). My project, drawing on Hart's conjunctural analysis, focuses on ambivalences as well as enduring meanings and sub-jectivities in order to open up possibilities otherwise foreclosed, as Hart notes so clearly in explicating her method (Hart 2018b). The book was partly aimed at critiquing two quite different orientations toward study-ing labour in South Africa. On the one hand, there are those that start from the assumption that workers enact labour politics and the question is to evaluate the 'successes' of these endeavours. These instrumental or strategic analyses of labour politics in South Africa have left unexplored all sorts of multiply determined, contradictory and historical reasons that explain why and when people act politically and collectively in spe-cific sites. On the other hand, others start from the premise that wage labour is anachronistic (especially in the global South) and therefore labour politics is increasingly less relevant. These can be grouped with others who analyse worker politics through an evaluation of the (a priori) impossibility of labour as a site of emancipatory politics. Broadly, this latter combined group can be seen as the nay-sayers.

Both positions – the yea and the nay – within South African labour sociology have in common a similar political logic. The instrumental approach that seeks to find empirical cases of successful organising to model future strategy takes as its focus an external object, removed from infiltrative relations that may complicate the story. Often such analy-ses may also begin with an encompassing framing (see Hart 2018b), with the 'case' being studied presented as the local manifestation of the transcendent totality (for instance, 'neo-liberalism'; see Hart 2008). Similarly, analysing the site of work either as anachronistic (because wage labour is less central to households) or (from the different per-spective) as anti-black subjugation, takes the deep imbrication of labour and race in South African history out of situated historical relations and, I suggest, following Hall and Hart, sidesteps a prior question about why people did (and do) struggle there and to what effect (not only for labour relations but, indeed, for social imaginaries). Ironically, both approaches – those that triumph labour politics and those that eschew it – meet the object of study as an abstraction; politics merely demonstrate the abstraction already demurred – the (prior) bargaining power of a situation tautologically explains the workers' politics; the (abstract prior) evaluation that the source of income predicts the site of politics (the 'kitchen table' not the factory floor); or, the (prior) anti-blackness of a set of relations explains an already foreclosed politics (Kenny 2018).

I ask instead why retail workers (with many women workers) continue to enact a labour politics under conditions of deepened precariousness (and, indeed, increasing wagelessness). By examining the historical and spatial specificity of the labour market of the greater Johannesburg area, I argue that the political subject *abasebenzi* was ruptural – it upended political imaginaries, at a specific time and within a specific set of relations, and contested specific forms of relationship (Kenny 2018). This political subject contested forms of personhood (not merely recognition), which were affectively resonant specifically at the site of work and concretely so in retail spaces, which relied on service labour to project meanings of modernity, nation and polity in ways that shifted with forms of contract, labour law and struggle. My book's analysis brings together language and meaning with structuring relations of capital, the organisation of retailing, consumption practices and collective politics. Exploring the changing politics of retail workers in greater Johannesburg over much of the twentieth century, then, I show how the contradictory and competing discourses of race, class, gender and nation – and recalling Hart's (2013) work on the contradictory processes of de-nationalisation and re-nationalisation – took effect to bolster workers' politics in different ways at different times.

Kobena Mercer writes of Hall's semiotics: 'It is precisely the possibility of breaking with oppressive regimes of racial meaning that is at stake in the polysemic agency of difference' (Mercer 2017, 17). My book argues for the situated relevance of collective political subjectivity of 'workers' for nation, as produced and re-articulated by workers through changing social relations of precariousness, neo-liberalism and democracy. Thus, the 'labour relation' itself was reinvested politically by precarious women retail workers in a post-apartheid context, even while the site of wage labour has reproduced deep forms of racialised subjugation (Kenny 2018). I posed this endurance of labour politics as a paradox that required explanation rather than predictive teleology.

More recently, I have been working on a 'relational comparison' of racial capitalism from two cities profoundly divided by race and class, Johannesburg and Baltimore, Maryland. The project examines the interrelated yet different histories of the workplace and of the marketplace in these two cities, as spaces of 'participation', as terrains of politics. I begin with a historical relational comparative focus on the service work of women in department stores. The shift in racial and gender composition of sales workers from white to black women in both contexts occurred in the same period. In both cases, this involved a similar temporality of women's life cycles and labour market opportunities, and in both was opposed by a white public (in quite different ways) (Kenny 2020). The project compares and interlinks differences between women's life cycle and labour market histories, trade union and civil rights movements, law and gender, and race and class relations of consumption in these divided cities. It examines the active processes of contesting (white and black) women's labour – what it is, where it belongs and what it demands – by a multiplicity of actors, including women workers, trade unions, social movements, the state, husbands and consumers within the semi-public spaces of department stores as evidence for how 'femininity', class respectability and racial relations of work extended expectations of political belonging. The project seeks to reconstruct theory on urban and racial formations by centring it around service labour – itself a place of intersection (of race, gender, age, class, of labour and consumption, of law, private property and labour rights).

This project furthermore extends to the character and effects of differences in 'intimate publics' materialised in mundane semi-public spaces, such as department stores, lifts, tea rooms, bioscopes, buses and city streets (Kenny 2020). It examines how such places, those semi-'publics' (on private property) became means through which the polity was debated. How have struggles around the market and the workplace related to each other or diverged? I problematise the terrain of the market and implicitly compare it to the workplace as space of action and politics (ultimately linking them). Through this conjunctural analysis, in which retail arenas (and other everyday social sites) become the site of comparison, themselves interconnected globally and imaginatively, this work seeks to explain how specific terrains and concrete places became contested as political.

In some ways, then, my current work examines how hegemonies operated on the plane of everyday racial (and class and gender) relations, from and within taken-for-granted sites, which often have not been deemed to be political. Hart deals with multi-varied political sites where state actors intervene, whereas my project seeks explicitly to stir up the ambivalences and gaps in those overburdened discourses of nationalism and belonging in precisely the locations where they were meant to play out seamlessly. In some ways, picking up on Hart's criticism of the study of labour in South Africa as disconnected from processes of dispossession, I explicitly link my ongoing interest in labour as a meaningful relation with changing regimes of private property – for instance, with department stores and malls (Kenny 2019) – and how private property has been instantiated through concrete relations and struggles in two places where such spatialised relations are obviously racialised (Kenny 2020).

Conclusion

In returning to Hart's pieces, I am reminded of how her analysis of articulated epistemologies, scales and relations is still so relevant today, particularly within South African sociology, enamoured as it is with institutional politics. My work for the past 20 years has been to try to show the meaning of the 'labour relation' as a site of politics. Hart has laid the groundwork to explain where, how and why politics emerge as they do, situated and yet multi-determined, and imbricating contradictions that open onto new questions. A central insight of Hart's feminism has been her understanding of politics. As she wrote in her article 'Engendering Everyday Resistance' in the *Journal of Peasant Studies*, grounding her work in that of others before her: 'Instead of referring simply to electoral politics and/or actions focused specifically on the state, politics has increasingly come to be used in a broader sense to refer to the processes by which struggles over resources and labour are simultaneously struggles over socially-constructed meanings, definitions, and identities' (Hart 1991, 95).

Michael Ekers, Stefan Kipfer and Alex Loftus (2020, 1590) ask of her recent work: 'Given that Hart's work has slowly put more weight on the couplet of race and class, rather than gender, how do we bring cross-cutting considerations of gender, sexuality, and reproduction back into these articulatory analytical frames?' Hart's earlier work on gendered labour reminds us of her long-standing method: to analyse the contradictory, situated everyday relations that people live through, to think through multiple, co-constituting scales, to explain connections and dissociations, and to attend to meaning and translation. That it is difficult to do both the 'micro' and the 'macro' – as Ekers, Kipfer and Loftus (2020, 1589) put it – in the same frame is one of the challenges. This is precisely the call that Gillian Hart's life work has sounded to us.

REFERENCES

Arizpe, Lourdes and Josefina Aranda. 1988. 'The Comparative Advantages of Women's Disadvantages: Women Workers in the Strawberry Export Agribusiness in Mexico'. In *On Work: Historical, Comparative and Theoretical Approaches*, edited by R.E. Pahl, 633–650. Oxford: Basil Blackwell.
Clarke, John. 2014. 'Conjunctures, Crises, and Cultures: Valuing Stuart Hall'. *Focaal* 70: 113–122.

Collier, Jane and Sylvia Yanagisako, eds. 1987. *Gender and Kinship: Essays towards a Unified Analysis*. Stanford: Stanford University Press.

Collins, Jane and Martha Gimenez, eds. 1990. *Work without Wages: Domestic Labor and Self-Employment within Capitalism*. Albany: State University of New York Press.

Ekers, Michael, Stefan Kipfer and Alex Loftus. 2020. 'On Articulation, Translation, and Populism: Gillian Hart's Postcolonial Marxism'. *Annals of the American Association of Geographers* 110, no. 5: 1577–1593.

Elson, Diane and Ruth Pearson. 1981. ' "Nimble Fingers Make Cheap Workers": An Analysis of Women's Employment in Third World Export Manufacturing'. *Feminist Review* 7: 87–107.

Fox, Bonnie, ed. 1980. *Hidden in the Household: Women's Domestic Labour under Capitalism*. Toronto: The Women's Press.

Fuentes, Annette and Barbara Ehrenreich. 1985. *Women in the Global Factory*. Boston: South End Press.

Hall, Stuart. 1980. 'Race, Articulation and Societies Structured in Dominance'. In *Sociological Theories: Race and Colonialism*, edited by Mary O'Callaghan, 305–345. Paris: UNESCO.

Hall, Stuart. 1985. 'Signification, Representation, Ideology: Althusser and the Post-Structuralist Debates'. *Critical Studies in Mass Communication* 2, no. 2: 91–114.

Hall, Stuart. 1986. 'The Problem of Ideology: Marxism without Guarantees'. *Journal of Communication Inquiry* 10, no. 2: 28–44.

Hart, Gillian. 1986a. 'Exclusionary Labour Arrangements: Interpreting Evidence on Employment Trends in Rural Java'. *Journal of Development Studies* 22, no. 4: 681–696.

Hart, Gillian. 1986b. 'Interlocking Transactions: Obstacles, Precursors or Instruments of Agrarian Capitalism?' *Journal of Development Economics* 23, no. 1: 177–203.

Hart, Gillian. 1988. 'Agrarian Structure and the State in Java and Bangladesh'. *Journal of Asian Studies* 47, no. 2: 249–267.

Hart, Gillian. 1989. 'Agrarian Change in the Context of State Patronage'. In *Agrarian Transformations: Local Processes and the State in Southeast Asia*, edited by Gillian Hart, Andrew Turton and Ben White, 31–52. Berkeley: University of California Press.

Hart, Gillian. 1991. 'Engendering Everyday Resistance: Gender, Patronage and Production in Rural Malaysia'. *Journal of Peasant Studies* 19, no. 1: 93–121.

Hart, Gillian. 1992. 'Household Production Reconsidered: Gender, Labor Conflict, and Technological Change in Malaysia's Muda Region'. *World Development* 20, no. 6: 809–823.

Hart, Gillian. 1997. 'From "Rotten Wives" to "Good Mothers": Household Models and the Limits of Economism'. *IDS Bulletin* 28, no. 3: 14–25.

Hart, Gillian. 2002. *Disabling Globalization: Places of Power in Post-Apartheid South Africa*. Pietermaritzburg: University of Natal Press.

Hart, Gillian. 2006. 'Denaturalizing Dispossession: Critical Ethnography in the Age of Resurgent Imperialism'. *Antipode* 38, no. 5: 977–1004.

Hart, Gillian. 2007. 'Changing Concepts of Articulation: Political Stakes in South Africa Today'. *Review of African Political Economy* 34, no. 111: 85–101.

Hart, Gillian. 2008. 'The Provocations of Neoliberalism: Contesting the Nation and Liberation after Apartheid'. *Antipode* 40, no. 4: 678–705.

Hart, Gillian. 2013. *Rethinking the South African Crisis: Nationalism, Populism, Hegemony*. Pietermaritzburg: University of KwaZulu-Natal Press.

Hart, Gillian. 2018a. 'Becoming a Geographer: Massey Moments in a Spatial Education'. In *Doreen Massey: Critical Dialogues*, edited by Marion Werner, Jamie Peck, Rebecca Lave and Brett Christophers, 75–89. New York: Columbia University Press.

Hart, Gillian. 2018b. 'Relational Comparison Revisited: Marxist Postcolonial Geographies in Practice'. *Progress in Human Geography* 42, no. 3: 371–394. First published online in 2016.

Hart, Gillian. 2020. 'Resurgent Nationalisms and Populist Politics in the Neoliberal Age'. *Geografiska Annaler: Series B, Human Geography* 102, no. 3: 233–238.

Hart, Gillian and Ari Sitas. 2004. 'Beyond the Urban–Rural Divide: Linking Land, Labour, and Livelihoods'. *Transformation* 56: 31–38.

Kenny, Bridget. 2001. ' "We Are Nursing These Jobs": The Impact of Labour Market Flexibility on South African Retail Sector Workers'. In *Is There an Alternative? South African Workers Confronting Globalisation*, edited by Neil Newman, John Pape and Helga Jansen, 90–107. Cape Town: ILRIG.

Kenny, Bridget. 2003. 'From Insurrectionary Worker to Contingent Citizen: Restructuring Labor Markets and Repositioning East Rand (South Africa) Retail Sector Workers'. *City & Society* 15, no. 1: 31–57.

Kenny, Bridget. 2004a. 'Divisions of Labor, Experiences of Class: Changing Collective Identities of East Rand Food Retail Sector Workers through South Africa's Democratic Transition'. PhD diss., University of Wisconsin-Madison.

Kenny, Bridget. 2004b. 'Selling Selves: East Rand Retail Sector Workers Fragmented and Reconfigured'. *Journal of Southern African Studies* 30, no. 3: 477–498.

Kenny, Bridget. 2007. 'Claiming Workplace Citizenship: "Worker" Legacies, Collective Identities and Divided Loyalties of South African Contingent Retail Workers'. *Qualitative Sociology* 30, no. 4: 481–500.

Kenny, Bridget. 2008. 'Servicing Modernity: White Women Shop Workers and Changing Gendered Respectabilities, 1940s–1970s'. *African Studies* 67, no. 3: 365–396.

Kenny, Bridget. 2009. 'Mothers, Extra-Ordinary Labour, and *Amacasual*: Law and Politics of Nonstandard Employment in the South African Retail Sector'. *Law & Policy* 31, no. 3: 282–306.

Kenny, Bridget. 2018. *Retail Worker Politics, Race and Consumption in South Africa: Shelved in the Service Economy*. Basingstoke: Palgrave Macmillan.

Kenny, Bridget. 2019. 'The Sprawl of Malls: Financialisation, Service Work and Inequality in Johannesburg's Urban Geography'. *Transformation* 101: 36–60.

Kenny, Bridget. 2020. 'Servicing "Intimate Publics": Johannesburg and Baltimore Department Stores in the 1960s'. *Safundi* 21, no. 2: 115–139.

Kenny, Bridget and Andries Bezuidenhout. 1999. 'Contracting, Complexity and Control: An Overview of the Changing Nature of Subcontracting in the South African Mining Industry'. *Journal of the South African Institute of Mining and Metallurgy* 99, no. 4: 185–191.

Kenny, Bridget and Edward Webster. 1999. 'Eroding the Core: Flexibility and the Re-segmentation of the South African Labour Market'. *Critical Sociology* 24, no. 3: 216–243.

Lamphere, Louise. 1987. *From Working Daughters to Working Mothers*. Ithaca: Cornell University Press.

Leacock, Eleanor and Helen I. Safa, eds. 1986. *Women's Work: Development and the Division of Labor by Gender*. South Hadley: Bergin and Garvey Publishers.

Massey, Doreen. 1984. *Spatial Divisions of Labour: Social Structures and the Geography of Production*. London: Macmillan.

Massey, Doreen. 1994. *Space, Place and Gender*. Minneapolis: University of Minnesota Press.

Mercer, Kobena. 2017. 'Introduction'. In *The Fateful Triangle: Race, Ethnicity, Nation: Stuart Hall*, edited by Kobena Mercer, 1–30. Cambridge, MA: Harvard University Press.

Murray, Colin. 1987. 'Class, Gender and the Household: The Developmental Cycle in Southern Africa'. *Development and Change* 18: 235–249.

Nash, June and Maria Patricia Fernandez-Kelly, eds. 1983. *Women, Men, and the International Division of Labor*. Albany: State University of New York Press.

Ong, Aihwa. 1987. *Spirits of Resistance and Capitalist Discipline*. Albany: State University of New York Press.

Scott, James. 1985. *Weapons of the Weak: Everyday Forms of Peasant Resistance*. New Haven: Yale University Press.

Scott, Joan Wallach. 1988. *Gender and the Politics of History*. New York: Columbia University Press.

Smith, Joan and Immanuel Wallerstein, eds. 1992. *Creating and Transforming Households: The Constraints of the World Economy*. Cambridge: Cambridge University Press.

Stolcke, Verena. 1984. 'The Employment of Family Morality: Labor Systems and Family Structure on Sao Paulo Plantations, 1950–1979'. In *Kinship, Ideology, and Practice in Latin America*, edited by Raymond T. Smith, 264–296. Chapel Hill: University of North Carolina Press.

Stoler, Ann Laura. 1985. *Capitalism and Confrontation in Sumatra's Plantation Belt, 1870–1979*. New Haven: Yale University Press.

Ward, Kathryn, ed. 1990. *Women Workers and Global Restructuring*. Ithaca: ILR Press, Cornell University.

Webster, Edward, Robert Lambert and Andries Bezuidenhout. 2008. *Grounding Globalization: Labour in the Age of Insecurity*. Oxford: Blackwell.

Zavella, Patricia. 1987. *Women's Work and Chicano Families: Cannery Workers of the Santa Clara Valley*. Ithaca: Cornell University Press.

2 | 'Interlocking Transactions': Micro-foundations for 'Racial Capitalism'

Sharad Chari

I first read Gillian Hart's article 'Interlocking Transactions' (1986a) in the mid-1990s. I found it field-changing with respect to debates on agrarian change. And it was here that I first encountered the concept of interlocking transactions, referring, in brief, to the problem of how transactions in land, labour and credit in rural Asia were usually intertwined, rather than separable as abstract markets. In other words, rural people often worked for specific landlords in their villages for low wages rather than working nearby for higher wages in the hope of accessing credit or other kinds of support, or they accepted usurious loans in the hope of future access to work, land or credit. In all these kinds of situations, poor people were forced to participate in land, labour and credit relations under extremely deleterious terms. Social scientists across the disciplines debated whether these relations were stubborn holdovers from a feudal past or whether they were on the verge of erasure by the inevitable advance of capitalism. Hart was among those who shied away from both radical and liberal wishful thinking to engage agrarian realities as they actually were.

In contemplating my intervention for this volume, I was led instinctively to this concept of praxis, 'interlocking transactions', as also important for our time of spiralling capitalist crises, exacerbated by the Covid-19 pandemic. I show how Hart's intervention in the Asian 'interlocking transactions' debates is key to deepening the theorisation of a concept that has seen renewed interest of late, also to explain specifically dire capitalist geographies, and this concept is 'racial capitalism' (Bhattacharyya 2018). There are many positions on 'racial capitalism', as we will see, but they converge on the importance of understanding how racialisation is closely intertwined with the workings of capitalism. The Black Marxist position goes deeper to argue that racialisation is not just a matter of ideology, but is immanent to capitalism's internal relations. Another way to put this position is that racialisation is not simply an addition to the workings of capitalism as we know it, but is foundational at the micro level to ways in which configurations of land, labour and credit relations emerge and transform everywhere. This is the line of argument I follow to show how Hart's intervention from Marxist agrarian studies points precisely to the micro-foundations necessary for a Black Marxist conception of racial capitalism.

In juxtaposing a forgotten category from Hart's early work and a seemingly novel category of our time, it is tempting to ruminate on how the later Hart is present in her earlier incarnation. We can read enduring commitments from Hart's early essay on 'interlocking transactions' (1986a) to her reading of Stuart Hall's intervention in the South African debates on race, racism and capitalism, which take her to the more supple Gramscian notion of 'articulation' (see chapter 8 in this volume). Just as Hall (2003) famously argues that we ought to read Marx's *oeuvre* as a whole, I suggest we read across Hart's work with the same generosity precisely for the richly materialist critical apparatus it offers for our time. I begin with a close reading of her important article published in the *Journal of Development Economics* (Hart 1986a).

'Interlocking transactions'

Hart begins her article of this name with the observation that 'recent empirical and historiographical studies are increasingly uncovering enormous variations in the forms of agrarian labour arrangements, often within the same area' (1986a, 177). These might 'range from simple, commercial transactions to many far more complex contracts in which labour is tied in with land, credit and other relations' (177). What is clear is that they are highly variable and changeable and do not appear to converge on impersonal, spot markets in 'free' labour in Karl Marx's sarcastic dual sense of freedom from the means of production and freedom from job security. Marx's conception of complete dispossession and proletarianisation does not appear to be or have been an eventuality. Rather, Hart argues, past and present evidence suggests that 'different forms of tied labour not only survive but are often adapted, reinforced and embellished in many ways' (177). The key question is how and why these 'interlocking transactions' in land, labour and credit have tied specific labourers to specific places and employers – for instance, through access to credit, land or other social institutions, all of which have implications for agrarian classes, income distribution and poverty.

Hart was responding to the 'interlinkage debate' in agrarian political economy of the 1970s, which she parses into three approaches. The first was an argument by Amit Bhaduri that the interlocking of tenancy and credit contracts presents an obstacle to investment and technological change in agriculture. Bhaduri (1973) argues that landlords shy away from innovation in order to maintain the indebtedness of their tenants at low levels of income. Hart reads this as a formalisation of Vladimir Lenin's (1899) argument that labour service is a feudal remnant, closely related to bondage and usury, and that the combination through interlocking contracts was an obstacle to the development of agrarian capitalism. In other words, this was an argument that presented interlocking transactions as 'semi-feudal', combining elements of the feudal past with a present that could not reach an ideal of full commodification of land, labour and credit. However, empirical studies in India by Pranab Bardhan, Ashok Rudra, Sheila Bhalla and others showed that interlocking contracts and forms of labour tying were evidently increasing also in contexts of technological change; parallel research in

Thailand, the Philippines and Java concurred. Another kind of critique Bhaduri proposes is historiographic; it shows that Bhaduri's teleology is refuted by historical research. Jan Breman's (1974) study of *hali*, a specific regime of bonded labour relations in South Gujarat, shows that the institution of *hali* sought to retain these relations in order to gain something from a position of comparative privilege. Ernesto Laclau's (1971) and Arnold Bauer's (1975) studies of the transition from the colonial *encomienda* system of labour service to the nineteenth-century *inquilino* system of interlinked land and estate labour contracts in Chile similarly refute the notion of a feudal hangover. Alan Richards' (1979) powerful comparative essay on nineteenth-century Chilean *inquilino* and Prussian *insten* concurs, showing also that landlords in these systems had even more power over estates and localities than the manorial feudal lords of the Western European past.

A second approach to interlocking transactions emerges from a kind of orthodox Marxist position, which sees them as a transitory precursor to the emergence of agrarian capitalism; the focus of much of this work is on sharecropping. For instance, Robert Pearce (1983) poses sharecropping as functional to the early stages of capitalist development, as a form of formal as opposed to real subsumption of labour, which keeps the costs of supervision low. Hart notes that apart from being dichotomous and undialectical, this position could not appreciate the resurgence of forms of labour tying, as in her own dissertation research in Java on the non-linear history of *kedokan* tied labour or in Miriam Wells' (1981) research on the resurgence of sharecropping in California's strawberry industry.

The third approach in the interlinkage debate was from mainstream economists who posed interlocking contracts as market relations, since they do not rely on 'extra-economic coercion' or on 'non-market' forms of obligation. Hart notes that this dualistic framework creates a raft of inconsistencies, not least that when these thinkers address how contracts are enforced, they turn to what they call 'extra-economic coercion'. Further, they cannot explain the dynamics of exclusionary or preferential relations noted by the historical and ethnographic studies cited above, nor can they explain why labour tying emerges under very different labour market conditions that show that interlocking transactions cannot simply be legible in non-Marxist terms as disguised market relations.

These three approaches in the interlinkage debate offer economistic models of 'obstacles, precursors or instruments of agrarian capitalism', the subtitle of the article I am offering a close reading of here. By separating the political from the economic, Hart shows that none of these approaches can explain the dynamics of labour tying or of interlocking transactions because they do not have a handle on social control, or 'the ways in which those who control the means of production attempt to exercise power in the non-labour spheres over those with little or no access to assets' (Hart 1986a, 190). Turning once more to Richards (1979) and Breman (1974) on agrarian change in Chile and Gujarat, Hart notes that 'in both cases, control over land and labor were primarily a means whereby the landowning elite gained access to wider spheres of accumulation' (Hart 1986a, 197). This parallels Hart's research in Java on the resurgence of exclusionary *kedokan* labour arrangements alongside the crackdown on agrarian mobilisation under the New Order regime, an insight key to Hart (1986b).

Hart's article ends with the tense dialectical relation between the politics of work discipline and social control. 'While apparently functional in the short run, such arrangements may well contain the seeds of their own destruction,' writes Hart (1986a, 200), with reference to the contradictory politics of exclusionary labour arrangements in Bhalla's analysis of Green Revolution in Haryana and in Wells' work (1981) on strawberry farming in California. While interlocking transactions are not inherently obstacles, precursors or instruments of agrarian capitalism, they illuminate the complex geography of power and powerlessness; power and struggle are decisive in this view. On this final point, Hart writes that 'those with little or no access to productive assets are not simply passive units of labor supply. Their efforts to secure a livelihood are part of a larger struggle in which they forge social and political relations with other direct producers and with those on whom their livelihood depends' (1986a, 201).

Indeed, one of the important insights of Hart's early article is that labour tying can be a way for women workers particularly to secure preferential terms of employment; this insight was picked up by parallel work in other parts of agrarian South and South East Asia. However, Hart was also a South African dissident in Ithaca, Indonesia, Bangladesh, Malaysia and Boston. The notion of preferential arrangements for some was absolutely untenable to the anti-apartheid critic. Her most precise term is 'exclusionary labour arrangements', which extend ' "privileges" to particular groups while deliberately excluding others' and therefore that 'exclusionary tactics tend also to have a demobilizing effect on agrarian organization' (Hart 1986a, 190). Recall that Hart's Java research was conducted in President Suharto's authoritarian Indonesia, built on the ruins of agrarian communist mobilisation (see the introduction to this volume). At best, exclusionary labour arrangements are politically ambiguous; in all probability, they are reactionary. They beg the critic to make political choices, to 'take sides in this game of the world' (Glissant 1997, 8).

Interpreting exclusionary land/labour/credit arrangements

The irony is that after Hart's departure from South Africa in 1971, the country was rocked by internal struggles, including the emergence of independent Black trade union movements linked to community struggles that refused the broader edifice of apartheid's social control. Central to these insurrectionary currents was an understanding of the mutually reinforcing exclusionary labour, land and credit arrangements that upheld apartheid capitalism, and the intersecting struggles necessary to abolish it. What I am suggesting is that apartheid South Africa was present throughout Hart's research in South and South East Asia, not directly in her published work, but in the margins of her biography. In Hart's hands, the notions of exclusionary labour relations and interlocking transactions held in their shadows the lived experience of apartheid.

When Hart returned to research and write about South Africa following the unbanning of liberation movement organisations in the 1990s, she did so overtly citing the lessons of her Asian agrarian experience. She brought to her work lived and scholarly understandings of Asian and South African capitalisms. In contrast to Asian agrarian transitions and industrialisation, Hart seized on the implications of deep levels of dispossession and proletarianisation for the possibility of a post-apartheid order. In the wake of the analysis of the Congress of South African Trade Unions (COSATU), in *Disabling Globalization* (2002), Hart theorised the importance of re-articulating 'land' as 'the social wage' as a way of attending to the legacies of racialised dispossession, segmented labour arrangements and grossly skewed access to the means of life. One might add that the political economy of modern South Africa has also been transformed in highly spatially uneven ways by the legacies of indirect rule and the ongoing dialectics of custom and capital, as Gavin Capps (2019) argues.

When I first read Hart's explication of interlocking transactions in land, labour, credit and other relations as forms of exclusion that were part of a broader structure of social control meant to demobilise subaltern political will, I read it in the context of broader debates of the 1990s about persisting forms of unfree labour and non-linear trajectories of capitalist change across the post-colonial and post-socialist world. By this time, alongside the shift in her research towards South Africa, Hart had also offered a powerful critique of metropolitan economic geographers who trumpeted the emergence of a new era of industrial decentralisation in which the Third Italy and Silicon Valley were harbingers of a new future. From the vantage of Marxist agrarian studies, Hart was decidedly sceptical on multiple counts (Hart 1998). While Anglo-American economic geographers and economic sociologists thought they had discovered a non-linear conception of capitalist change, Hart and others offered the reminder that radical agrarian studies scholars of the 1970s and 1980s had already proposed non-linear, non-teleological, multi-stranded and geographical conceptions of capitalist social change. This agrarian studies perspective was deeply suspicious that the 1990s marked a new age of industrial democracy anywhere, rather than a reconfiguration of the social division of labour, and of geographies of capital and power.

My own dissertation research of the 1990s, very much inspired by Hart's thinking at the time, took the insights of this agrarian Marxism to critique the agrarian origins of industrial flexibility in the town of Tiruppur in South India (Chari 2004). From Hart (1986a), I retained a sense that exclusionary labour arrangements can be quite important to a fraction of the organised working class that might not see itself as a labour aristocracy, but might be central to the workings of hegemony. In Tiruppur, for instance, the division of labour in the knitwear industry and the revival of older forms of work discipline made space for some male workers of the regionally dominant Gounder caste to forge exclusionary labour arrangements that offered a route to class mobility for 'self-made men'. These accumulation strategies produced a class fraction, a Gounder fraternity of decentralised capital, which effectively took over the industrial town from the old guard of capitalists of patrician caste backgrounds.

In the book emerging from this research, I argue (Chari 2004) that these subalterns could accumulate capital, but only through the domination of the workforce as a whole, specifically through a shifting gendered hegemony over an increasingly differentiated workforce. Their form of exploitation and social domination hinged on what they called their propensity to 'toil', an ideology that interpellated their subjectivation as subaltern capitalists. Consequently, they forged an industrial form that was, at least by the turn of the millennium, difficult for other fractions of capital to break into. In effect, Gounder 'self-made men' articulated a particular gendered/caste politics of work through an exclusionary geography of class mobility and capital accumulation, all on the backs of deepening immiseration and environmental despoliation. In parallel to Hart's work in Java, Tiruppur's fraternal capital forged this intricate form of hegemony in the wake of a long and persisting history of communist trade union activism.

Politically, my argument in *Fraternal Capital* is similar to Hart's on Java in that both studies see the transformative power of exclusionary labour arrangements, differently in different contexts, and we do not find them acceptable anywhere precisely because of their demobilising effects in relation to struggles for social justice. We did not name the exclusionary power of interlocking transactions as the work of 'racism' in the general sense proposed by Ruth Gilmore (2002, 16; emphasis in original): 'Racism is a practice of abstraction, a death-dealing displacement of difference into hierarchies that organize relations within and between the planet's sovereign political territories. Racism functions as a limiting force that pushes disproportionate costs of participating in an increasingly monetized and profit-driven world onto those who, due to the frictions of *political* distance, cannot reach the variable levers of power that might relieve them of those costs.' That is, however, precisely what Hart's research in Java in the 1970s and my own research in South India in the 1990s was about, albeit through racisms that do not work through 'race' but through gender, caste, ethnicity and class.

Reading, however, is also a way of taking a path not taken.

Code shift: 'Racial capitalism' with micro-foundations

Read alongside Hart's early work in 2020, the concepts of interlocking transactions and exclusionary labour arrangements appear immediately relevant to the concept of racial capitalism (Bhattacharyya 2018). Both sets of concepts are revisions of liberal and Marxist conceptions of capitalism that presume an inexorable tendency towards the full commodification of land, labour and money, turning each into impersonal 'markets' that bulldoze established forms of social power. Both sets of concepts try to attend to geographies of social power and exclusion as intrinsic to the way in which capitalism works. By the end of this chapter, I will make a stronger argument that the notion of interlocking and exclusionary land, labour and credit arrangements provides necessary micro-foundations for an analysis of capitalism as mediated by 'death-dealing displacement of difference into hierarchies' (Gilmore 2002, 16).

Central to my argument is a path not taken by perhaps the most important contemporary progenitor of 'racial capitalism', Cedric Robinson, who developed a critique of Western Marxism and of the transition to capitalism in Europe, but without engaging with the insights of the agrarian Marxist tradition. To be clear, Robinson does not refute or decline this tradition, but its occlusion provides an opportunity to rethink what might yet bolster the concept's contemporary possibilities.

First, what is the provenance of the concept 'racial capitalism' that has returned with a vengeance in scholarship and activism in our time? At roughly the same period as Hart's Java and Bangladesh research, Robinson was working on 'racial capitalism', building on the work of Black American Marxist sociologist Oliver Cromwell Cox. Robinson's *Black Marxism* does several things: it indicts Marxism as 'indisputably Western' at its philosophical foundations and charges 'European Marxists' as myopic about the 'racialism' at the heart of the 'ordering ideas which have persisted in Western civilization' (Robinson [1983] 2000, 2). By racialism, Robinson clarifies that he means 'the legitimation and corroboration of social organization as natural by reference to the "racial" components of its elements' and he adds that this was 'hardly unique to European peoples', but was 'codified, during the feudal period, into Western conceptions of society' with 'enduring consequences'. In other words, his concern was with racial consciousness (see Gilmore 2019), but 'as a material force' that 'would inevitably permeate the social structures emergent from capitalism' (Robinson [1983] 2000, 2). He calls the consequence of this process 'racial capitalism'.

Robinson clearly lambastes historical materialists who presume that capitalism was a negation of the feudal past. Instead, he offers a complex historical argument that the bourgeoisie at the helm of the development of capitalism in Europe emerged from specific cultural and ethnic groups, as did workers, mercenaries, peasants and slaves. This led him to conclude that the racialised classes of European capitalism were prefigured in pre-capitalist forms of difference:

> The tendency of European civilization through capitalism was thus not to homogenize but to differentiate – to exaggerate regional, subcultural and dialectical differences into 'racial' ones. As the Slavs became the natural slaves, the racially inferior stock for domination and exploitation during the early Middle Ages, as the Tartars came to occupy a similar position in the Italian cities of the late Middle Ages, so at the systematic *interlocking* of capitalism in the sixteenth century, the peoples of the Third World began to fill this expanding category of a civilization reproduced by capitalism. (Robinson [1983] 2000, 26; emphasis added)

Fortuitously, Robinson uses the language of the 'systematic interlocking of capitalism', but he does not elaborate on what this might mean concretely. Indeed, this might be an artefact of what Yousuf Al-Bulushi (2020) usefully identifies as Robinson's inclination to the world-systems approach and to the broad sweep of *Annales* school of historiography, as well as more specifically to the arguments of historian Henri Pirenne. What Al-Bulushi does not note is that Pirenne's position in the heated debates on the transition to capitalism in Europe centred on the key role of towns, burghers and migrants. In counterpoint, Maurice Dobb argued that the transition to capitalism in agriculture had been decisive for diverse trajectories of social change. In the 1970s, Robert Brenner's interventions in these debates, and his geographically sensitive analysis of agrarian transitions was key within the revival of agrarian Marxism; indeed, for agrarian Marxists, Dobb and Brenner effectively concluded this debate.

By relying on Pirenne without engaging this debate substantively, Robinson misses the opportunity to engage with the agrarian revival on the uneven geographies of capitalism. This is why agrarian Marxism falls out of his critique of what he sees as Western Marxism. We might wonder what Robinson might have made of the agrarian Marxists as they ventured out to study exactly the phenomenon he points to in the quote above, with a differentiated understanding of 'the peoples of the Third World'. What might Robinson have made of Hart's interlocutors in the 'interlinkage debate' who were concerned precisely with the revival and transformation of social institutions as they sought to determine the specific land, labour, capital and state relations that produced diverse forms of 'systematic interlocking of capitalism' across the colonial and post-colonial world – forms that were always tenuous and prone to produce new rounds of struggle?

Robinson ([1983] 2000) makes several other key arguments in *Black Marxism*. He contrasts what he sees as Western Marxist and liberal traditions with 'the Black Radical Tradition' emerging from histories of struggle against slavery, colonialism and decolonisation; he argues that the violence of primitive accumulation and forced labour in the Americas produced 'the Negro', but also a militant Black intellectual tradition. The second half of his book turns to its exemplars – W.E.B. Du Bois, C.L.R. James and Richard Wright – each engaged in different ways with the tensions between Marxism and Black radicalism. Recall Du Bois' ([1935] 1998, 700–701) historiographically audacious argument that after watching the advance of Northern armies, slaves downed their tools and joined the advancing forces in an armed general strike; but also recall the powerful argument about the multifaceted exclusionary arrangements that supported 'the wages of whiteness'. These were, in Robinson's hands, the product of a revisionist reading of Marxism in relation to Black radicalism.

Robinson's arguments have become iconic; that is, they are often pointed to with reverence rather than grappled with in comradely debate. Yet, there is considerable disagreement about the concept of racial capitalism, both in readings of Robinson and in general. Is it meant as a reminder that capitalism is always racial, as Gilmore (2017, 225; 2020, 171) repeatedly insists? I have tended to this view, to think of the compound term as a categorical aid that signifies that capitalism always involves forms of racial differentiation, though not always through race and often through gender, sexuality and other means (Boyce-Davies 2007; Davis 2020; Vergès 2020). Consider again Gilmore's (2002, 16) expansive conception of racism as 'a practice of abstraction' or 'a death-dealing displacement of difference into hierarchies' or 'a limiting force that pushes disproportionate costs of participating … onto those who, due to the frictions of *political* distance, cannot reach the variable levers of power'. Nothing in this definition limits itself to abstraction through 'race' or to Blackness, a point that Gilmore often makes. Rather, it allows us to consider how capitalism works racially, as a difference-producing machine that always attempts to displace the differences it creates through the production of capitalist space.

Michael Ralph and Maya Singhal (2019) offer a sceptical review of racial capitalism, faulting what they call 'this literature' for imprecision about race and capitalism, a tendency to African-American exceptionalism, and an attention to the violence of accumulation, but not to its transformative power. These critiques are important, but they hinge on an ungenerous reading of many of the thinkers reviewed here and in their article in *Theory and Society*. I agree with their critique of Robinson on Marx's attentiveness to social difference and that his choice of exemplars of the Black Radical Tradition is narrow and masculinist (Ralph and Singhal 2019, 860–861 and footnote 21). Yet, I disagree that 'Robinson sees Marx's influence on the Black Radical Tradition as a kind of straightjacket it must ultimately escape from in order to be free' (863). Most importantly, Ralph and Singhal do not appreciate that the concept of racial capitalism has been useful for interrogating the dialectics of racism and capitalism, when both terms are considered historical, mutable and simultaneously material and cultural/ideological.

This is the position Arun Kundnani (2020) takes, arguing that 'the promise of the term [racial capitalism] lies in its apparent bridging of the economic and the cultural, of the class struggle and the struggle against white supremacy ... It promises a way to close the race-class gap on the Left, a gap through which marched Trump and Brexit, with their nationalist constructions of a white working class.' Kundnani usefully reconstructs the specific conjuncture of late 1970s and early 1980s Britain on the verge of neo-liberalism yet still shaped by active anti-colonial, Black and working-class struggles. Robinson, working at Cambridge University at the time, encountered these struggles through engagement with the journal *Race & Class*, edited by Sri Lankan revolutionary exile and Marxist theorist of the British racial state Ambalavaner Sivanandan (1976). *Race & Class* also published the race–class debates among South African exiles, some of whom used the term 'racial capitalism'. Alongside these thinkers, Hall was actively reworking his understanding of race, racism, Marxism and capitalism in important ways (Hall 2021a, 2021b). These thinkers would have come into contact with Martin Legassick and David Hemson's (1976) pamphlet for the Anti-Apartheid Movement, which critiqued the South African liberal argument that boycotts against the apartheid regime were unnecessary and that capitalism would dissolve the anachronism of apartheid. Peter Hudson (2018) notes that this argument was seriously debated among South African exiles – and, it is worth noting, also by writers such as Sivanandan, Hall and Robinson.

However, Legassick and Hemson's *Foreign Investment and the Reproduction of Racial Capitalism in South Africa* and the critiques it unleashed were a small part of a much broader set of works in the 1970s revisiting the past and present of the South African predicament.

The South African Communist Party (SACP) Central Committee representative for Europe, Vela Pillay, had been writing Marxist critiques of the apartheid economy in the mid-1960s in *African Communist* (Padayachee and Van Niekerk 2019, 51), well before the 'revisionist' historians Shula Marks, Stanley Trapido, Leonard Thompson, Harold Wolpe and others effectively rewrote the radical historiography of segregation and apartheid (Legassick and Hemson 1976; Wolpe 1972). In parallel, Bernard Magubane, who had worked politically with Legassick in Los Angeles in the 1960s, was developing his own Marxist critique (Magubane 1979); in Durban, Rick Turner, fresh from the Sorbonne, brought a particular blend of radical Christianity and critical theory to bear on engaging with the 1972–1973 Black workers' strikes alongside the Black Consciousness Movement and the charismatic Bantu Stephen Biko, whose writings were also in wide circulation (Biko 1978; Turner 1978); and, after his release from Robben Island in 1974, Neville Alexander as 'No Sizwe' was forging his particular blend of Leon Trotsky, Rosa Luxemburg, Paulo Freire and Ivan Illich (No Sizwe 1979). All these thinkers were deeply engaged with the relationship between racism and capitalism as specifically institutionalised in apartheid South Africa.

In his intellectual history of what he calls 'the dialectical tradition in South Africa', Andrew Nash (2009) notes the increased circulation of the term 'racial capitalism' in the late 1970s because it epitomised the analysis of a generation of apartheid's critics. Nash discusses the circulation of the term in the National Union of South African Students (NUSAS) in the late 1960s, citing Marx's 1844 manuscripts, Herbert Marcuse, Jean-Paul Sartre, Frantz Fanon and *New Left Review*; later citations in the 1970s were to Louis Althusser and to Hall's revision of the South African race–class debates in his essay of 1980 (republished in Hall 2021b). Nash insists, I think correctly, that these arguments in South African intellectual life were crucially linked to the struggles of the oppressed; in Robinson's terms, they were already a product of the encounter of Marxism and Black radicalism.

In the 1970s and 1980s, social historians and political economists thinking about and working on South Africa reflected carefully on Brenner's interventions in the debates on transitions to agrarian capitalism. Helen Bradford (1990) argues that Mike Morris, Tim Keegan, Colin Bundy, Henry Slater, William Beinart and others of this burgeoning agrarian scholarship were sensitive to sociocultural and historical variation, as well as to the politics of the time.

Since the 1990s, the standard bearer for South African agrarian studies has been the Programme in Land and Agrarian Studies (PLAAS) at the University of the Western Cape, through the work of Ben Cousins, Lungisile Ntsebeza, Ruth Hall, Andries du Toit and others, including Henry Bernstein in London. Another key strand were scholar activists engaged in documenting rural dispossession through the Association for Rural Advancement (AFRA) and the Surplus Peoples' Project, including Cherryl Walker. A proper accounting of these fields of agrarian study and advocacy is well beyond the scope of this chapter.

Returning to Robinson's *Black Marxism*, much hinges on how one interprets the other compound category that is its title. The 1983 edition does not state clearly what 'Black Marxism' connotes. Robinson's preface to the 2000 edition tries to answer this with: 'Black Marxism [the concept] was not a site of contestation between Marxism and the [Black Radical] tradition, nor a revision', but rather 'a new vision centred on a theory of the cultural corruption of race' (Robinson [1983] 2000, xxxii), but this does not exactly grapple with whether and how the 'new theory' is Black *and* Marxist, as the term implies. Robinson ends the preface modestly: 'I suspect the Black Radical Tradition extends into cultural and political terrains far beyond my competence to relate. In short, as a scholar it was never my purpose to exhaust the subject, only to suggest that it was there.' Robin D.G. Kelley's (2000, xxi) generous foreword to this edition picks up on Robinson's invitation by reflecting on his own work on African diaspora intellectuals and artists drawn to the international surrealist movement: 'I think it could be argued that surrealism served as a bridge between Marxism and the Black Radical

Tradition' (see also Kelley and Rosemont 2009). Kelley has, to my mind, taken Robinson's argument in the spirit intended, and offered a useful way of thinking of the compound term 'Black Marxism' as an invitation for what is to be done.

In a parallel spirit, Angela Y. Davis notes that while Robinson may have initially intended racial capitalism to be a critique of Marxism from the point of view of Black radicalism, 'it can also be a generative concept for new ways of holding these two overlapping intellectual and activist traditions in productive tension' (2020, 205). The key, Davis argues, is to refuse the dichotomy of adherence versus disavowal to Marxism as doctrine, and to rather treat Marxism as open to ongoing internal critique, an 'implicit invitation to push it in new directions' (206). Such an open Marxism is consistent with the way in which Antonio Gramsci saw the work of the militant intellectual as always translating subaltern and Marxist languages of critique. This is also, of course, how Marxist feminists and Marxists of the global South have approached 'Marxism'.

This also is exactly what Hall's 1980 chapter 'Race, Articulation and Societies Structured in Dominance' is driven by, the search for 'a new theoretical paradigm which takes its fundamental orientation from the problematic of Marx, but which seeks by various theoretical means to overcome certain of the limitations – economism, reductionism, "a priorism", a lack of historical specificity – which have beset certain traditional appropriations of Marxism' (Hall 2021b, 233). Unlike Robinson, Hall reconstructs Marxism by attending to 'historically specific racisms' and decidedly not by 'extrapolating a common and universal structure to racism' (234). Historically specific racisms – for instance, in slave plantations or in apartheid Israel – work in relation to other social relations, which leads to Hall's important formulation: 'One must start, then from the concrete historical "work" which racism accomplishes under specific historical conditions – as a set of economic, political and ideological practices, of a distinctive kind, concretely articulated with other practices in a social formation' (236).

While Hall's chapter was a response to South African debates, it is clear that he reflects at this crucial point in the argument on his collective work in *Policing the Crisis* with Chas Critcher, Tony Jefferson, John Clarke and Brian Roberts (Hall et al. 1978), which explains the sudden hue and cry about 'the mugger' in the British press as a symptom of multi-scalar crises ramifying through Britain's 'internal colonies' in which many Black descendants of its former empire live, if not always labour. The powerful final chapter of *Policing the Crisis* recasts criminalised Black youth 'as a class fraction' like the lumpenproletariat valorised by Fanon, Malcolm X and the Black Panthers, a class not only loathed in the realm of ideology but through 'interlocking structures which *work through race* … through the education system, the housing market, the occupational structure and the division of labour'; racism is not just ideological, in other words, it is this complex set of 'interlocking structures' that reproduces racialised classes over time (Hall et al. 1978, 389; emphasis in original). After reflecting on the insights from *Policing the Crisis*, Hall (2021b, 239) offers his now-famous formulation: 'Race is … the modality in which class is "lived", the medium through which class relations are experienced, the form in which it is appropriated and "fought through".' The power of racism is that 'it has performed the function of that cementing ideology which secures a whole social formation under a dominant class' and part of its power is in its ability to refuse its historicity through 'the timeless language of nature' (240–241).

Hall's work of the late 1970s and early 1980s continues on a path not taken in Robinson's *Black Marxism* and it moves beyond a functionalist argument about the relationship between race and class, or racism and capitalism, by attending to lived experience and struggle. The next generation of scholars from the Birmingham Centre for Contemporary Cultural Studies elaborated on this argument through new layers of theoretical and political complexity, brilliantly demonstrated in contributions by Paul Willis, as well as by Paul Gilroy, Hazel Carby and others in *The Empire Strikes Back* (Centre for Contemporary Cultural Studies 1982).

Gilmore is the figure who connects the dots between Robinson, Hall, Sivanandan and Davis, not all of whom appeared to engage with one another through their decades of parallel work. Gilmore's complex material and ideological argument about the attempt to forge hegemony through the racial geography of the prison industrial complex in California, and her focus with Craig Gilmore on rural–urban activism to call this structure into question, shows us that bridging Marxism and Black radicalism is always also geographical work (Gilmore 2007). There is an affinity between Gilmore's carefully theorised and empirically rich analysis of racial capitalist geographies, not all structured by race, and the agrarian Marxist tradition that has shaped Hart's work. Both are premised on rigorous historical and ethnographic research, and both seek to bridge an open Marxism with the traditions of the oppressed. What distinguishes the Black intellectuals I have considered from their agrarian Marxist counterpoints, however, is the imperative with which they foreground the work of subaltern intellectuals in forging critical consciousness, a point that takes us back to the value of Robinson's contributions not only to understanding racial capitalism, but also to opposing it.

Openings: Micro-foundations in practice and consciousness

I would like to conclude with some thoughts for scholars to pick up in new ways, openings emerging from the insights of Hart's critique of the interlocking transactions debate in relation to the Black Marxist tradition that was reconsolidated in important ways in the 1970s. I argue that, in conjunction with a Black Marxist attention to consciousness-raising praxis, the concept of interlocking transactions offers tools to interrogate the micro-foundations of exclusion. More precisely, it reminds us of the importance of a more granular understanding of geographies of racial capitalism, by helping us get at the specific ways in which exclusionary land, labour and credit arrangements interlock with broader social power relations, including relations of the state, military, police, corporations, universities, hospitals, families and other institutions of social domination, which collectively work to reproduce – but also perhaps at times to undermine – the workings of racial capitalism.

What would it mean for Black Marxist scholarship to attend to micro-foundations in ways that I suggest the agrarian Marxism of the last quarter of the twentieth century models for us? Notice that both Robinson and Hall use the metaphor of interlocking elements in the making of capitalism. What the agrarian scholarship I have alluded to – on the revival of bonded labour in late-twentieth-century Gujarat or nineteenth-century Chile, or on the persistence of village-specific tenancy contracts linked to landlord power over land, labour and credit in rapidly transforming rice-farming systems in India, or on the revival of sharecropping in California's strawberry fields in the 1990s – points to is the diversity of ways in which the institutionalisation of land, labour and credit relations might be understood in their concrete articulations, which also involve the reproduction of specific forms of social differentiation and exclusion. With this work in mind, Black Marxist attention to geographies of social change ought not presume to homogenise 'capitalism' or 'the market', but rather attend with this kind of political-economic sensitivity to micro-level institutional mechanisms through which specific forms of power and exclusion in the making of land, labour and credit relations 'interlock' in specific capitalist geographies. Indeed, this is what the critical ethnographic approach offers – a grounded understanding of concrete articulations of power and exclusion.

This is where Hall's 'articulation' emerges as a better concept than 'interlocking' or 'interlinking', as it carries an engagement with the expressive aspect of social relations that the Black Radical Tradition has engaged with consistently. 'Articulation' is the concept that assumes the place that the working concepts 'interlocking' and 'interlinking' sought to grasp (see chapter 8 in this volume).

Two scholars who have produced important scholarship in this vein point to how we might think about engaging in this kind of critical ethnographic research. First, Taneesha Mohan's (2015) insightful doctoral dissertation, inspired by Hart's framework, shows how labour-tying arrangements have intensified in dynamic agricultural areas in Tamil Nadu and West Bengal in India in recent years, and how they reproduce exploitative labour contracts, particularly with Dalit women. Mohan shows how attempts at progressive state intervention in the countryside through the Public Distribution System and the National Rural Employment Guarantee Act have not transformed the social power relations that support the persistence of agrarian unfreedom. Mohan thinks with the categories of Hart (1986a), of labour tying, exclusionary labour arrangements, interlocking transactions and the social power relations that maintain them. I suggest that this work, like my own work in South India and Hart's in Java and Malaysia, is also about socially and spatially distinctive forms of exclusion as immanent to the dynamics of these capitalist geographies. These were always already forms of racial capitalism differentiated through means other than race. The important point here is that race, gender, class and other aspects of differentiation are not treated in Weberian fashion as separable categories, but rather as always only apprehended in their articulation. Extending Hall's formulation, we might say that all forms of social difference are modalities in which class is lived and the notion of modality must be thought in a fully dialectical sense of interrelation, completion and non-identity, so as not to convey a sense of hierarchies of separable oppressions (Hall 2003).

Second, Erin Torkelson's equally insightful research on what she calls 'racial finance capitalism' in past and present South Africa shows how another seemingly progressive state intervention, a post-apartheid cash-transfer programme, has worked to empower a coercive and monopolistic financial system, and how proprietary technology has in fact undermined the cash-transfer programme by deepening racialised indebtedness. Torkelson's work (2020a, 2020b) is on a society saturated by race, where the concept of racial capitalism trips off the tongue with the ease it does in the contemporary United States. Yet, her research also shows that racial finance capitalism is not the product of racial ideology disrupting a race-/class-/gender-neutral landscape of debt, credit and cash transfer to the poor. Rather, Torkelson's insights are indebted to the agrarian Marxist tradition for its complex approach to exclusionary relations of land, labour and credit that take different shape through different geographical histories.

What I am suggesting, by directing the reader to Mohan's and Torkelson's thoughtful research, is that in both studies, under very different conditions, geographies of racial capitalism are reinforced rather than undermined by seemingly value-neutral instruments of state and capital that in fact reproduce very different geographies of racial capitalism (Torkelson 2020a, 2020b).

Inspired by these scholars, I would like to ask a more general question about capitalism in the current moment. We live in a time in which capitalist ideologues cannot argue anywhere, in any society, that capitalism can offer full employment, housing, education, health and access to the means of life to the denizens of any society. After the end of what was called the 'golden age of welfare capitalism' in the North Atlantic world, which was never particularly golden for large numbers of working-class, women, Black, Indigenous and otherwise subaltern people; after the end of twentieth-century state socialisms through 'shock therapy' or capitalist transformation under one-party rule, might we be seeing a renewal of interlocking and exclusionary land, labour and credit arrangements? Rather than a world of capitalist convergence, might we see a return to the kinds of uneven geographies of land, labour and capital noted by agrarian scholars of the global South in the 1970s? Might these interlocking relations tie people into place-specific forms of social domination that prevent spatial and political movement? And might those who dispense insecure work, housing, land, credit and other services accrue a kind of emplaced 'racial' power not unlike the agrarian landlord-moneylender of 1970s agrarian studies?

Perhaps this is the phenomenon that racial capitalism ought to name: the breakdown of the hope of spatially uniform markets in land, labour and capital and a return to a much more spatially differentiated order in which interlocking oppressions force people to agree to super-exploitative wages in exchange for relatively stable housing, life-shortening working conditions in exchange for consumption credit, or periodic credit in exchange for political patronage, and so on, buttressed by notions of differential humanity expressed in a variety of forms of racialisation.

Central to the agrarian Marxist debates of the 1970s was a refusal of a unilinear conception of 'transition to capitalism'. Today, after the end of the mirage of a golden age, contemporary neo-liberal capitalist societies might continue to deploy the rhetoric of individual opportunity and discipline, painting a convergent world in which everything is always for sale, at a bargain, including the value of life. The hegemonic apparatus might also deploy the repressive apparatus against dissent from labour unions, civic organisations and specifically oppressed groups – Black people, Uighurs, Muslims, Palestinians and any worker unsatisfied with a life of precarity. After decades of periodic capitalist crises, and with prolonged, multifaceted crises associated with the Covid-19 pandemic, scholars of contemporary capitalism might attend more carefully to the possibility that we might be in a time of increasingly fragmented, differentiated and exclusionary land, labour and credit arrangements.

Indeed, in contexts of spiralling consumer debt, impermanent and precarious labour, transient housing and perpetually insecure conditions of emplaced livelihood, personalised and exclusionary arrangements might hold out to some the means of fixing the appearance of security. This is where we might return to Hart's warning in 'Interlocking Transactions' (1986a) that exclusionary labour/land/ credit arrangements come with generally demobilising effects for other working-class people. What this reading of Hart on interlocking transactions with Robinson and others on racial capitalism points to is that the interlocking arrangements that create geographies of inequality and exclusion are sustained, and undermined, in everyday ways. We must attend to the latter in order to retain the hope of challenging a fragmenting and differentiating enemy. If there is a final lesson from the Black Radical Tradition about the future's capitalism, it is summarised in one word it has brought into critical consciousness: abolition.

REFERENCES

Al-Bulushi, Yousuf. 2020. 'Thinking Racial Capitalism and Black Radicalism from Africa: An Intellectual Geography of Cedric Robinson's World-System'. *Geoforum*. In press. https://doi.org/10.1016/j.geoforum.2020.01.018.

Bauer, Arnold J. 1975. *Chilean Rural Society from the Spanish Conquest to 1930.* Cambridge: Cambridge University Press.

Bhaduri, Amit. 1973. 'A Study in Agricultural Backwardness under Semi-feudalism'. *Economic Journal* 83, no. 329: 120–137.

Bhattacharyya, Gargi. 2018. *Rethinking Racial Capitalism: Questions of Reproduction and Survival.* London: Rowman and Littlefield.

Biko, Steve. 1978. *I Write What I Like: A Selection of His Writings.* Edited by Aelred Stubbs. London: Bowerdean Press.

Boyce-Davies, Carol. 2007. *Left of Karl Marx: The Political Life of Black Communist Claudia Jones.* Durham: Duke University Press.

Bradford, Helen. 1990. 'Highways, Byways and Cul-de-Sacs: The Transition to Agrarian Capitalism in Revisionist South African History'. *Radical History Review* 46, no. 7: 59–88.

Breman, Jan. 1974. *Patronage and Exploitation.* Berkeley: University of California Press.

Capps, Gavin. 2019. 'Custom and Exploitation: Rethinking the Origins of the Modern African Chieftaincy in the Political Economy of Colonialism'. In *Agrarian Marxism*, edited by Michael Levien, Michael Watts and Yan Hairong, 117–141. London: Routledge.

Centre for Contemporary Cultural Studies. 1982. *The Empire Strikes Back: Race and Racism in 70s Britain.* London: Hutchison & Co.

Chari, Sharad. 2004. *Fraternal Capital: Peasant-Workers, Self-Made Men, and Globalization in Provincial India.* Stanford: Stanford University Press.

Davis, Angela Y. 2020. 'Angela Davis'. In *Revolutionary Feminisms: Conversations on Collective Action and Radical Thought*, edited by Brenna Bhandar and Rafeef Ziadah, 203–215. London: Verso.

Du Bois, W.E.B. (1935) 1998. *Black Reconstruction in America, 1986–1880*. New York: The Free Press.

Gilmore, Ruth Wilson. 2002. 'Fatal Couplings of Power and Difference: Notes on Racism and Geography'. *Professional Geographer* 54, no. 1: 15–24.

Gilmore, Ruth Wilson. 2007. *Golden Gulag: Prisons, Surplus, Crisis, and Opposition in Globalizing California*. Berkeley: University of California Press.

Gilmore, Ruth Wilson. 2017. 'Abolition Geography and the Problem of Innocence'. In *Futures of Black Radicalism*, edited by Gaye Theresa Johnson and Alex Lubin, 225–240. London: Verso.

Gilmore, Ruth Wilson. 2019. 'Foreword'. In *Cedric J. Robinson: On Racial Capitalism, Black Internationalism, and Cultures of Resistance*, edited by H.L.T. Quan, xi–xiii. London: Pluto Press.

Gilmore, Ruth Wilson. 2020. 'Ruth Wilson Gilmore'. In *Revolutionary Feminisms: Conversations on Collective Action and Radical Thought*, edited by Brenna Bhandar and Rafeef Ziadah, 161–178. London: Verso.

Glissant, Edouard. 1997. *The Poetics of Relation*. Translated by Betsy Wing. Ann Arbor: University of Michigan Press.

Hall, Stuart. 2003. 'Marx's Notes on Method: A "Reading" of the "1857 Introduction"'. *Cultural Studies* 17, no. 2: 113–149.

Hall, Stuart. 2021a. *Selected Writings on Marxism*. Edited by Gregor McLennan. Durham: Duke University Press.

Hall, Stuart. 2021b. *Selected Writings on Race and Difference*. Edited by Paul Gilroy and Ruth Wilson Gilmore. Durham: Duke University Press.

Hall, Stuart, Chas Critcher, Tony Jefferson, John Clarke and Brian Roberts. 1978. *Policing the Crisis: Mugging, the State, and Law and Order*. London: Macmillan.

Hart, Gillian. 1986a. 'Interlocking Transactions: Obstacles, Precursors or Instruments of Agrarian Capitalism?' *Journal of Development Economics* 23, no. 1: 177–203.

Hart, Gillian. 1986b. *Power, Labor and Livelihood: Processes of Change in Rural Java*. Berkeley: University of California Press.

Hart, Gillian. 1998. 'Multiple Trajectories: A Critique of Industrial Restructuring and the New Institutionalism'. *Antipode* 30, no. 4: 333–356.

Hart, Gillian. 2002. *Disabling Globalization: Places of Power in Post-Apartheid South Africa*. Berkeley: University of California Press.

Hudson, Peter James. 2018. 'To Remake the World: Slavery, Racial Capitalism, and Justice – Racial Capitalism and the Dark Proletariat'. *Boston Review*, 20 February. http://bostonreview.net/ (accessed 27 January 2020).

Kelley, Robin D.G. 2000. 'Foreword'. In *Black Marxism: The Making of the Black Radical Tradition*, by Cedric Robinson, xi–xxvi. Raleigh: University of North Carolina Press.

Kelley, Robin D.G. and Franklin Rosemont, eds. 2009. *Black, Brown & Beige: Surrealist Writings from Africa and the Diaspora*. Austin: University of Texas Press.

Kundnani, Arun. 2020. 'What is Racial Capitalism?' Talk at the Havens Wright Center for Social Justice, University of Wisconsin, Madison, 15 October. https://www.kundnani.org/what-is-racial-capitalism/ (accessed 12 January 2021).

Laclau, Ernesto. 1971. 'Feudalism and Capitalism in Latin America'. *New Left Review* 67: 19–38.

Legassick, Martin and David Hemson. 1976. *Foreign Investment and the Reproduction of Racial Capitalism in South Africa*. London: Anti-Apartheid Movement. https://www.sahistory.org.za/archive/foreign-investment-and-reproduction-racial-capitalism-south-africa-martin-legassick-and (accessed 27 January 2021).

Lenin, Vladimir I. 1899. *The Development of Capitalism in Russia*. Moscow: Progress Publishers.

Magubane, Bernard Makhosezwe. 1979. *The Political Economy of Race and Class in South Africa*. New York: Monthly Review Press.

Mohan, Taneesha Devi. 2015. 'Labour Tying Arrangements: An Enduring Aspect of Agrarian Capitalism in India'. PhD diss., London School of Economics.

Nash, Andrew. 2009. *The Dialectical Tradition in South Africa*. New York: Routledge.

No Sizwe [Neville Alexander]. 1979. *One Azania, One Nation: The National Question in South Africa*. London: Zed Press.

Padayachee, Vishnu and Robert van Niekerk. 2019. *Shadow of Liberation: Contestation and Compromise in the Economic and Social Policy of the African National Congress, 1943–1999*. Johannesburg: Wits University Press.

Pearce, Robert. 1983. 'Sharecropping: Towards a Marxist View'. *Journal of Peasant Studies* 10, no. 2–3: 42–70.

Ralph, Michael and Maya Singhal. 2019. 'Racial Capitalism'. *Theory and Society* 48: 851–881.

Richards, Alan. 1979. 'The Political Economy of *Gutwirtschaft*: A Comparative Analysis of East Elbian Germany, Egypt and Chile'. *Comparative Studies in Society and History* 21: 483–518.

Robinson, Cedric. (1983) 2000. *Black Marxism: The Making of the Black Radical Tradition*. Raleigh: University of North Carolina Press.

Sivanandan, Ambalavaner. 1976. 'Race, Class and the State: The Black Experience in Britain'. *Race & Class* 17, no. 4: 347–368.

Torkelson, Erin. 2020a. 'Collateral Damages: Cash Transfer and Debt Transfer in South Africa'. *World Development* 126: 1–11.

Torkelson, Erin. 2020b. 'Sophia's Choice: Debt, Social Welfare, and Racial Finance Capitalism'. *Environment and Planning D: Society and Space*. https://journals.sagepub.com/doi/abs/10.1177/0263775820973680.

Turner, Richard. 1978. *Eye of the Needle: Toward Participatory Democracy in South Africa*. New York: Orbis Books.

Vergès, Françoise. 2020. *The Wombs of Women: Race, Capital, Feminism*. Durham: Duke University Press.

Wells, Miriam. 1981. 'Social Conflict, Commodity Constraints and Labor Market Structure in Agriculture'. *Comparative Studies in Society and History* 23: 679–704.

Wolpe, Harold. 1972. 'Capitalism and Cheap Labour-Power in South Africa: From Segregation to Apartheid.' *Economy & Society* 1, no. 4: 425–456.

3 | Relational Comparison and Contested Educational Spaces in Durban

Mark Hunter

'Relational comparison' has roots going back to Gillian Hart's work in South East Asia in the 1970s, although she developed the concept in her book *Disabling Globalization* (2002) and subsequent journal articles. It is a method that compares places, but also recognises connections between these places. Gillian Hart was my PhD supervisor and the concept of relational comparison exemplifies one of the most important lessons I learnt at graduate school, which was the inseparability of method and theory (the latter I had assumed would be a main focus at the University of California, Berkeley). However, research methods have not, on the whole, been central to the discipline of geography, at least compared to ongoing discussions by anthropologists about ethnography and sociologists on theory and method. While radical geographers' strong critique of positivism in the 1970s fundamentally shaped the discipline and its theoretical developments (Castree 2000) when it comes to method, 'doing rather than talking about it has been the dominant intellectual culture' (Barnes et al. 2007, 1). Important exceptions are feminist and anti-racist geographers, who have long emphasised the inseparability of theory and the embodied practices of researchers (see, for example, Pulido 2002; Sangtin Writers Collective and Nagar 2006).

As other contributions to this volume show, relational comparison is part of a dialectical theoretical approach that drew Hart into close engagement with the work of Antonio Gramsci (see particularly chapter 7). However, this chapter foregrounds how Hart's relational comparison approach grew out of her empirical research that centred on Java, Malaysia and, in particular, South Africa from the 1990s onwards. The primary focus is on the situated practices through which methods are constructed. While I hope to show that the relational comparison method has particular strengths, anyone who has worked with Hart knows that she does not impose a strict methodological regime on her students. After reviewing how Hart's own research trajectory gave rise to the relational comparison approach, I show how my study of schooling markets in South Africa uses a research approach with broad affinities to the relational comparison method.

Hart describes the concept of relational comparison in an article titled 'Relational Comparison Revisited' in *Progress in Human Geography*:

> I posited relational comparison in opposition to two other methods of comparison. First, by far the most common approach is based on pre-given bounded units or 'cases'; it includes Weberian ideal-types, but much else besides. Second is the sort of approach that asserts an overarching general process, and sees comparative cases as variants of this process. Instead of comparing pre-existing objects, events, places, or identities – or asserting a general process like globalisation and comparing its 'impacts' – I argued that the focus of relational comparison is on how key processes are constituted in relation to one another through power-laden practices in the multiple, interconnected arenas of everyday life. (Hart 2018, 374–375)

The relational comparison approach thus conceives of places as always connected and stresses how social processes are constructed at multiple scales. As we shall see, this approach both draws from and extends geographical thinking in important ways. How, then, did Hart come to advance this model?

The East Asian roots of relational comparison: From econometrics to power, local to global

Hart began her PhD fieldwork in rural Java in 1975, a decade after President Suharto's New Order government came into power. Key questions economists grappled with at this time included the reasons for the country's high rate of economic growth and its main beneficiaries. Hart had trained at Cornell University in econometrics, an approach that prioritises large household surveys and sophisticated statistical techniques. Yet, as she explains, in the field this method 'soon disintegrated' (Hart 1986b, xiii). Econometrics had no vocabulary to explain gender struggles and class differentiation or connections between household production and the policies of the New Order state. By the time she finished her PhD dissertation on Java, Hart's work was grounded in a single village and the study of 'power, labor and livelihood' (the title of her 1986 book).

While we should be wary of tracing neat origins of relational comparison, two aspects of Hart's turn from econometric methods are instructive: the first is her attention to power and social relations, especially labour and gender; the second is her rejection of the local as a bounded entity. In the 1970s, Marxist political economy placed class relations at the heart of agrarian studies, a movement reflected in the launch of the *Journal of Peasant Studies* in 1973. On the ground in rural South East Asia, struggles over labour and debt forced Hart to reject a view of farm-households as apolitical units of production and consumption (Hart 1992). Hart's approach to power was processual in the sense that she showed how social structures of class and gender were derived from everyday contestations and actions. She writes about Malaysia, her second major area of study: 'The rules defining property rights, labor obligations, resource distribution, and so forth are potentially subject to contestation, and must be constantly reinforced and reiterated' (811).

It was Hart's attention to gendered power relations, however, that animated one of her most well-known articles, her incisive critique of James Scott's influential book *Weapons of the Weak* (1985). Scott, like Hart, worked in rural Malaysia. As the title of his book suggests, Scott foregrounded how peasants engaged in everyday forms of resistance such as foot-dragging and pilfering. In her response in the article 'Engendering Everyday Resistance', Hart (1991) revealed how women – less tied than men to subservient political patronage relationships – developed *collective* social identities that had critical political consequences. A year later, in an article titled 'Household Production Reconsidered', Hart elaborated a wider critique of Malaysia's agricultural take-off as being a gender-neutral 'green revolution', arguing that mechanisation was 'also part of an effort by large landowners and the irrigation authorities to bring recalcitrant women workers under control' (Hart 1992, 810).

Though Hart abandoned the use of large survey data early on in favour of more detailed local research in one village, she did not conceive of the local as a bounded entity. She interrogated 'the connections between macro political-economic forces and processes of institutional change at the local level' (Hart 1986a, 196). Gender too, she argued later, could not be confined only to the household, 'but is invoked and contested in a variety of institutional arenas as part of many kinds of struggles for power' (Hart 1997, 15).

In theorising gender and class in a way that emphasises spatial connections, Hart was increasingly drawn to the work of Doreen Massey. Massey's relational approach to space revealed the importance of understanding the local and global as mutually constituted; that is to say, social relations are always 'stretched out' across multiple scales. Massey's scholarship is illustrative of the rich theoretical and methodological geographical questions in the 1980s and 1990s, some swirling around the study/theorisation of the 'local' (see, for example, Massey 1994;

Sayer 1991). When making sense of her research sites in Asia, Hart was influenced by these critical geographers, whom she says 'blew my mind' (Hart 2018, 373). And in the 1990s, Hart made two critical changes to her own location: she returned to studying her native South Africa and took up a geography position at the University of California, Berkeley, in the United States.

The South African roots of relational comparison

Hart returned to South Africa in 1990, the year that Nelson Mandela was released from prison and four years before the first democratic elections. The liberation movement had defeated apartheid, but the country's economy had suffered from negative real growth for two decades. Educational facilities and property and land ownership were all massively skewed toward white South Africans. Black workers, who had played a major role in defeating apartheid, demanded jobs, skills and high wages – but big business held the keys to the economy. Yet, soon after winning political power in 1994, the African National Congress (ANC) adopted the broadly neo-liberal plan GEAR, which emphasised fiscal discipline and the need for foreign investment (GEAR stands for Growth, Employment and Redistribution, but as many have pointed out, it delivered none of these).

Eager to kickstart the economy, influential writers of South Africa's early industrial policy became attracted to strategies that promised to benefit both labour and capital. Claims that fragmenting consumer markets signalled a new era of 'flexible specialization' (Piore and Sabel 1984) appeared to offer the possibility of a high-skill/high-wage industrial path. A second, widely celebrated model exampled by the 'Asian Tigers' (Hong Kong, Singapore, South Korea and Taiwan) stressed the opportunities offered to developing countries by export-orientated industrialisation. Yet both the 'flec-spec' and Asian Tigers models glossed over South Africa's racialised conflicts and ignored the literature on agro-industrial links in Asia and elsewhere.

Affiliated with what came to be called the University of KwaZulu-Natal, Hart's early work (some of which was undertaken with Alison Todes) explored the rapid growth of small industries in the towns of Ladysmith and Newcastle, located in north-western KwaZulu-Natal. Beginning in the 1970s, the apartheid regime had used generous incentives to lure industries into semi-rural sites in an ambitious attempt to prevent black people from migrating to 'white' cities. This policy attracted numerous small, Taiwanese-owned factories, especially those in the textile and clothing industries, in addition to South African businesses. Hart's point of departure, gained from her Asian experience, was that rural industrialisation could not be separated from questions of land redistribution, household organisation, gender relations and technological implementation.

Ladysmith and Newcastle, like all South African towns and cities, bore the deep scars of racialised dispossession. After 1948 the National Party government embarked on a massive programme of forced removals that extended and ordered colonial patterns of land ownership. Of particular significance was the removal in the Ladysmith/Newcastle region of thousands of families from 'black spots' where black people had bought freehold land. The apartheid state viewed the rightful place of black Africans as being in ethnic 'homelands' like KwaZulu. The history of dispossession and unequal land distribution in South Africa had far-reaching economic and political consequences.

In contrast to her experience in parts of Asia, where she argued that land redistribution had lowered the cost of living and underpinned a social wage, Hart (1998) was struck by how racialised land dispossession, and the attendant agricultural decline, had rendered KwaZulu-Natal's factories unable to lower wages beyond certain levels. Gender relations also differed. In Taiwan, industrial growth rested on patriarchy within households, 'whereby senior males exercise considerable (although not unilateral) power through control of inherited and acquired property' (Hart 1996, 256). In South Africa, Taiwanese industrialists often failed in their efforts to control female factory workers. In the face of growing unemployment, women embarked on complex migration patterns to urban and peri-urban areas. Modern industries, especially in low-wage sectors, often preferred women workers. In South Africa, 'a few Taiwanese industrialists in Newcastle have sought to reconstruct paternalistic labour relations in new ways. The majority, however, resort to varying degrees of gendered and racially charged coercion in their relations with women workers' (267).

As one of the few South African scholars with direct research experience in Asia, Hart saw stark differences between the two regions. In other words, she was critical of flawed comparisons, including the application to South Africa of oversimplified models of Asian export-oriented growth. This was especially important at a time when seemingly inexorable forces of globalisation were used to justify free-market policies in South Africa, as elsewhere. In her article 'Multiple Trajectories', she wrote: 'Comparative Asian trajectories are salient not because they represent "models" to be emulated, but rather because the multiple histories of redistribution together with the diversity of institutional forms – here I particularly have in mind the township and village enterprises in parts of China – provide a means for contesting the disabling discourses of globalisation and market triumphalism' (Hart 1998, 350).

As Hart's long-term research deepened in Ladysmith and Newcastle, the relational comparison approach took firmer shape. The two proximate research sites had similar racial demographics, spatial forms and dependencies on Taiwanese-owned factories. However, Hart showed how different histories of dispossession and contemporary politics affected the two areas' divergent trajectories. Compared to Newcastle, Ladysmith had more contested land removals and militant township politics. There was a lesser tradition of activism in Newcastle, a point underlined when a Taiwanese business leader stood for mayor in Newcastle as a supporter of the Inkatha Freedom Party. Inkatha, revitalised in the 1970s as a Zulu nationalist party, governed the KwaZulu homeland and opposed independent unions in a bid to attract capital to the region.

However, Hart's study was relational, not simply comparative, because it conceptualised the local as connected to wider processes and places. Hart's insistence on 'multiple trajectories ... of socio-spatial restructuring' (see chapter 4 in this volume) provided a powerful critique of what she saw as the 'impact model', in which global capitalism bears down on passive 'locals' (Hart 1998, 2002). Hart's relational analysis considered these two towns' different trajectories in the context of their relationship to each other and to the outside world, including Taiwan and China. This analysis culminated in her 2002 book *Disabling Globalization*. Thus, to return to Hart's description of her approach quoted at the beginning of this chapter, Ladysmith and Newcastle were not just two separate cases, nor were they just cases that illuminated a general process. A relational comparison approach allowed Hart to explore the divergent trajectories of Ladysmith and Newcastle in relation to each other and to outside places.

In 2016 Hart used the *Progress in Human Geography* lecture at the Association of American Geographers conference to return to the concept of relational comparison. One motivation for rethinking relational comparison was to position the approach 'more explicitly as part of a spatio-historical method of Marxist postcolonial analysis' (Hart 2018, 372). Since the original presentation of relational comparison, debates in geography about how to conceptualise the local and the global had receded without resolution. David Harvey remained a central figure in geography, prioritising class divisions, but feminist scholars and scholars of colour continued to 'mess with the project' by showing that capital accumulation depends in part on the production of difference (Katz 2006).

Hart's Marxist post-colonialism contributes not only to efforts to recognise articulations between class and other social relations, but also to going beyond Western-centred approaches. From around the early 2000s, post-colonial geography established itself as a small sub-field, one written off by many geographers as relevant only to those studying the global South (Blunt and McEwan 2003). However, post-colonial urban studies, as it came to be called, intentionally parked post-colonial critiques at the front door of urban studies, a bastion of critical geography.

Jennifer Robinson's book *Ordinary Cities* (2006) casts all cities as 'ordinary' and draws intellectual guidance from non-Western sources, including the Rhodes Livingstone Institute in Zambia, and her native South Africa. This built on her earlier arguments, positing, for example, that a 'spatialized account of the multiple webs of social relations which produce ordinary cities could help to displace some of the hierarchizing and excluding effects of this approach' (Robinson 2002, 545). Debates among urban scholars that include Jennifer Robinson and Marxists that include Neil Brenner have illuminated many a conference in recent years (see Brenner and Schmid 2015; Robinson 2016). Post-colonial urban studies, in its insistence that theory can come from 'ordinary' places and its use of a relational understanding of space, have many similarities to Hart's relational comparison approach (see Ward 2010).

First published online in 2016, Hart's article 'Relational Comparison Revisited' sought to clarify and extend relational comparison and its theoretical, political and empirical aspects (Hart 2018). First, she explains that her use of 'relational' is a dialectic one, referring to David Harvey and Bertell Ollman's use of dialectics. She uses this to build bridges between Marxism and post-colonial urban studies. A second point she makes is the importance of undertaking critical ethnographic methods; here, 'methods' means undertaking work through participant observation in the field. This takes her back to her own research trajectory, beginning in a rural village in Java. Third, she draws from her work on populism in India and South Africa to think through 'spatio-historical conjunctures'. Hart notes how the rise of Hindu nationalism and economic liberalisation in India in the 1990s had strong parallels with Jacob Zuma's rise in South Africa. Her approach remains multi-scalar but begins, in this more recent analysis, at the national rather than the local scale.

Relational comparison and schooling in South Africa

From 2009 to 2019 I studied schooling marketisation in Durban, culminating in my book *Race for Education* (Hunter 2019). The study is not strictly comparative, but it is relational in the sense that it considers changing connections among a number of schools and residential areas. The project's point of departure was that tens of thousands of South African learners do not attend their local schools. Every weekday morning, in every city, scores of taxis, buses and cars move children, black and white, long distances to attend school. When children leave one school, they leave an empty desk for others to use and they take with them resources, including fees. Indeed, in the last three decades, South Africa has moved from having one of the most spatially and racially planned education systems to one of the most marketised systems in the world.

Schooling provides insights into long-standing 'race–class' debates in South Africa that rested on the question of whether inequalities were anchored in racial or class discrimination. The salience of race and class did not disappear when apartheid ended. While the black middle class came to surpass the size of the white middle class, there was not a simple move from 'race apartheid' to 'class apartheid' (Bond 2004). In the educational world, beginning in the mid-2010s, black students led a wave of protests at universities that propelled race to the foreground of South African politics. These were led by the 'born-free' generation (those born after the fall of apartheid), individuals who were 'increasingly disillusioned by and … push[ing] back against the notion of the Rainbow Nation' (Chigumadzi 2015, 1). Moreover, continued racism in schools and society clearly showed that apartheid segregation had not given way to 'non-racialism' – a guiding concept of the liberation movement and the post-1994 Rainbow Nation.

Wider afield, over the last 30 years one of the biggest changes to public schooling worldwide is its subjection to market principles. 'School choice policies are sweeping the globe,' argue David Plank and Gary Sykes (2003, vii). 'In countries on every continent, governments have decided that giving parents more choices among schools is an appropriate policy response to local educational problems.' As Stuart Woolman and Brahm Fleisch (2006) argue, South Africa was an 'unintended experiment' in schooling choice. A crucial turning point came in the dying years of apartheid, when the white minority state encouraged white schools to desegregate classrooms but introduce school fees – in part as a way for schools to retain control over admissions. After winning power in 1994, the ANC ended formal discrimination in schools and passed education legislation that eventually converted two-thirds of public schools into 'no fee' institutions. However, it continued to allow better-off schools to charge fees that financed the employment of extra teachers and facilities such as libraries and computer rooms. Parents with the means, therefore, chose schools in the marketplace.

The background to my study in Durban is as follows: the 1950 Group Areas Act divided South African cities into racial zones based on one of four 'races' (which by the end of apartheid were called white, Coloured, Indian and African/black African). Figure 3.1 shows the three different parts of Durban (or, more specifically, eThekwini Municipality) considered in my study. The first is the township of Umlazi, one of many huge urban townships that apartheid planners built for black Africans, who were barred from living in (and often removed from) 'white' towns. The second is the Bluff, a formerly white, working-class/lower-middle-class suburb located in south Durban. Though privileged by apartheid policy, the Bluff area gained a rough-and-tough image because its early residents typically worked at the nearby port or railway yards and in other local industries. The third comprises the upper parts of the Berea ridge that represent the heartland of 'traditional' upper-middle-class white schools that modelled themselves on British private schools.

Durban, like all South African cities, is marked by massive economic and educational divisions. Umlazi's average per capita income is only R1 900 a month (around £115 or $150).[1] Typical annual school fees in Umlazi total around R200. In contrast, the formerly white Bluff and Berea have monthly per capita incomes of over R10 000. Annual school fees range from R10 000 to over R50 000. These fees equate to formerly white schools' employing on average nine privately funded

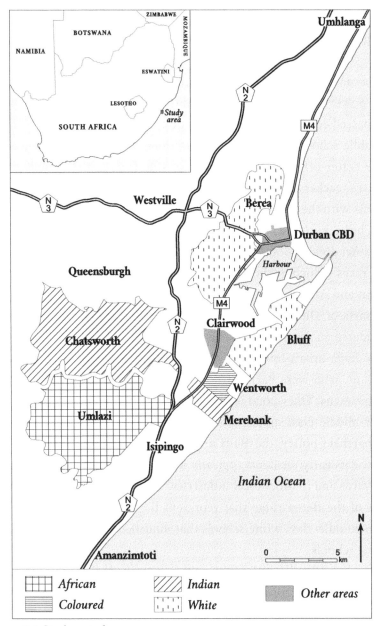

Figure 3.1: Durban study area

Source: Author

Note: In the apartheid period, the townships and suburbs were racially classified as follows: Umlazi (black African); Merebank and Chatsworth (Indian); Wentworth (Coloured); Bluff, Berea, Hilary, Seaview, Montclair, Woodlands and Westville (white).

('governing body') teachers, in addition to those provided by the state on the basis of the school's enrolment.

Because of the profound spatiality of urban inequalities, a learner from Umlazi who climbs the schooling hierarchy today will almost inevitably travel north or west – whether to benefit from better facilities and higher average pass rates or (as noted below) from the 'cultural capital' of a more prestigious English accent. A second pattern I examine appears to be anomalous: white children leaving the residentially whiter Bluff, where half of the residents are still white, to attend school in Berea, where fewer than one in three residents is white. This pattern took some time to evolve, but accelerated in the early 2000s when some Berea schools aggressively poached white students and when Bluff residents put more value on accessing what one parent called, in an interview, 'Harry Potter schools' (implying their fidelity to the British private schooling model).

How then do we study such schooling dynamics? Indeed, why should we? A well-known method for studying schooling is participant observation at one or several schools. Paul Willis' *Learning to Labor* (1977) famously used ethnography to reveal how the rebellion of working-class 'lads' propelled them into working-class jobs. Pamela Perry's *Shades of White* (2002) demonstrates how whiteness is constructed differently in two high schools in the United States, one predominantly white and suburban and the other urban and multiracial. For South Africanists, Nadine Dolby's *Constructing Race* (2001) is an indispensable account of the early period of desegregation in a formerly white Durban school, showing how music and other popular culture mediated racialised interactions.

I conducted 90 interviews with school staff, usually principals or deputy principals, and was often shown around the school. I also interviewed, and in some cases got to know well, members of more than 200 families. However, I did not follow the well-trodden path of conducting an ethnography in a single school for three related reasons. First, South Africa's colonial history makes the differences among schools much more significant than those within a single school. Willis, among others, pioneered critical educational research in the post-Second World War period when divisions among secondary schools were deliberately flattened (in the United Kingdom most became 'comprehensive schools'). Many scholars like Willis showed that a learner's school is immensely important to her or his future and how, within the same school, middle-class learners did better than working-class learners. In South Africa, however, differences among groups of racially designated schools continue to be bigger than differences within particular schools. In 1969–1970, white children were funded nearly 18 times more than black African children, with the gap narrowing to 4 times by 1989–1990 (SAIRR 1992, lxxxv). Today, in the era of school marketisation, one can find in the same city a school charging no fees and another charging R50 000 a year.

A second reason for an approach that considers groups of connected schools is that it captures the dynamic processes shaping the marketised system. Whereas government funding formulas do direct extra resources to poorer schools, when children move to better schools, they take with them fees that enhance the quality of these schools. Schoolchildren's movement is therefore a countervailing force to state redistribution and can, in fact, naturalise divisions in society. In contrast to classic work such as Willis' *Learning to Labor*, which locates hegemony-making processes *within* schools, a focus on marketised schooling foregrounds what we might call 'hegemony on a school bus'.

In other ways, analysis of the schooling market shows the active politics of race and class at work. Race did not wither away in South Africa's new democracy; nor can racism be simply cast as a legacy of what is sometimes called the 'apartheid mindset'. To more than just illuminate the 'fact of inequality', a relational comparison approach to race shows how racism is constituted through links between places (Goldberg 2009). In South Africa, such an approach can provide new insights into how race and class are spatially constituted phenomena that are always changing.

A third reason for my method is that learners' daily movement shines a light on apartheid's racial–cultural hierarchies – that is, it conceptualises schools as bestowing more than simply qualifications or credentials. Apartheid society valued 'white' cultural practices gained in schools – for instance, fluency in the official languages of English and Afrikaans. In contrast, the state established ten ethnic homelands for Africans and made African languages the language of instruction at Bantu Education's primary schools. These cultural hierarchies have enduring legacies. Today, compared to someone attending a historically black school, a white or black learner attending one of the formerly white schools (constituting 7 per cent of all schools) has an advantage in finding work because many new jobs are English-intensive jobs in the service sector and 'white' English has high prestige in South African society.

What my project highlights, then, is the process of hierarchisation among schools and learners. The empirical study is not meant to be comprehensive, but rather to provide an entry point into key processes at work. For this reason, I chose the bottom and the top of the educational market – that is, formerly black African schools in Umlazi (the vast majority) and formerly white schools (the most prestigious and high performing). I discuss only formerly white schools below. When I first began research on these institutions in 2009, I sought to emphasise their very different trajectories and I developed a typological approach – for instance, noting how some schools raised fees to enhance facilities, whereas others made a huge effort to enrol as many white pupils as possible. As I dug deeper, however, I found that most schools had attempted the same tactics at some stage. The difference was often a matter of degree or success.

Specifically, among formerly white schools, five interconnected changes have occurred. First, schools came to compete for 'desirable' students who could increase the prestige of the school – in general these tended to be white, better-off and athletic students. While in the 1990s formerly white schools generally cooperated among themselves, in the 2000s, competition intensified and became increasingly acrimonious as schools used bursaries to attract desirable students – sometimes explicitly to 'poach' certain students.

Second, desegregation among schools became increasingly uneven. By this I mean that it unfolded very differently across the white schooling system. Some schools enrolled predominantly white students, whereas others admitted a majority of black students. This dynamic was not simply a reflection of the residents who lived near a school. For instance, the upper-middle-class Berea suburb desegregated more quickly than the lower-middle-class Bluff area. However, in terms of the schools, the opposite pattern unfolded. This pattern resulted because white children moved from lower-class areas like the Bluff into schools in Berea, and most black students were kept out and pushed into lower-class white schools.

Third, whiter, more upper-middle-class schools charged higher fees. By 2012, schools in the working-class Bluff area charged on average R10 000 a year, whereas those in the more upper-class Berea charged R30 000.

Fourth, spatially, in the late 1990s and 2000s, formerly white schools significantly increased the scale at which they recruited learners. Whereas in the 1960s it was taken for granted that children would attend their local school, by the early 2000s around half of the school advertisements in south Durban's free local newspaper *Southlands Sun* were from schools located outside the newspaper's distribution area. Some advertisements were from schools as far away as Pietermaritzburg (80 kilometres away). Berea schools began to advertise in the Bluff's local paper in the 2000s, and Bluff residents also recall seeing posters on lamp posts advertising Berea schools. From the perspective of Berea's 'traditional' schools, the Bluff was no longer a place of undesirable rough-and-tough working-class whites; instead, it was a pool of potential white learners.

Finally, boys' schools used sports aggressively to promote their status. Though soccer was popular among south Durban's working-class whites, rugby had long been played in elite schools and was the accepted national white sport. After apartheid, some schools made huge investments to improve the performance of their rugby teams. From around 2000, a number of rugby scandals erupted across South Africa that ranged from schools poaching rugby players to sports stars faking their ages. One marketing officer at a rugby-centred school told me that his job was created in 2000 and that his duties include travelling as far as Pretoria (more than 500 kilometres away) to 'buy' rugby stars. A number of boys' schools now invest large sums of money in bursaries to attract desirable students; at one sports-focused boys' secondary school, a teacher told me that 60 per cent of its students had some kind of scholarship. Most of these scholarships were aimed at luring students who are good at sports, notably rugby. Even a referee of schoolboy rugby matches, I was told by the referee's brother (a teacher I interviewed), was on the payroll of a prominent school; he was paid to look out for talent. Schools with more successful rugby teams have remained notably whiter than other schools: their reputations are of fidelity to whiteness and, related but not equivalent, they enrol a higher proportion of white children.

Conclusions: Thinking with relational comparison

As other chapters in this book show, 'relational comparison' works alongside other key concepts that Hart deploys, including multiple trajectories, articulation, populism and translation. In this chapter, however, I stress how Hart developed the relational comparison approach in the context of her empirical work in Java, Malaysia and South Africa. It might seem mundane to note that fieldwork can drive methodological innovations, but one reason this point needs to be made is because of the difficulty many graduate students face today in undertaking long-term fieldwork. As academic jobs have become scarcer, graduate students face intense pressures to become professionalised very early on in their careers – for instance, by writing articles and attending conferences.

As someone with a tenured job, I had the privilege of being able to undertake decade-long fieldwork on schooling in Durban. An established ethnographic approach to studying schools might have involved ethnographic research in a single school or several schools. Given that racial segregation still marks much of the country, this approach could easily be justified. The limitation of this method, however, is that it is unable to fully grasp the *dynamic connections* between schools and place. Central to my approach was therefore to 'follow the children' to show the workings and consequences of the tremendous daily movement of learners in a marketised schooling system. These dynamics have parallels with but also connections to those unfolding elsewhere. In varied ways, most schooling systems around the world have amplified or introduced marketised mechanisms, as a result of which schools have more powers to choose learners and parents to choose schools. To fully understand the way that race, class and other social relations are mutually constituted necessitates a relational approach, rather than one that considers a single school in isolation.

This relational comparison approach to schooling demonstrates how race is never static and always being reworked and sometimes contested. The racial hierarchies that remain today are not a 'legacy of apartheid' – to choose a phrase that is commonly evoked to describe South Africa – but actively produced in relation to class and gender and struggles over space. A relational approach to race in fact has a long history that, in some cases, is only now being recognised within mainstream social theory. Cedric Robinson's *Black Marxism* (2000), discussed in chapter 2, is a unique study of the development of racial hierarchies within Europe, and how these shaped the rise of Atlantic slavery and the black radical tradition. Activists against apartheid themselves influenced and drew from anti-colonial and anti-racist struggles elsewhere on the continent and in the United States, as well as elsewhere. In the contemporary period, Donald Trump's rise is often studied through an American lens but in a recent essay Hart (2021) challenges American exceptionalism by drawing connections to Hindu nationalism in India and populism in South Africa. The strength of the relational comparison approach, as a point of departure rather than a rigid method, is that it encourages researchers to simultaneously focus on everyday situated practices and their relation to forces and contestations taking place in multiple other places.

NOTE

1   Statistics in this paragraph are 2011 census data calculated using Supercross software provided by Statistics South Africa.

REFERENCES

Barnes, Trevor, Jamie Peck, Eric Sheppard and Adam Tickell. 2007. 'Methods Matter: Transformations in Economic Geography'. In *Politics and Practice in Economic Geography*, edited by Adam Tickell, Eric Sheppard and Jamie Peck, 1–24. London: Sage.

Blunt, Alison and Cheryl McEwan. 2003. *Postcolonial Geographies*. London: Bloomsbury.

Bond, Patrick. 2004. 'From Racial to Class Apartheid: South Africa's Frustrating Decade of Freedom'. *Monthly Review* 55, no. 10: 45–59.

Brenner, Neil and Christian Schmid. 2015. 'Towards a New Epistemology of the Urban?' *City* 19, no. 1: 151–182.

Castree, Noel. 2000. 'Professionalisation, Activism, and the University: Whither "Critical Geography"?' *Environment and Planning A* 32: 955–970.

Chigumadzi, Panashe. 2015. 'Of Coconuts, Consciousness and Cecil John Rhodes'. 14th Annual Ruth First Memorial Lecture, Johannesburg, 17 August, University of the Witwatersrand. http://wits.journalism.co.za/wp-content/uploads/2019/03/Ruth-First-Lecture-by-Panashe-Chigumadzi-2015.pdf (accessed 10 January 2022).

Dolby, Nadine. 2001. *Constructing Race: Youth, Identity, and Popular Culture in South Africa*. New York: SUNY Press.

Goldberg, David Theo. 2009. 'Racial Comparisons, Relational Racisms: Some Thoughts on Method'. *Ethnic and Racial Studies* 32: 1271–1282.

Hart, Gillian. 1986a. 'Interlocking Transactions: Obstacles, Precursors or Instruments of Agrarian Capitalism?' *Journal of Development Economics* 23, no. 1: 177–203.

Hart, Gillian. 1986b. *Power, Labor, and Livelihood*. Berkeley: University of California Press.

Hart, Gillian. 1991. 'Engendering Everyday Resistance: Gender, Patronage and Production Politics in Rural Malaysia'. *Journal of Peasant Studies* 19, no. 1: 93–121.

Hart, Gillian. 1992. 'Household Production Reconsidered: Gender, Labor Conflict, and Technological Change in Malaysia's Muda Region'. *World Development* 20, no. 6: 809–823.

Hart, Gillian. 1996. 'The Agrarian Question and Industrial Dispersal in South Africa: Agro-Industrial Linkages through Asian Lenses'. *Journal of Peasant Studies* 23: 245–277.

Hart, Gillian. 1997. 'From "Rotten Wives" to "Good Mothers" : Household Models and the Limits of Economism'. *IDS Bulletin* 28, no. 3: 14–25.

Hart, Gillian. 1998. 'Multiple Trajectories: A Critique of Industrial Restructuring and the New Institutionalism'. *Antipode* 30, no. 4: 333–356.

Hart, Gillian. 2002. *Disabling Globalization: Places of Power in Post-Apartheid South Africa*. Berkeley: University of California Press.

Hart, Gillian. 2018. 'Relational Comparison Revisited: Marxist Postcolonial Geographies in Practice'. *Progress in Human Geography* 42, no. 3: 371–394.

Hart, Gillian. 2021. 'Decoding "the Base": White Evangelicals or Christian Nationalists?' *Studies in Political Economy* 102, no. 1: 61–76.

Hunter, Mark. 2019. *Race for Education: Gender, White Tone, and Schooling in South Africa*. Cambridge: Cambridge University Press.

Katz, Cindi. 2006. 'Messing with "the Project" '. In *David Harvey: A Critical Reader*, edited by Noel Castree and Derek Gregory, 234–246. London: Blackwell.

Massey, Doreen. 1994. *Space, Place and Gender*. Cambridge: Polity.

Perry, Pamela. 2002. *Shades of White: White Kids and Racial Identities in High School*. Durham: Duke University Press.

Piore, Michael and Charles Sabel. 1984. *The Second Industrial Divide: Possibilities for Prosperity*. New York: Basic Books.

Plank, David and Gary Sykes. 2003. *Choosing Choice: School Choice in International Perspective*. New York: Teachers College Press.

Pulido, Laura. 2002. 'Reflections on a White Discipline'. *The Professional Geographer* 54, no. 1: 42–49.

Robinson, Cedric. 2000. *Black Marxism: The Making of the Black Radical Tradition*. Chapel Hill: University of North Carolina Press.

Robinson, Jennifer. 2002. 'Global and World Cities: A View from off the Map'. *International Journal of Urban and Regional Research* 26, no. 3: 531–554.

Robinson, Jennifer. 2006. *Ordinary Cities: Between Modernity and Development*. New York: Routledge.

Robinson, Jennifer. 2016. 'Thinking Cities through Elsewhere: Comparative Tactics for a More Global Urban Studies'. *Progress in Human Geography* 40, no. 1: 3–29.

SAIRR (South African Institute of Race Relations). 1992. *Race Relations Survey 1991/2.* Johannesburg: SAIRR.

Sangtin Writers Collective and Richa Nagar. 2006. *Playing with Fire: Feminist Thought and Activism through Seven Lives in India.* Minneapolis: University of Minnesota Press.

Sayer, Andrew. 1991. 'Behind the Locality Debate: Deconstructing Geography's Dualisms'. *Environment and Planning A: Economy and Space* 23, no. 2: 283–308.

Scott, James. 1985. *Weapons of the Weak: Everyday Forms of Peasant Resistance.* New Haven: Yale University Press.

Ward, Kevin. 2010. 'Towards a Relational Comparison Approach to the Study of Cities'. *Progress in Human Geography* 34, no. 4: 471–487.

Willis, Paul. 1977. *Learning to Labor: How Working-Class Kids Get Working-Class Jobs.* New York: Columbia University Press.

Woolman, Stuart and Brahm Fleisch. 2006. 'South Africa's Unintended Experiment in School Choice: How the National Education Policy Act, the South Africa Schools Act and the Employment of Educators Act Create the Enabling Conditions for Quasi-Markets in Schools'. *Education and the Law* 18, no. 1: 31–75.

4 | Multiple Trajectories of Globalisation: Deforestation in Guatemala's Protected Areas

Jennifer A. Devine

The current geopolitical context of rising nationalism, climate crisis and the Covid-19 pandemic has reinvigorated long-standing debates about the costs and benefits of globalisation. Gillian Hart's theorisation of globalisation in *Disabling Globalization* (2002) provides a valuable approach to understanding these pressing global challenges, among others. She defines globalisation as 'multiple inter-connected trajectories of social and spatial change taking shape in a context of global economic integration' (Hart 2002, 13). This chapter argues that multiple trajectories of globalisation remains a vital concept to think alongside Hart, for three primary reasons. First, the concept explains how socio-spatial change occurs across time and space in multi-scalar processes in politically enabling ways. Second, I show how her analysis of multiple trajectories of globalisation illus-trates her philosophy of praxis at work and can be used as a concept and method elsewhere. Third, I 'translate' the concept to think along-side Hart in Guatemala's northern forests where I study the multiple trajectories of globalisation driving deforestation in protected areas, which include centuries of indigenous land dispossession, civil war violence and the US-led war on drugs. Exploring these trajectories denaturalises pathologising discourses that depict Central American people and places as inherently prone to violence and as environmentally destructive. Rendering clear the trajectories of globalisation that produce places in historically and geographically situated ways provides political ammunition to refute anti-globalisation discourses that are fuelling the resurgence of nationalism, populism and isolationism around the world.

Multiple trajectories of socio-spatial change

Multiple trajectories of globalisation as a concept is not solely about globalisation per se, but is rather a theory of socio-spatial change. The concept originates in Hart's work in a 1998 article in which she develops the term 'multiple trajectories' to describe diverse experiences of industrial restructuring in South East Asia and South Africa, focusing in particular on a comparison of land redistribution in China and Taiwan to black land dispossession and segregation in apartheid South Africa. These multiple, divergent yet interconnected trajectories of rural industrialisation serve as evidence to challenge the hegemony of neo-liberal development 'models'. In particular, Hart critiques the new institutionalism literature that homogenises the diverse experiences of rural industrialisation of the so-called East Asian Tigers by focusing on models of institutional structures and norms that shape people's behaviours (Hart 1998, 333–337). The new institutionalism literature, according to Hart, is 'severely limited in its capacity to illuminate the questions of socio-spatial change posed by contemporary processes of industrial dispersal' (334). She refers to the relocation of manufacturing to the global South, starting in the 1960s, which connected places in China and Taiwan to rural areas in South Africa through the circulation of capital, bodies and commodities. In contrast to the new institutionalism's models, Hart's concept of multiple trajectories of socio-spatial change requires identifying the trans-local historical flows and connections that explain diverse experiences of rural industrialisation: 'Multiple trajectories of rural industrialization … exemplify the multiplicity of capitalisms taking shape in different regions of the world economy' (333).

Rather than producing development models that 'only hold at a very broad and abstract level, the key question … is how to come to grips with the multiple … trajectories through which industrial capital … encounters and intersects with enormously varied agrarian conditions' (Hart 1998, 333). To meet this analytical task, Hart turns to the agrarian literature to illustrate how historically specific 'interlocking dynamics of [land] dispossession and industrialization have been constituted and experienced in locally specific ways that bear directly on future possibilities for reconstruction' (335). She uses the method of relational comparison (Hart 2002, 13–14; 2016) to show how differences in South East Asia and South Africa bear directly on future political possibilities for rebuilding South Africa after the end of legal apartheid. Industrialisation in China and Taiwan followed the redistribution of land and other resources and acted as a 'social wage' for South East Asian industrialists and workers, thus enabling the mobilisation of low-wage labour (Hart 2002, 10, 198–231). Rather than a miracle or a model to emulate, comparative histories of South African, Chinese and Taiwanese development reveal 'trajectories of industrial accumulation *without* dispossession … that enable us to see dispossession not as a "natural" precursor of capitalist accumulation' or something relegated to the past, but as 'an ongoing process that continues to define the conditions of existence for huge numbers of black South Africans' (Hart 2002, 10–11; emphasis in original).

In challenging neo-liberal models, Hart makes a political call for land redistribution as a precursor to rural industrialisation in South Africa. She argues that 'comparative Asian trajectories are salient *not* because they represent "models" to be emulated, but rather because the multiple histories of redistribution together with the diversity of institutional forms … provide a means for contesting the disabling discourses of globalization and market triumphalism' (Hart 1998, 350; emphasis in original).

Hart's critique of neo-liberal models found in the new institutionalism literature has methodological implications. Rather than
modelling geographic and historical specificity away, Hart advo-
cates for a 'processual approach' that 'grounds the exercise of power
in specific institutional and political-economic contexts' (1998, 340).
This processual approach, in contrast to abstract models, 'requires
in-depth ethnographic and historically grounded understandings'
(340). Understanding socio-spatial change calls 'for explicitly spatialized understandings of how local and trans-local processes continually
constitute and reconstitute one another within an increasingly interconnected global system' (341).

Hart's article 'Multiple Trajectories' (1998), focusing on rural
industrialisation and multiple capitalisms, laid the groundwork for
her theory of globalisation in *Disabling Globalization* (2002). Hart's
definition of globalisation brings together various dimensions of her
spatial thinking, which is deeply informed by Henri Lefebvre's ([1974]
1994) theory of the production of space. She defines 'globalization in
terms of the multiple, divergent, but ... interconnected *trajectories* of
socio-spatial change taking place in the context of intensified global
integration' (Hart 2002, 13; emphasis in original). Trajectories are the
'ongoing *processes* through which sets of power-laden practices in the
multiple, interconnected arenas of everyday at different spatial scales
constantly rework place and identities' and 'actively *produce* and drive
the processes we call "globalization"' (13–14; emphasis in original).

Drawing on Doreen Massey's article 'A Global Sense of Place' (1991),
Hart emphasises the 'importance of understanding place and the "local"
not as bounded units, but as nodal points of interconnection in socially
produced space' (2013b, 230). Thinking about rural industrialisation
unfolding in 'multiple, intersecting arenas' (1998, 347; 2002, 2013b)
enables Hart to draw connections across places and to think about scale
in terms of the geographical reach of these connections, rather than
a hierarchical notion of scale that defines the local as particular and
opposed to the global, which is universal.

Globalisation, defined as such, is a discursive project as well as a material one, and is shot through with power relations (Hart 2002, 12, 48–49). How people think about and talk about globalisation and industrial restructuring holds implications for people's lives and shapes political imaginaries and possibilities. Identifying and analysing multiple trajectories of rural industrialisation and globalisation is the means by which Hart challenges the hegemony of neo-liberal one-size-fits-all models. Doing so is critical to enabling alternative practices of knowledge production and political possibilities, and is the focus of *Disabling Globalization* (2002), which illuminates her philosophy of praxis at work.

Disabling globalisation and the philosophy of praxis

One of the main dialectical forces driving Hart's analysis in *Disabling Globalization* and her concept of multiple trajectories of globalisation is not the interplay of global and local processes, but the relationship between power and possibility, between disabling/enabling discourses and practices.

The term 'disabling' in her book's title flags a 'central question of the book: what is it that renders these discourses so disabling, and what might be entailed in more politically enabling understandings?' (Hart 2002, 12). To answer this question, Hart defines and takes to task the 'impact model of globalization'. This model for Hart is one of the most disabling discourses 'defining and delimiting the terrain of political action and the formation of political identities'. She defines the 'impact model' as 'typically framed in terms of the impact of "the global" on "the local"' and argues that it 'conjure[s] up inexorable market and technological forces that take shape in the core of the global economy and radiate out from there' (49). She notes that a number of other power-laden binaries map on the global/local dichotomy – dynamic/static, active/passive, economic/culture, general/specific, abstract/concrete – as well as time/space, where time is seen as an active force and space as a merely passive backdrop or container (13, 49). In doing so, she makes explicit the implications of positivist, binary understandings of space and the ways they connect with and reproduce other violent ways of knowing, being and acting in the world. The impact model is disabling because it suggests that local places have no power, agency or constitutive role in global processes. Rather than suggesting multiple trajectories and paths of socio-spatial change, the impact model suggests that, as Margaret Thatcher (in)famously stated, there is no alternative to neo-liberalism (Flanders 2013).

To contest the impact model, *Disabling Globalization* uses the concept of multiple trajectories to examine the divergent outcomes of neo-liberal reforms in two places, Ladysmith-Ezakheni and Newcastle-Madedeni in South Africa. These neighbouring sites in the province of KwaZulu-Natal experienced political reforms in the 1990s that decentralised state power to local government agencies in the context of the national government's neo-liberal Growth, Employment and Redistribution (GEAR) austerity programmes and Taiwanese and Chinese-led industrialisation. Hart shows how the unique histories of racialised land dispossession (in South Africa), agrarian reform (in China, Taiwan) and the African National Congress (ANC) party politics in the townships ultimately produced disparate socio-spatial outcomes in what appear to be, superficially, similar places.

In analysing the multiple trajectories of globalisation connecting South East Asia and South Africa, Hart denaturalises racialised land dispossession in South Africa by illustrating the centrality of agrarian reform in the success of the Asian Tigers. Hart suggests that the dire conditions of landlessness for many black South Africans constitute an articulating set of issues that can bring together people from different political factions, regions and ethnicities to advocate for redistributive policies and the provision of a 'social wage' (Hart 2002, 10, 302–303). In doing so, she puts the question of land redistribution front and centre in industrial restructuring and neo-liberal debates to create more enabling and politically progressive understandings of globalisation and development possibilities.

This example of her use of multiple trajectories of globalisation as a concept and a method of analysis illuminates her philosophy of praxis at work, which functions as a two-edged sword – providing cutting critiques and suggesting strategies for reconstruction. Her work does not provide a model to follow; rather, she shows us what the philosophy of praxis looks like in practice. The philosophy of praxis is the combination of theory and social activism; it is the production of knowledge to transform the world, starting with the actually existing relations of power defining the present and working to transform them (Marx [1845] 1978). The philosophy of praxis enables many critical thinkers to strengthen and explain their integrated scholarship and activism. Hart defines the philosophy of praxis as 'the collective practices and processes through which fragmentary common sense becomes coherent, enabling new critical understandings and actions' (Hart 2013a, 308).

Rather than abstract utopias, the philosophy of praxis is grounded in the material and discursive conditions of the day and foregrounds contradictions in power relations and 'common sense' as points of political entry. Contradictions are important because they illuminate weaknesses in hegemonic relations of force, weaknesses that can serve as starting points to create change. Hart, citing Antonio Gramsci, argues, 'the philosophy of praxis does not aim at the peaceful resolution of existing contradictions in history and society but is rather the very theory of these contradictions' (2013a, 308). Hart's philosophy of praxis shows how disabling moments can enable alternatives; they produce them, relationally and dialectically. The philosophy of praxis seeks out these enabling moments with the aim of collectively developing and pursuing alternatives.

In *Disabling Globalization*, Hart identifies local government as a key site of contradictions in the first phase of post-apartheid neo-liberal restructuring (Hart 2002, 12). In her 2013 book *Rethinking the South*

African Crisis, she argues that local government has become *the* key site of contradictions and an important terrain of the ANC's efforts to manage poverty and deprivation in a capitalist society defined by massive inequalities (2013b, 5). In this book, Hart shows how Nelson Mandela's Rainbow Nation platform and neo-liberal reforms worked at odds: while the ANC's identity politics tried to weave South Africans together, neo-liberal levels of austerity, inequality and dispossession tore them apart. These contradictions are not only the product of transnational neo-liberal reforms, but also their intersection with two dialectical trajectories of socio-spatial change occurring in South Africa: de-nationalisation and re-nationalisation (Hart 2013b). On the one hand, processes of de-nationalisation further integrate South Africa into global financial markets, while on the other hand, the ANC's identity politics breed re-nationalisation and xenophobia at the same time. In the context of these dialectical forces, the ANC's populist promises have fallen subject to betrayal and backfire, thus enabling a moment to articulate alternative readings of the past in order to craft a more equitable vision of the future, particularly in relation to redistributive policies. Hart (2013b) argues this political path is a viable alternative to the nationalism and xenophobia characterising Jacob Zuma's populism that emerged from the contradictions in the ANC's passive revolution.

In both the 2002 and 2013 books, Hart argues that 'any possibility for an alternative politics must be grounded in local historical geographies and must also be capable of forging connections with dynamics beyond the local' (Hart 2013b, xx). Thus, in contrast to the impact model, the 'local' is not a 'powerless place' (Hart 2002, 49). Recovering the agency of local people and places in processes of globalisation is part of the enabling project the 2002 book's title alludes to. Hart's analysis of globalisation breathes political life back into people and places that are no longer seen as passive victims of the forces of globalisation, but are active, albeit unequally empowered, participants in the formation of trans-local relations.

Multiple trajectories of globalisation driving deforestation in Guatemala's protected areas

Appropriating and employing the concept of multiple trajectories of globalisation requires a process that Stefan Kipfer and Hart (2013), drawing on Gramsci, call 'translation'. 'From a Gramscian perspective,' they argue, 'the chief task of politics is to engage in a practice of translating – elaborating, modifying, and transforming meaning from context to context' (2013, 326). Hart reminds us that 'Gramsci's concepts are not 'abstract model[s] that can simply be applied or against which specific "cases" can be measured. The challenge, both analytical and political, is to rework – or as Gramsci might have said, "translate" – it in relation to the forces thrown up by a different set of circumstances' (2013b, 9–10). Once again we see how multiple trajectories of globalisation is not just a theoretical concept; it is also a methodological framework, a concept-method.

I take Hart's concept of multiple trajectories of globalisation into Guatemala's Maya Biosphere Reserve to identify systemic drivers of environmental degradation. This allows me to denaturalise discourses of 'ungovernability' (*ingobernabilidad*) circulating among reserve stakeholders and policymakers who define the reserve as lawless and criminalise residents in ways that obscure the trajectories of socio-spatial change driving deforestation. I further use the concept to identify political possibilities for transformative change in Guatemala's post-war era that have failed to bring peace by illustrating how Maya Biosphere residents have leveraged conservation contradictions in order to contest and redefine post-war land tenure and resource usufruct rights and create one of the world's largest communally managed forests. Following Hart's lead, my translation also employs the philosophy of praxis' dual practice of providing critical insights about the present by rereading the past, while focusing on slippages and contradictions within existing power structures to advocate for more democratic and equalitarian modalities of rule and forms of governance.

Guatemala's immense Maya Biosphere Reserve spans 21 602 square
kilometres and comprises half of Guatemala's border with Mexico
(see figure 4.1). Since the Maya Biosphere Reserve's creation in 1990,
a spatial paradox or contradiction has defined conservation efforts.
The western half of the reserve is home to two large national parks,
Laguna del Tigre and Sierra del Lacandón, where land use change is
prohibited (see figure 4.2); yet the national parks have experienced
some of the world's highest deforestation rates since their creation
(Carr 2008; Hodgdon et al. 2015). In contrast, the eastern half of the
reserve that is home to nine community forest concessions, managed
by reserve residents and neighbouring communities, has fared much
better, although conservation outcomes between concessions are
uneven (Hodgdon et al. 2015).

I use the concept-method of trajectories of globalisation to unpack
this conservation paradox, identify drivers of land use change and
deforestation, and challenge disabling discourses that blame these
dynamics on the reserve's residents and neighbours. I examine the
multiple trajectories of globalisation producing the Maya Biosphere
to illuminate how deforestation of the reserve is the spatial product
of interconnected dynamics unfolding at national and global scales.
In part, Maya Biosphere deforestation is the product of Guatemala's
perversely unequal and racist political and economic system. In short,
'illegal' settlement in the reserve is the product of landlessness and
poverty in the rest of the country (Grandia 2012). In 2006, 16 years
after the Maya Biosphere's creation, these two western parks, total-
ling 8 786 square kilometres, had five legally residing communities,
with an estimated population of 2 800 people (CONAP and WCS
2018). These communities were granted legal residency while a congressional decree prohibited future settlement in the 'core zones' of
the national parks (Nations 1996). In 2015, there were an estimated
25 550 people living in 37 communities, 32 of which the government designates as illegal settlements that are vulnerable to eviction
(CONAP and WCS 2018).

Figure 4.1: The Maya Biosphere Reserve
Source: Author

This 'illegal' population growth in the national parks can only be explained by a critical reading of the past, by excavating the multiple trajectories of globalisation that have produced this contemporary critical conjunction that I am describing as a conservation paradox. These multiple trajectories include centuries of indigenous land dispossession (Grandia 2012), the reversal of the 1952 land reform, state-sanctioned wartime colonisation of the department (province/state) of the Petén (Schwartz 1990), decades of civil war violence (Jonas 2000; REHMI 1998) and failed market-assisted land reform (Alonso-Fradejas 2012; Gauster and Isakson 2007) – to name a few of the most prominent issues. These key historical moments, collectively, in mutually reinforcing ways, have created a situation of structural landlessness, inequality and poverty that endures today and drives colonisation in the Maya Biosphere Reserve. However, this trajectory of socio-spatial change, my colleagues and I argue, is responsible for only a small percentage of deforestation in the parks (Devine et al. 2020a, 2020b).

Rather, we argue that the US-led war on drugs is responsible for most of the deforestation in the Maya Biosphere Reserve (Devine et al. 2020a, 2020b). Drug trafficking's environmental impacts during the war on drugs in Guatemala are not anomalous. Emerging research on the topic describes how drug trafficking, as a trajectory of socio-spatial change, correlates (Sesnie et al. 2017) and causes (Tellman et al. 2020) forest loss in Central America, drives narco-deforestation in the Honduran Mosquitia (McSweeney et al. 2014) and threatens regional conservation efforts and ecosystems (Wrathall et al. 2020). Drug traffickers are deforesting to plant pasture and ranch cattle as a means of laundering money and claiming drug-smuggling territory (Devine et al. 2020b; McSweeney et al. 2017). There are over 200 clandestine airstrips in the Maya Biosphere, which makes up 50 per cent of Guatemala's border with Mexico (Devine et al. 2020b). Our collaborative mixed-method work draws on critical ethnography (Hart 2004) and relational comparison (Hart 2002) to foreground the multiple trajectories of globalisation producing narco-deforestation and systematic landlessness in Guatemala (Devine et al. 2020a). We also use remote sensing and geographic information system (GIS) analysis to provide evidence that illegal cattle ranchers, not indigenous farmers, are responsible for an estimated 65 per cent of deforestation in the Maya Biosphere's western national parks (Devine et al. 2020a). Figure 4.2 illustrates

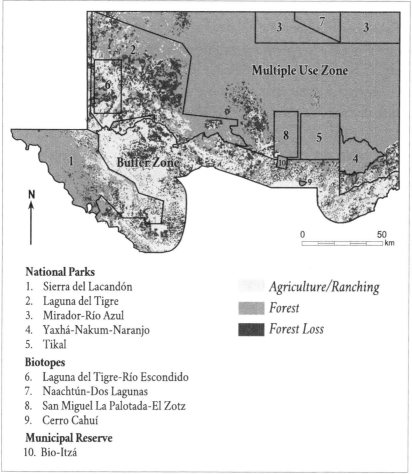

Figure 4.2: Forest loss in the Maya Biosphere Reserve, 2015
Source: Devine et al. 2020a

the Maya Biosphere's conservation paradox: narco-trafficking cattle ranchers are driving deforestation in the reserve's west where national park status should prevent land use change, while in the east, community foresters live and sustainably manage natural resources and forest cover remains.

Cocaine trafficking in Guatemala surged in the early 2000s, following the re-routing of cocaine-trafficking routes away from the Caribbean to Mexico, and then through Central America (Grillo 2012).

The US-led war on drugs in Colombia in the 1990s resulted in the death of Pablo Escobar, but it did not end the cocaine trade; it just changed its geography, as Colombians began offloading the risk and profit of smuggling cocaine into the United States to Mexican cartels (Dudley 2010). The Mexican cartels' profits soared, as did their political power and public visibility (Tuckman 2012). When Felipe Calderón was elected president of Mexico in 2006, he declared war on 'narcos' and the resulting so-called drug wars have claimed the lives of an estimated 200 000 people in Mexico alone (Lakhani and Tirado 2016). The Mexican drug wars spurred another balloon effect and the cartels hopped over the remote and forested Guatemalan border into the Maya Biosphere Reserve (Dudley 2010).

Rather than addressing the structural forces operating at connected national and global scales driving deforestation in the reserve, dominant explanations blame deforestation in the national parks on landless indigenous and non-indigenous farmers. Many reserve actors discuss this combination of the region's most powerful and most precarious both illegally living and working in the reserve as a problem of *ingobernabilidad*, a lack of reserve governance (Alvarez 2017; CONAP 2006; CONAP and WCS 2018). Reserve stakeholders collapse these two very different drivers of reserve colonisation into the shared discursive frame of ungovernability for two primary reasons. First, when powerful reserve actors from the military, government and conservation organisations gather to discuss security and conservation policy in the Maya Biosphere Reserve, there are most likely people present that have ties to narco-trafficking organisations. These individuals are happy to let peasants take the blame for deforestation activities as narco-traffickers fund their financial campaigns and retirements. Second, for everyone else – the vast majority of state, military and conservation workers – denouncing narco-trafficking activities is life threatening. Rather than calling out narco-capitalised 'powerful ranchers' as drivers of deforestation in the reserve in mixed company, reserve actors evoke the discourse of ungovernability. The ambiguity built into this euphemism lumps poor landless squatters and drug traffickers into the same criminal category, thus muddling the different means, motivations and impacts of these actors and their activities (Devine et al. 2020b).

The ungovernability discourse further delimits and contains the drivers of deforestation in the Maya Biosphere to the area enclosed in the reserve's boundaries in ways that analytically cut the constituting ties between the US-led war on drugs and reserve deforestation. Reserve discourses of ungovernability pathologise people and places in ways that render local, biological and apolitical the trans-local, structural forces driving socio-spatial change. Regardless of the intentions of people who use the term, the *ingobernabilidad* discourse criminalises park residents because it puts them in the same category and discursive frame as narco-affiliated cattle ranchers who are driving environmental degradation in the park (Devine et al. 2020b).

Denaturalising pathologising discourses, like reserve ungovernability and the impact model of globalisation, is part of translating the concept-method of multiple trajectories of socio-spatial change. For Hart, denaturalising globalisation (2002), denaturalising dispossession (2006, 2013b) and denaturalising nationalisms (2013b, 225) means questioning 'common sense', taken-for-granted understandings and histories to produce new insights. In *Disabling Globalization*, Hart identifies the ways orthodox economics assigns qualities of nature and natural phenomena to render teleological, technical and apolitical the winds and tides of the market (2002, 13). Denaturalising often means literally questioning 'scientific' knowledge production, the social construction of 'nature' and the multiplicity of binary ways of knowing (that is, global/local, nature/culture, male/female) that undergird unequal power relations.

The practice of translating multiple trajectories of globalisation into my own work functions more as a method rather than a model, and has, perhaps not surprisingly, led to my own engagement with the philosophy of praxis. Unpacking the Maya Biosphere's multiple trajectories of globalisation that inform the present enables me to disable and denaturalise pathologising discourses and at the same time advocate for politically enabling alternatives. Reading alongside Hart reminds me to seek out contradictions and political possibilities, even in moments of crisis like these, which point to community-based resource management as a viable and proven strategy to build a more democratic, equitable and environmentally sustainable future in the Maya Biosphere (Devine 2018; PRISMA 2014).

Reserve residents experienced the 1990 creation of the Maya Biosphere as an act of land dispossession (Sundberg 1998). In response, they organised themselves politically to defend their land rights. Community forestry was not part of the Guatemalan state's original plans for the Maya Biosphere; the state planned to grant private, industrial concessions in the eastern half of the reserve, designated as a 'multiple use zone' where sustainable forestry would be permitted. Reserve residents became aware of these plans at the same moment a central contradiction in reserve governance emerged. The Guatemalan government was unable to enforce the new conservation laws, particularly in the reserve's western national parks, and deforestation, poaching and trafficking activities occurred with impunity (Monterroso and Barry 2012). It became obvious to conservationists and state officials that reserve residents needed to play a role in conservation and governance efforts.

With the support of the global conservation organisations, residents seized this moment of conservation crisis to call for the creation of a community forestry system in the eastern part of the reserve. They further leveraged a key clause in the 1995 Peace Accord on 'the agrarian and socio-economic question' to campaign for their territorial and resource rights. The Accord stipulates that the Guatemalan government would grant 100 000 hectares of communally managed lands to organised peasants (Jonas 2000). For ten years, residents fought for and established community forestry concessions that gave them the exclusive right to sustainably harvest timber and non-timber products in their concession territories (Cortave 2003). Today, 20 years later, despite many threats to the process, including the murder of four leaders who defended their concession lands from narco cattle-ranchers, community forestry successfully conserves the forest and alleviates poverty (Monterroso and Barry 2012). It economically benefits 35 000 people a year and deforestation rates are much lower in communally managed lands than in the national parks in the western half of the reserve (Hodgdon et al. 2015).

Elsewhere, I argue that the success of this social and environmental justice movement has depended on the articulation of a rights-bearing subject, the forest concessionaire, which brings reserve residents together across racial, ethnic, religious and class differences, as well as ex-members of both the army and the guerrillas (Devine 2018). The articulation of this identity took place through several key moments of political struggle over land rights. The forest concessionaire as a rights-bearing subject was forged in response to lost usufruct rights at the Maya Biosphere's creation in 1990, through political organising and activism in the 1990s, as well as during a three-year legal battle that threatened the integrity of the concession system in the early 2000s (Devine 2018). Through the political struggle to create and defend their movement, Guatemalan forest concessionaires have appropriated conservation efforts to create a powerful platform of transformative change. Today, Maya Biosphere community foresters play a leading role in reserve governance, policy formation and the re-territorialisation of contemporary power in northern Guatemala, albeit not always under conditions of their own choosing (Devine 2018).

While I have translated the concept of multiple trajectories of globalisation into the northern forests of Guatemala, this concept-method is also useful to understand the rise of contemporary right-wing nationalist movements around the world. In the United States, Donald Trump, like many of his nationalist counterparts in Europe, ran his political campaign under the mantra of 'anti-globalism', defined by policy promises of border building, deporting immigrants and diplomatic and military isolationism (Saval 2017). Hart's concept-method of trajectories of globalisation can be used to denaturalise the 'anti-globalism' discourses fuelling these movements by making clear the historical and geographical connections producing places and contemporary crises. Hart (2013a) insists this is not a project for historians, but an integral part of the philosophy of praxis, in which denaturalising discourses and practices of anti-globalism are a collective practice and process occurring among 'organic intellectuals' (Gramsci 1971) in everyday life.

Hart's research on populism and nationalism in South Africa in her book *Rethinking the South African Crisis* further provides a framework for understanding the rise of right-wing populism around the world (2013b). In 'Gramsci, Geography, and the Languages of Populism' she challenges us to think carefully about the allure of populism, to denounce simplistic claims that the supporters of right-wing populists are 'manipulated mindless masses' (Hart 2013a, 302) and to critically analyse the process, experiences and memories fuelling the rise of 'exclusionary nationalisms and right wing populist politics' (Hart 2020, 239). Hart's book *Rethinking the South African Crisis* (2013b) aims to do just that by situating the rise of right-wing nationalism in what she calls a 'global conjunctural frame', which focuses on 'major turning points when interconnected forces at play at multiple levels and spatial scales in different regions of the world have come together to create new conditions with worldwide implications and reverberations' (242). Her project challenges readings of the rise of right-wing nationalism as a response to the 2008 economic crisis, or as emanating from Europe and the United States, or the election of Trump in the United States as an aberration to liberal democracy (240–241), by unpacking the multiple historical-geographical trajectories of socio-spatial change that produce them.

In doing so, Hart rejects simplistic, economistic and Eurocentric explanations regarding the contemporary rise of right-wing nationalisms. She argues that the fallout of what she calls 'Cold War Era' projects – that is, the creation of secular, socialist democracies in the global North, the 'Development' in the global South, as well as their antecedents in settler colonialism, imperialism and processes of nation formation – are 'crucial to understanding the intensification of exclusionary forms of nationalism and right-wing politics in the post-Cold War era' (Hart 2020, 243). Her 'global conjunctural frame' builds on, rather than replaces, her earlier theorisation of multiple trajectories of globalisation and thus further illustrates the enduring utility of this concept-method to understanding how Hart theorises socio-spatial change to face evolving political demands (2020, 239).

Conclusion

Multiple trajectories of globalisation remains a vital concept for contemporary critical scholarship and activism for three key reasons. First, the concept elucidates Hart's theorisation of socio-spatial change. Hart's analytical concepts are not easily separated from one another because they form part of an interconnected web of analytical categories that define one another in mutually constituting ways. The concept of multiple trajectories of globalisation provides a way into this totality and illuminates how she theorises the social production of space, the local–global dialectic and how trans-local, neoliberal reforms and capitalist development articulate with places to rework both simultaneously.

Second, her use of the concept of multiple trajectories of globalisation illustrates her philosophy of praxis at work when she disables the 'global impact model' of globalisation in order to identify potential paths of political change in post-apartheid South Africa (2002, 49). Hart's theorisation of multiple trajectories of globalisation breathes political life and possibility back into local spaces and actors who participate in the processes producing globalisation and other forms of socio-spatial change.

Third, I suggest the concept of multiple trajectories of globalisation is also a method that can be translated to study other trajectories of socio-spatial change constituting other places. Hart, drawing on

Gramsci, argues that the philosophy of praxis calls for translation, both as a method that translates concepts to other geographical-historical contexts, and as the practice of building political alliances across space through the work of political organising (Kipfer and Hart 2013). In this chapter, I have illustrated how I translate the concept of multiple trajectories of globalisation into my own work and into the forests of northern Guatemala to intervene in academic and policy debates regarding the paradoxical outcomes of conservation efforts. Using the concept-method of multiple trajectories of globalisation enables me to denaturalise the political pathologies operating in the Maya Biosphere Reserve that render individual, local, biological and apolitical the structural forces driving deforestation. I show how the pathologising discourses of 'ungovernability' render invisible the roles that enduring landlessness and the US-led war on drugs play in driving deforestation. I further translate the concept of multiple trajectories of globalisation to do the work of critically rereading the past in northern Guatemala, which points to the political potential of community-based forestry as a political platform for the redistribution of resources, territory and political power.

Lastly, this concept still has a lot of work left to do. Unpacking the multiple trajectories of socio-spatial change enabling the rise of nationalist, populist movements around the world is the focus of Hart's book *Rethinking the South African Crisis* (2013b), in which she elaborates a 'global conjunctural framework' that illustrates the enduring centrality of the concept of multiple trajectories of globalisation and the philosophy of praxis in her work. She argues that 'calls for the electoral defeat of the right through a politics of left populism … are dangerously simplistic' (Hart 2020, 258). Rather, the task requires analytically unearthing the deep-seated, historical-geographical trajectories of globalisation and socio-spatial change articulating expressions of nationalism today with the aim of deepening our understanding of 'the challenges, opportunities, and possibilities for alliances and creative political action' (Hart 2020, 258).

ACKNOWLEDGEMENT

I would like to thank Melanie Samson, Jenny Baca and Kimberly Kinder for their comments on this chapter, and Melanie Samson, Sharad Chari and Mark Hunter for editing this collection. Last, but not least, I would like to thank Gillian Hart for the inspiration.

REFERENCES

Alonso-Fradejas, Alberto. 2012. 'Land Control-Grabbing in Guatemala: The Political Economy of Contemporary Agrarian Change'. *Canadian Journal of Development Studies/Revue canadienne d'études du développement* 33, no. 4: 509–528.

Alvarez, Carlos. 2017. 'Selva Petenera Muere sin que Nadie Haga Nada'. *Prensa Libre*, 30 April. http://www.prensalibre.com/guatemala/comunitario/selva-petenera-muere-sin-que-nadie-haga-nada (accessed 12 January 2022).

Carr, David L. 2008. 'Farm Households and Land Use in a Core Conservation Zone of the Maya Biosphere Reserve, Guatemala'. *Human Ecology* 36, no. 2: 231–248.

CONAP (Consejo Nacional de Áreas Protegidas). 2006. *Estudio Tecnico Integral Asentamientos Humanos Parque Nacional Laguna del Tigre-Biotopo Protegido Laguna del Tigre – Rio Escondido, Petén, Guatemala*. San Benito, Guatemala: CONAP.

CONAP (Council of National Protected Areas) and WCS (Wildlife Conservation Society). 2018. 'Monitoreo de la Gobernabilidad en la Reserva de la Biosfera Maya.' https://conap.gob.gt/monitoreo-de-la-gobernabilidad-en-la-reserva-de-la-biosfera-maya-actualizacion-2017/ (accessed 7 January 2020).

Cortave, Marcedonio. 2003. *La Experiencia de ACOFOP en Petén, un Proceso Arduo de Gestión Política, Asociación de Comunidades Forestales de Petén*. San José, Costa Rica: Centro de Derecho Ambiental y de los Recursos Naturales (CEDARENA).

Devine, Jennifer. 2018. 'Community Forest Concessionaires: Resisting Green Grabs and Producing Political Subjects in Guatemala'. *Journal of Peasant Studies* 45, no. 3: 565–584.

Devine, Jennifer A., Nathan Currit, Yunuen Reygadas, Louise I. Liller and Gabrielle Allen. 2020a. 'Drug Trafficking, Cattle Ranching and Land Use and Land Cover Change in Guatemala's Maya Biosphere Reserve'. *Land Use Policy* 95. https://doi.org/10.1016/j.landusepol.2020.104578.

Devine, Jennifer A., David Wrathall, Nate Currit, Beth Tellman and Yunuen Reygadas Langarica. 2020b. 'Narco-Cattle Ranching in Political Forests'. *Antipode* 52, no. 4: 1018–1038.

Dudley, Steven S. 2010. *Drug Trafficking Organizations in Central America: Transportistas, Mexican Cartels and Maras.* Washington, DC: Woodrow Wilson International Center for Scholars, Mexico Institute.

Flanders, Laura. 2013. 'At Thatcher's Funeral, Bury TINA, Too'. *The Nation,* 12 April. https://www.thenation.com/article/thatchers-funeral-bury-tina-too/ (accessed 12 January 2022).

Gauster, Susana and S. Ryan Isakson. 2007. 'Eliminating Market Distortions, Perpetuating Rural Inequality: An Evaluation of Market-Assisted Land Reform in Guatemala'. *Third World Quarterly* 28, no. 8: 1519–1536.

Gramsci, Antonio. 1971. *Selections from the Prison Notebooks of Antonio Gramsci.* Edited and translated by Quintin Hoare and Geoffrey Nowell Smith. New York: International Publishers.

Grandia, Liz. 2012. *Enclosed: Conservation, Cattle, and Commerce among the Q'eqchi' Maya Lowlanders.* Seattle: University of Washington Press.

Grillo, Ioan. 2012. *Narco: Inside Mexico's Criminal Insurgency.* New York: Bloomsbury.

Hart, Gillian. 1998. 'Multiple Trajectories: A Critique of Industrial Restructuring and the New Institutionalism'. *Antipode* 30, no. 4: 333–356.

Hart, Gillian. 2002. *Disabling Globalization: Places of Power in Post-Apartheid South Africa.* Berkeley: University of California Press.

Hart, Gillian. 2004. 'Geography and Development: Critical Ethnographies'. *Progress in Human Geography* 28, no 1: 91–100.

Hart, Gillian. 2006. 'Denaturalizing Dispossession: Critical Ethnography in the Age of Resurgent Imperialism'. *Antipode* 38, no. 5: 977–1004.

Hart, Gillian. 2013a. 'Gramsci, Geography, and the Languages of Populism'. In *Gramsci: Space, Nature, Politics,* edited by Michael Ekers, Gillian Hart, Stefan Kipfer and Alex Loftus, 301–320. Malden: Wiley-Blackwell.

Hart, Gillian. 2013b. *Rethinking the South African Crisis: Nationalism, Populism, Hegemony.* Athens: University of Georgia Press.

Hart, Gillian. 2016. 'Relational Comparison Revisited: Marxist Postcolonial Geographies in Practice'. *Progress in Human Geography* 42, no. 3: 371–394.

Hart, Gillian. 2020. 'Why Did it Take so Long? Trump-Bannonism in a Global Conjunctural Frame'. *Geografiska Annaler: Series B, Human Geography* 102, no. 3: 239–266.

Hodgdon, Benjamin D., David Hughell, Victor Hugo Ramos and Roan Balas McNab. 2015. 'Deforestation Trends in the Maya Biosphere Reserve, Guatemala (2000–2013)'. *Rainforest Alliance,* 19 February. https://www.rainforest-alliance.org/impact-studies/deforestation-trends-maya-biosphere-reserve (accessed 12 January 2022).

Jonas, Susanne. 2000. *Of Centaurs and Doves: Guatemala's Peace Process.* Boulder: Westview Press.

Kipfer, Stefan and Gillian Hart. 2013. 'Translating Gramsci in the Current Conjuncture'. In *Gramsci: Space, Nature, Politics*, edited by Michael Ekers, Gillian Hart, Stefan Kipfer and Alex Loftus, 321–343. Malden: Wiley-Blackwell.

Lakhani, Nina and Erubiel Tirado. 2016. 'Mexico's War on Drugs: What Has it Achieved and How Is the US Involved?' *The Guardian*, 8 December. https://www.theguardian.com/news/2016/dec/08/mexico-war-on-drugs-cost-achievements-us-billions (accessed 12 January 2022).

Lefebvre, Henri. (1974) 1994. *The Production of Space*. Oxford: Blackwell.

Marx, Karl. (1845) 1978. 'Theses on Feuerbach'. In *The Marx-Engels Reader*, 2nd edition, edited by Robert C. Tucker, 143–145. New York: W.W. Norton and Company.

Massey, Doreen. 1991. 'A Global Sense of Place'. *Marxism Today* 35, no. 6: 24–29.

McSweeney, Kendra, Erik A. Nielsen, Matthew J. Taylor, David J. Wrathall, Zoe Pearson, Ophelia Wang and Spencer T. Plumb. 2014. 'Drug Policy as Conservation Policy: Narco-Deforestation'. *Science* 343, no. 6170: 489–490.

McSweeney, Kendra, Nazih Richani, Zoe Pearson, Jennifer Devine and David J. Wrathall. 2017. 'Why Do Narcos Invest in Rural Land?' *Journal of Latin American Geography* 16, no. 2: 3–29.

Monterroso, Iliana and Deborah Barry. 2012. 'Legitimacy of Forest Rights: The Underpinnings of the Forest Tenure Reform in the Protected Areas of Petén, Guatemala'. *Conservation and Society* 10, no. 2: 136–150.

Nations, James D. 1996. *The Maya Tropical Forest: People, Parks, and Ancient Cities*. Austin: University of Texas Press.

PRISMA (Programa Salvadoreño de Investigación sobre Desarrollo y Medio Ambiente). 2014. 'Pueblos Indígenas y Comunidades Rurales Defendiendo Derechos Territoriales'. https://www.prisma.org.sv/publicaciones/pueblos-indigenas-y-comunidades-rurales-defendiendo-derechos-territoriales/ (accessed 12 January 2022).

REMHI (Recuperación de la Memoria Histórica, Proyecto Interdiocesano). 1998. *Guatemala: Nunca Más – The Official Report of the Human Rights Office of the Archbishop of Guatemala*. New York: Orbis Books.

Saval, Nikil. 2017. 'Globalization: The Rise and Fall of an Idea that Swept the World'. *The Guardian*, 14 July. https://www.theguardian.com/world/2017/jul/14/globalisation-the-rise-and-fall-of-an-idea-that-swept-the-world (accessed 12 January 2022).

Schwartz, Norman B. 1990. *Forest Society: A Social History of Petén, Guatemala*. Philadelphia: University of Pennsylvania Press.

Sesnie, Steven E., Beth Tellman, David Wrathall, Kendra McSweeney, Erik Nielsen, Karina Benessaiah, Ophelia Wang and Luis Rey. 2017. 'A Spatio-Temporal Analysis of Forest Loss Related to Cocaine Trafficking in Central America'. *Environmental Research Letters* 12, no. 5: 1–19.

Sundberg, Juanita. 1998. 'NGO Landscapes in the Maya Biosphere Reserve, Guatemala'. *Geographical Review* 88, no. 3: 388–412.

Tellman, Beth, Steven E. Sesnie, Nicholas R. Magliocca, Erik A. Nielsen, Jennifer A. Devine, Kendra McSweeney, Meha Jain, David J. Wrathall, Anayasi Dávila, Karina Benessaiah and Bernardo Aguilar-Gonzalez. 2020. 'Illicit Drivers of Land Use Change: Narcotrafficking and Forest Loss in Central America'. *Global Environmental Change* 63. https://doi.org/10.1016/j.gloenvcha.2020.102092.

Tuckman, Jo. 2012. *Mexico: Democracy Interrupted*. New Haven: Yale University Press.

Wrathall, David J., Jennifer A. Devine, Bernardo Aguilar-González, Karina Benessaiah, Elizabeth Tellman, Steve Sesnie, Erik Nielsen, Nicholas Magliocca, Kendra McSweeney, Zoe Pearson, John Ponstingel, Andrea Rivera Sosa and Anayansi Dávila. 2020. 'The Impacts of Cocaine-Trafficking on Conservation Governance in Central America'. *Global Environmental Change* 63. https://doi.org/10.1016/j.gloenvcha.2020.102098.

5 | A Conversation with Gillian Hart about Thabo Mbeki's 'Second Economy'

Ahmed Veriava

Gillian Hart is my teacher, although I have never been a formal student of hers. The lessons she has offered have come through our (real and imagined) conversations, especially as these have unfolded in my engagement with her work. As master–student relationships go, ours is therefore an unorthodox one, enabled by the intellectual generosity of a teacher who refuses her title as master, so that teaching can start as conversation between militants.

One of the consequences of this unorthodox master–student relationship, however, is that what I take from Hart is not in the first place any concept. Instead, the deepest point of influence and inspiration has been in a style of intellectual engagement that exceeds the concepts she puts to work. In Hart's work, concepts are always a rich totality of many determinations and relations, constantly and painstakingly reworked in relation to engagements with the concrete. And in this work, conversation – with all its productive tensions – is an additional support for tracing the paths between abstract forms and ever-finer determinations, and one mode through which this praxis finds its spaces of intervention (and sometimes also students).

In this chapter I try to make this style of intellectual engagement thematic by focusing not on a 'Gill concept', but one that she adopts a critical relationship to: Thabo Mbeki's 'second economy'. Reflecting my enormous debt to Hart's work, I argue that the development and deployment of the concept of the second economy tells us a lot about how the technical and political practices of neo-liberal governmentality were *articulated* with official nationalism (see chapter 8 in this volume for a discussion of the concept of articulation). Rather than repay the debt, however, this chapter marks out a slightly different path to the one Hart took – my paradoxical way of showing her influence.

Field notes on the crisis

Rethinking the South African Crisis (Hart 2013) is an important left-academic statement on the transition from apartheid for its suggestion that we focus on the interlocking practices and processes of de-nationalisation and re-nationalisation. The virtue of Hart's conceptual reworking of the narrative of transition is to draw our attention to the articulation of practices and processes in different spheres, such that her account of 'the South African crisis' now shows it simultaneously anchored in the political, economic and cultural domains, with thick historical-spatial sediments. Hart's concept of de-nationalisation draws together shifting class composition, capital flight, discursive forms and governmental practices: '[De-nationalisation] signals ... the simultaneously economic, political and cultural practices and processes that are generating ongoing inequality and "surplus" populations, and the conflicts that surround them. De-nationalisation focuses attention on the historical and geographical specificities of South African racial capitalism and settler colonialism, their interconnections with forces at play in other parts of the world, and their modes of reconnecting with the increasingly financialised global political economy in the post-apartheid period' (Hart 2013, 7).

And if the 'forces of de-nationalisation' can only be understood in their relation to the 'practices and processes of re-nationalisation', the latter too are linked to a wide spectrum of phenomena, including discursive interventions, expressions of official xenophobia, pogroms and popular protest. It is, however, important to note that Hart's appreciation of the complex unfolding of these processes was in the first place enabled by exactly the kinds of conceptual reworkings that I highlight at the beginning of this chapter, and her critique of Mbeki's concept of the 'second economy' is an important part of this story: a critique that develops in conversations on the left.

In 2006 Hart challenged the audience gathered at a colloquium of left academics and activists to think about how the Mbeki-led 'ruling bloc in the ANC [African National Congress] articulated shared meanings and memories of the struggles for national liberation to its hegemonic project – and how a popular sense of betrayal is playing into support for Jacob Zuma' (Hart 2007, 85). The colloquium was partly centred on the intellectual work and legacy of Harold Wolpe and at the heart of Hart's presentation was a 'return' to the race–class debate, framed as a search for 'analytic tools' for grappling with the 'dangerous conjuncture' signalled by the rise of Zuma, and the new fractures this was opening up in the ANC-led Alliance. What she retrieves from this debate is a Gramscian concept of articulation, worked out and developed by Stuart Hall and shown to be at work in the late Wolpe's writing (but differentiated from his earlier Althusserian concept of articulation).

Working from Hall's concept of articulation (see chapter 8 in this volume), Hart shows that something like race has to be understood in its historicity, which is to say, 'in terms of relations and practices that have tended to erode and transform – or preserve – [racial] distinctions through time' (Hart 2007, 89) as structuring principles of social life and the forms of class relations that characterise it. The take-away from this discussion was therefore an analytic practice centred on the historical formation and transformation of the 'economic, political and ideological practices' that underlie particular social relations and categories and the ways these practices have been articulated with other practices within a social formation.

Rethinking the social in this way has real implications for conceptual work, as Hart (2007, 90) suggests with explicit reference to Karl Marx's 'the method of political economy' in his *Grundrisse* and Hall's engagement with it. It means that conceptual work must necessarily be undertaken in relation to, and must keep pace with, concrete empirical points of reference. Armed with this concept of articulation, with its deep methodological and ontological implications, when Hart now turns to offer a concrete analysis of concrete situations, something important happens. In the final sections of her presentation, where she reflects on the concept of the second economy, we can already see Hart reworking her field notes on the crisis, now with local government at the centre, and in terms of conceptual coordinates that include populism and nationalism. And it is in these notes, developed through a 'concrete analysis' of the South African context, that Hart recasts the left narrative of the transition, highlighting 'simultaneous practices and processes of *de-nationalisation* and *re-nationalisation*' (Hart 2013, 6; emphasis in original).

More than a decade 'late', what follows is the story of how I took up Hart's challenge in her 2006 presentation. The virtue of her reworked perspective on the transition, that is, the way it draws together practices and processes unfolding in different spheres, also means that all of these elements ultimately must be related to one another at an extraordinarily high level of abstraction. What I ended up focusing on then was some of the stuff happening 'lower down', centring Hart's analysis of the 'concrete situation' that opened with Mbeki's introduction of a concept of the second economy. But, for me, taking up Hart's challenge (as a returning graduate student) also meant misreading it (with all her support) and reworking her questioning of the articulation between political economy and nationalism within a different conceptual framework.

Hart and the two economies debate

In his 2003 'State of the Nation' address, Mbeki (re)introduced a distinction between a first and second economy as the terms of a narrative that explained the persistence of poverty. His speech began, however, as an affirmation of progress. He reminded those listening of the people's 'long march against the system of white minority domination' and their eventual 'transition to democratic majority rule' (Mbeki 2003). A 'tide had turned,' he said; lives were changing for the better and the 'economy is demonstrating resilience … that is the envy of many across the world'. But when he turned to the question of poverty, he added:

> With regard to the accomplishment of the task of ensuring a better life for all … government is perfectly conscious of the fact that there are many in our society who are unable to benefit from whatever our economy is able to offer … This reflects a structural fault in our economy and society as a result of which we have a dual economy and society. The one modern and relatively well developed. The other is characterised by underdevelopment and an entrenched crisis of poverty. (Mbeki 2003)

And the implications of this disjuncture were that the ('correct') interventions made at the level of the 'first economy' did not have corresponding (poverty-alleviating) outcomes at the level of the 'second economy', necessitating a realignment of governmental action.

Mbeki's statement coincided with a wide-ranging review of the first ten years of democratic rule and a renewed emphasis on the governmental discourse on poverty and social assistance for the poor. In this context, the two economies thesis provided a simplified grid that explained the persistence of poverty while at the same time acting as a statement of political will that committed governmental agencies to renewed action targeting the poor. This idea of the second economy, however, also provoked a barrage of criticism and at the 2006 colloquium discussed above it was the subject of more than one polemical intervention. For all the work devoted to understanding and critiquing it, however, the ways Mbeki's thesis reframed a nationalist representation of 'the people' and their 'political project' were generally ignored.

Focusing on the assertion of an impassable blockage between the first and second economies, the dominant line of critique worked to show the links between formal and informal economic activity and in this way also the deleterious unity of economic processes under policies sponsored by the executive. Alternatively, for other critics, second economy measures were shown to produce the very inequalities they were meant to address. Generally, however, what was emphasised about the thesis on this side of the political spectrum was its instrumentalism in deflecting criticism over 'bad' policy decisions.

In this political context, Hart made her intervention, and with a Gramscian eye on the political, she transformed the terms of the debate:

> First/Second Economy discourses can be seen as part of an effort to contain the challenges from oppositional movements that reached their zenith at the time of the WSSD [World Summit on Sustainable Development, in 2002] and render them subject to government intervention. What is significant about this discourse is the way it defines a segment of society that is superfluous to the 'modern' economy, and in need of paternal guidance – those falling within this category are citizens, but second class. As such they are deserving of a modicum of social security, but on tightly disciplined and conditional terms. (Hart 2007, 96)

In a parallel article that develops this line of argument, Hart centres on emerging municipal indigent management frameworks, shown to be paradigmatic for second economy measures (Hart 2006).

Two enduring themes of Hart's rethinking of the South African crisis surface here: popular protest and 'the government of the poor'. And if these are shown here in their dialectical relation, Hart draws into her analysis a wider field of practices in order to show how the concept of the second economy was genealogically bound to a mutating conception of the 'national democratic revolution' (NDR). On the one hand, Hart's analysis drew attention to the ways in which (public) invocations of the NDR by the ruling bloc within the ANC paralleled, and in part grew out of, a 'drive' to contain increasingly antagonistic challenges to 'the ANC's hegemonic project' after 2002 with the emergence of new movements (Hart 2007, 95). On the other hand, taking the public statements of ANC officials seriously, she read successive expressions of governmental policy as a re-articulation of a conception of the NDR.

In this account, the adoption of the Growth, Employment and Redistribution (GEAR) programme in 1996 was therefore more than simply a shift away from the 'benign Keynesianism' of the government's earlier Reconstruction and Development Programme (RDP) towards 'harsh neoliberalism'. It also represented, Hart insists, 'a redefinition of the NDR in terms of a re-articulation of race, class and nationalism, along with the assertion of new technologies of rule' (Hart 2006, 58). And to the extent that the second economy concept marked a new shift in discursive representations of the ANC's governmental project, it represented a further redefinition of the NDR in relation to the problem of the surplus population.

This account came to serve as the initial scaffolding for my own research on the concept of the second economy. Following the paths opened up by Hart's work, my own contribution to this conversation was to slow things down, showing the governmental significance of the concept as well as the antinomies of post-apartheid political practices that sit behind it.

The governmental significance of the concept of the second economy

Following Mbeki's first statements on the second economy, this concept was given a less literal meaning that was responsive to the objections made to it, and by 2007 officials were insisting that the 'second economy' was a 'metaphor'. What is important, however, is that at a governmental level the concept of the second economy functioned as a discursive emblem for a social security framework aimed at offering basic social support to the poor. Its various elements (described as second economy measures) included, crucially, a set of targeted cash grants, lifeline allocations for water and electricity, municipal indigent management strategies, and (less crucially) jobs through public works campaigns.

These measures, along with the roll-out of basic services and housing, continue to represent the broad means through which post-apartheid governmental authorities administer to the poor, connecting them to an evolving social security framework as specific subject categories. Although the history of this framework cannot be read from Mbeki's statements, the introduction of the concept of the second economy did mark an important moment in the post-apartheid government of the poor, characterised not only by an increase in spending on 'second economy measures', but also an attempt to deepen state knowledge of poverty, and to conceptualise and align measures targeting it as part of an 'overall strategy'.

Setting aside my interest in the political genealogy of second economy measures targeting the poor, what intrigued me about official statements on the second economy was the ways they came to operate on two levels. On the one hand, they model a symbolic grammar for representations of the people and their will and, on the other, a practical grammar bifurcating modes of governmental practice. With respect to the concept of the second economy, then, it is crucial to ask how this way of conceptualising the social problem of poverty enabled, supported or clarified the modes through which officials attempted to govern a particular reality.

Focusing on discursive representations of the second economy, what became apparent was that in the end government officials were less concerned with insisting on the impassable singularity of distinct economic formations than with framing a governmental approach in terms of two seemingly opposed models of governmental practice. So, within the idiom of the two economies, the ideal of governmental action was presented as a form of 'economic management', conceived as a mode of indirect government through market effects. For this form of 'economic management' (corresponding to a 'first economy'), governmental interventions were represented as the work of creating 'the right deposition of things' (Foucault 2007) (for instance, appropriate laws and an enabling framework for a market-centred allocation of infrastructure and resources) to bring about a higher order of political ends (equality, redistribution, social inclusion and so on). On the other hand, the discourse of the two economies suggested that, in the specific/distorted circumstance of South Africa, this mode of action was also insufficient to address the problem of poverty. For this reason, the political end of mitigating poverty required direct intervention and support by governmental agencies, and through means standing apart from market mechanisms (such as targeted cash transfers and concessions for accessing decommodified water and electricity through lifeline allocations).

In this narrative, the second mode of practice stands as the exception to the normal run of things. In addition to the various social security interventions undertaken by governmental agencies, and economic interventions aimed at growing the first economy, what was also needed were 'catalytic' programmes to encourage 'mobility' between the second economy and the first (Netshitenzhe 2007; Republic of South Africa 2006), such as education and measures for fostering entrepreneurial habits and the conditions for the development of enterprise. It is important to see that this approach was not so much a departure from neo-liberal governmentality as a refocusing of local social security frameworks in line with a specific mode of representing the problem of poverty. And whether explicitly stated or presupposed, the problem animating governmental discourse on the second economy was exactly what Hart characterised as the presence of a 'segment of society that is superfluous to the "modern" economy' (Hart 2007, 96).

In a telling address, Joel Netshitenzhe, at the time in Mbeki's Office of the Presidency, explained that the idea of the second economy emerged with the examination of data on employment, inequality and growth as part of government's ten-year review process (that is, exam-ination of statistics focused on the population) and a growing sense that 'even as the economy grew by 6% and more, there would still be a large sediment of an "under-class" imprisoned in the poverty trap' (Netshitenzhe 2007). In this account, it is this specific governmental problem and 'the need to define the phenomenon of the under-class' that the metaphor of the second economy was attempting to capture.

The problem indicated by the numbers Netshitenzhe was looking at is well known. Simply stated, it was the fact that a large section of popu-lation is unlikely to ever find a place in formal economic activity, given the shape of capitalist development in South Africa. What the emergence of second economy discourse represented, as Hart spotted, was a gov-ernmental orientation to this problem. All the same, the imagined res-olution for the Presidency remained within a framework in which the poor's entry into the formal labour market was to be the basis of their social inclusion. In this context, measures for administering to the poor were necessarily represented as temporary, stopgap measures to help them on their (impossible) journey to the first economy.[1]

Between neo-liberal governmentalisation and the resistance of the poor

At the centre of the governmental problem to which Hart connects the concept of the second economy is a subject that must be 'identified and registered', '(re)defined' as 'indigent' and drawn into the state's 'struc-tures of social security' on 'tightly disciplined and conditional terms' (Hart 2007, 96). But there is also in Hart's account the suggestion that the moment in which this subject appeared politically mobilised – in the wave of social movement struggles that unfolded in the early 2000s – was the same moment this subject entered the gaze of the state as needing to be rendered subject to governmental intervention.

Drawing on Prishani Naidoo's reflection (see 2007, 2009) on the development of indigent management policies in Johannesburg, and my own work on the commodification of basic services, I wanted to highlight how tightly interwoven the development of the struggles of the poor in Johannesburg were with the measures and institutional forms for administering to them. And as Hart was beginning to speak about 'a dialectic of protest and containment' (Hart 2007, 96), my own research was describing 'a double movement between neoliberal governmentalisation and the resistance of the poor'.

On one side of these arguments was a reflection of the rationality that underlies measures targeting the poor and the ways it moved in the direction of making a life lived under the sign of indigence as unattractive as possible in order to ensure that the poor should rather look to the market for any lasting escape from the condition of poverty … should rather look to themselves to empower themselves. Measures like indigent management strategies and water and electricity lifeline allocations had to therefore be at an 'optimum minimum' – warding off welfare dependency at the same time as they sought to ward off resistance. Rather than working to secure a dignified existence for those belonging to the surplus population, for a neo-liberal governmentality, dignity is precisely what governmental measures must work to avoid. And the measures to meet the 'extreme needs' of the poor must themselves work to ensure that the poor are turned to a life conditioned by market relations.

Apparatuses for governing the poor are, however, machines that work by constantly breaking down, forcing a constant process of reconstitution. The principle of change for these rapidly morphing forms is often opposition, resistance, counter-conduct. On the other side of the argument was therefore an account of how the struggles of the poor constantly worked to push concessions offered by governmental agencies across new thresholds as they acted for a life beyond bare existence. But even with their 'successes', they often become increasingly subject to new modes of surveillance and control.

In linking the development of indigent management policies to the social movements' resistance of the early 2000s, both Hart and Naidoo opened the way for my account of a double movement of neo-liberal governmentalisation and the resistance of the poor. However, the resistance that shaped Johannesburg frameworks targeting the poor also included less organised forms of action, undertaken independently of the social movements referenced in Hart's account (2007).

As I turned to deployments of a conception of the NDR, I again emphasised the operation of NDR discourse, before 2002, in underwriting state policy through the inscription of a set of limits on the content and forms of dissent *within the Alliance*. In fact, the political deployment of the NDR within the Alliance, in the name of an ostensibly neo-liberal policy framework, is threaded through the mesh of tensions out of which the new movements of Hart's account spring (2007). What the post-2002 public deployments of the NDR conception highlighted was the growing dysfunctionality of the Alliance in containing popular forces, and a concomitant drive to generalise the discursive frames and disciplinary models of the ANC-led nationalist movement over a wider area – its ironic response to cracks in its hegemonic project. The failures of this drive are apparent today inside and outside the ANC.

The NDR and the problem of nationalism

One of the important steps taken by Hart is to shift beyond various modes of denunciation of duplicity in order to recentre the question of post-apartheid nationalism and the discursive figures that characterise public representations of the ANC's project in government. In her work, what is important is not simply the ways in which deployments of NDR are instrumentally directed towards soliciting hegemony for a ruling elite as they pursue a programme of neo-liberal restructuring – a talking left that enables a rightward step. Now it becomes important to understand how the conception is made to work to particular ends and how it in fact bends to those ends. Hart's analysis points to the possibility of constructing something like a political genealogy of the

NDR conception that makes its changing shape, the contingencies that mark its deployments in different contexts and times, and the political imperatives it accumulates, the subject of critique (2007). In connecting the NDR conception to Mbeki's two economies thesis – with its extension of a dualistic conception of the social formation, and an expression of a will towards the social inclusion of the black poor and thus the ends of the struggle – Hart also allows us to see Mbeki's statement as a crucial moment in this genealogy.

It is important to note (as Hart reminds us) that Mbeki's two economies thesis was a reworking of his earlier 'two nations' speech (Hart 2007). Presenting on the questions of 'reconciliation and nation building' during a 1998 session of the general assembly, Mbeki (then the deputy president) developed a conception bearing many of the marks of his later two economies thesis, but to a different end: 'South Africa is a country of two nations … One of these nations is white, relatively prosperous … It has ready access to a developed economic, physical, educational, communication and other infrastructure … The second and larger nation of South Africa is black and poor … This nation lives under conditions of a grossly underdeveloped economic, physical, educational, communication and other infrastructure … And neither are we becoming one nation' (Mbeki 1998).

The pessimism of the two nations' speech marked a significant shift from the language of 'a new South Africa' in which Nelson Mandela had cast his image of reconciliation and stood in stark contrast to the dualism of Mbeki's 2003 'State of the Nation' address that announced the 'turning of the tide'. Part of what marks the space between Mbeki's statements in 1998 and his later formulation, is that in this 1998 iteration it is the 'material base' (that is, the singular economy) that both structures the division between the two nations and acts as the motor that drives and enables the project of national reconciliation. In 1998, with challenges to the ANC coming from the parliamentary right, whose leadership and support were drawn largely from white, middle-class constituencies, the remnants of the past are represented as going beyond the 'objective' forms through which the legacy of the past is imprinted on the present, to take on a 'subjective' dimension as well.

In the later two economies thesis, (re)presented for an altered political context, the division is no longer between two nations, but structures a split in the body of the people; between those who can participate in all the nation 'has to offer' (the benefits of national wealth and progress) and those who cannot. The image of the first economy, vibrant and robust, holds the promise of citizenship, democracy and progress. By contrast, the second economy belongs to another temporal form, figured as the stubborn imprint of the past on the present. In both characterisations, however, the dualistic 'image of the past' persists, becoming the point and motivation for state action expressed as national will – whether as threat against the 'agents of the old order', or in reproducing bare life.

Beyond how it operated at a governmental level, stepping back to a different level of abstraction, the two economies thesis was another way of imagining the nation and its people, a narrative that modelled a grammar to reconcile the nationalist principle of progress with the growing material inequities of the national population. But why then did government need the two economies thesis? As we have seen, this characterisation marked a moment of consolidation and extension of governmental approaches, but the latter could just as easily take on less metaphorical, more practical terms. Moreover, intergovernmental communication and institutional structuring gain little from the pomp and ceremony with which the characterisation was passed into the public realm, dressed, we might add, in the imaginings of 'a nation' and 'the history of the struggle' (as in Mbeki's 'State of the Nation' address).

Intersecting questions

The questions that inspired me in Hart's interventions in the debates on the concept of the second economy have, over time, morphed into a slightly esoteric theoretical problem, but one I believe we should take seriously if we are to understand the nationalism of the Congress tradition as it has come to be articulated with the government of the state. In its most abstract form, this is a question of how to think the relationship between government(ality) and popular sovereignty.

Motivated by a similar set of concerns, Partha Chatterjee's *The Politics of the Governed* characterises the relationship between government(ality) and popular sovereignty in terms of an antinomy: 'The classical idea of popular sovereignty, expressed in the legal-political facts of equal citizenship, produced the homogenous construct of the nation, whereas the activities of governmentality required multiple, cross-cutting and shifting classifications of the population as the targets of multiple policies, producing a necessary heterogeneous construct of the social. Here, then, we have the antinomy between the lofty political imaginary of popular sovereignty and the mundane administrative reality of governmentality' (Chatterjee 2004, 35).

Chatterjee's statement owes a debt to Michel Foucault. As is well known, Foucault's lecture (2007) that introduces the concept of governmentality does so in relation to his genealogical reflection on the entry of the concept of economy into political discourse, and in this sense, on the birth of 'political economy'. And in this lecture, Foucault presents the development of modern governmental practices as a transition away from the traditional modality to sovereignty (Foucault 2007). However, he also insists that, in this context, the question of sovereignty came to be even 'more sharply posed'. And for Foucault, it was in Jean-Jacques Rousseau's work that a *diagram* for relating the new arts of government with a conception of sovereignty began to emerge.

It is in fact in Rousseau that we find – from a genealogical perspective – an important formulation of the problem of the articulation of political economy and civic nationalism. Speaking about Rousseau's article 'Political Economy', Foucault says that Rousseau had already shifted from a notion of economy conceived along the model of the family, so that when he turns to the question of sovereignty in

The Social Contract, his question now is how, 'with notions like those of "nature," "contract," and "general will," one can give a general principle of government that will allow for both the juridical principle of sovereignty and elements through which an art of government can be defined and described?' (Foucault 2007, 107). But apart from these brief remarks on *The Social Contract*, Foucault gives us little sense of the form of relation that characterises the space between modern government and a re-articulated conception of sovereignty.

What should follow our perception of the kind of 'antinomy' that Chatterjee highlights? After all, the most sacred artefact of post-apartheid nationalism, the Freedom Charter, leads with the Rousseauian signature, 'no government can just claim authority unless it is based on the will of the people' (Congress of the People 1955). If we assume an antinomy then, what are its effects, both for how 'government' and 'the people' come to be *represented*?

The second economy concept is not new to South African theoretical debates. However, what separated Mbeki's characterisation is that the second economy comes to be imagined as a singular level of governmental intervention, corresponding spatially with sites of mass poverty. As is well known, Foucault's research on neo-liberalism drew attention to practices working at 'recoding of the social as the economic' (Foucault 2008; Lemke 2001, 2002). In a paradoxical way, two economies discourse did this as well. In Mbeki's mouth, what belonged to the social (as the problem of the surplus population) appeared in the frame of 'the dysfunctional economic'. At the same time, from a Foucauldian perspective, the great emphasis placed by governmental agencies on establishing an indigent register, developing the analytic and statistical models to gather information on the 'second economy' (or, more precisely, on the poor) and extending institutional frameworks to administer to this section of the population might be seen as less about finding ways of penetrating a second economy, than of creating one – that is, the constitution of a particular field of knowledge and governmental management and the designation of a specific (which is to say, exceptional) tactical approach towards it.

The quick answer, then, to the question of why officials needed the two economies thesis is that a neo-liberal governmentality needed a popular frame as it was articulated with official nationalism, or rather the technical-political mechanisms targeting the poor needed a narrative that drew them together as resolution to an imagined national problem. In this sense, what the two economies conception worked to do was (re)code a neo-liberal rationality for the progressive 'will' of the nationalist imaginary.

Conclusion

In his re-articulation of the NDR in the form of the two economies thesis, Mbeki was working at one mode, however crisis ridden, of discursively relating two poles – government and popular sovereignty. To be sure, Mbeki's statement offered an admission of the emptiness of the landscape of post-apartheid citizenship for the poor. However, it did so only by connecting this deficiency to the unexhausted legacy of apartheid and national oppression, and thus to the persistence of the 'structural faults' and barriers it created, while reaffirming the ideal of transcending such limits as the ongoing work of the liberation movement in government.

In this narrative, growth in the economy (as a consequence of 'correct' policy) that could absorb the poor carries real symbolic weight. In the two economies discourse it was given the work of (progressive) realisation of citizenship, imagined as an outcome of the integration of the poor into the formal economy and the activation of the entrepreneurial agency of the population, with *basic* support along the way. Like the working of the god of providence, here enabling interventions and administrative capacities engender 'collateral effects' through which the will of the people is to be realised, that is, as an indirect outcome of the good (economic) government of the state.[2] And it is in this way govern-mental decision-making and its field of causality are linked to a broader set of political ends coded in the nationalism of the Congress tradition.

Today officials seldom talk about second economy measures, but the social security framework that was described in these terms reflects the persistence of the Mbeki-era rationality with respect to the government of the poor. The frames for linking the government of the state with a set of aspirations coded in the nationalist discourse of ANC officials have also been shifting (from the second transition, through economic free-dom, to, more recently, radical economic transformation). Ironically, with the decline of the hegemony of the ANC, there is also a remarkable nos-talgia for the Mbeki era with its highpoint in the early 2000s; seen as the golden era of the post-apartheid government of the state in middle-class publics. As Hart has shown, however, the 'incurable structural contradic-tions' that underlie the present crisis were already there. One thing that did mark Mbeki's presidency as different, however, was the depth of his sense of a governmental project whose popular frame became the two economies thesis. Today, new frames like 'radical economic transforma-tion' are now more prominent in the nationalist vocabulary, but they also point to a deeper crisis of connecting discursive forms of the Congress tradition to the practical rationality for the government of the state.

NOTES

1   In making all this explicit I am, of course, doing little more than offering a supporting appendix to Hart's statement, one that delineates how the two economies thesis worked at a *governmental level* as a discourse or rationality for expressing a broad approach to the government of the state. What is far more interesting, however, is what Hart's 2006 account and later writing fix on – the second economy measures themselves and the ways in which they came to be shaped by the political action of the poor.

2   Giorgio Agamben's (2011) discussion of the relationship between the concept of providence and liberal government helped inspire this formulation.

REFERENCES

Agamben, Giorgio. 2011. *The Kingdom and the Glory: For a Theological Genealogy of Economy and Government*. Translated by L. Chiesa and M. Mandarini. Stanford: Stanford University Press.

Chatterjee, Partha. 2004. *The Politics of the Governed: Reflections on Popular Politics in Most of the World*. New York: Columbia University Press.

Congress of the People. 1955. 'The Freedom Charter'. https://en.wikipedia.org/wiki/Freedom_Charter (accessed 7 February 2022).

Foucault, Michel. 2007. *Security, Territory, Population: Lectures at the Collège de France, 1977–78*. New York: Palgrave Macmillan.

Foucault, Michel. 2008. *The Birth of Biopolitics: Lectures at the Collège de France, 1978–79*. New York: Palgrave Macmillan.

Hart, Gillian. 2006. 'Post-Apartheid Developments in Comparative and Historical Perspective'. In *Development Decade? Economic and Social Change in South Africa, 1994–2004*, edited by Vishnu Padayachee, 13–32. Cape Town: HSRC Press.

Hart, Gillian. 2007. 'Changing Concepts of Articulation: Political Stakes in South Africa Today'. *Review of African Political Economy* 34, no. 111: 85–101.

Hart, Gillian. 2013. *Rethinking the South African Crisis: Nationalism, Populism, Hegemony*. Pietermaritzburg: University of KwaZulu-Natal Press.

Lemke, Thomas. 2001. 'The Birth of Bio-Politics: Michel Foucault's Lecture at the Collège de France on Neo-liberal Governmentality'. *Economy and Society* 30, no. 2: 190–207.

Lemke, Thomas. 2002. 'Foucault, Governmentality, and Critique'. *Rethinking Marxism* 14, no. 3: 49–64.

Mbeki, Thabo. 1998. 'Statement of Deputy President Thabo Mbeki at the Opening of the Debate in the National Assembly on "Reconciliation and Nation Building"'. 29 May. http://www.dirco.gov.za/docs/speeches/1998/mbek0529.htm (accessed 13 January 2022).

Mbeki, Thabo. 2003. 'Mbeki: State of the Nation Address at the Opening of Parliament'. 14 February. http://www.info.gov.za/speeches/2003/03021412521001.htm (accessed 13 January 2022).

Naidoo, Prishani. 2007. 'Struggles around the Commodification of Daily Life in South Africa'. *Review of African Political Economy* 34, no. 111: 57–66.

Naidoo, Prishani. 2009. 'The Making of "The Poor" in Post-Apartheid South Africa: A Case Study of the City of Johannesburg and Orange Farm'. DPhil diss., University of KwaZulu-Natal.

Netshitenzhe, Joel. 2007. 'Opening Address'. Paper presented at Living on the Margins: Vulnerability, Social Exclusion, and the State in the Informal Economy Conference, Cape Town, South Africa, 26 March.

Republic of South Africa. 2006. 'Brief Synopsis Clarifying the Second Economy Concept'. www.thepresidency.gov.za/docs/pcsa/social/briefsynopsis.pdf (accessed 1 December 2013).

6 | 'D/developments' after the War on Terror, post 9/11

Jennifer Greenburg

In 2003, I was an undergraduate student in Gillian Hart's large lecture course, DS100, at the time titled 'History of Development and Underdevelopment' (the course has since morphed into 'Global Developments: Theory, History, Geography'). This was my first exposure to Hart's concept of D/development, or the intertwined nature of the development of capitalism with 'Development' projects of intervention in the 'Third World'. The US invasion of Iraq occurred while I was taking this class, the war in Afghanistan raged on, and the post-9/11 wars began expanding into today's global geography of war and militarism. This chapter thinks with Hart through her concept of 'big D' and 'little d' D/development, which I have engaged with since 2003 to understand the weaponisation of D/development in the post-9/11 wars. Reflecting Hart's writings on keeping 'big D' and 'little d' in tension with one another and understanding their situated practices, my ethnography of military training reveals how, far from their intention to strengthen military operations, privatised forms of militarised D/development introduce new tensions and contradictions into the terrain of global militarism. In contrast to what is often a popular and academic interpretation of military institutions as monolithic, this ethnographic approach reveals how changes in military policy come into conflict with aspects of military culture.

Concept and genealogy of D/development

Hart's concepts are deeply entangled with the political-economic context in which she writes. The concept of 'D/development' grew out of the necessity to establish concepts adequate to the challenges of the moment in which she was working. In her 2009 *Antipode* article, 'D/developments after the Meltdown', Hart defines 'big D' Development as 'the multiply scaled projects of intervention in the "Third World" that emerged in the context of decolonisation struggles and the Cold War. "Little d" development refers to the development of capitalism as a geographically uneven but spatially interconnected process of creation and destruction, dialectically interconnected with discourses and practices of Development' (Hart 2009, 119). Yet the origins of the concept go back to Development debates in the 1990s, spawned by the demise of the Washington Consensus by the early 2000s. Hart (2001) notes the convergence of neo-liberal and post-Development critiques, both of which take aim at 'big D' Development, understood as a post-war project of international intervention in the 'Third World' (see Lal 1985; Sachs 1992). The notion of D/development as formed *both* through the development of capitalism *and* through post-war international interventions in the 'Third World' grew out of the need for a way out of what Hart calls 'the intellectual and political *cul de sac*' formed by responses to neo-liberal and post-Development critiques that invoke problematic conceptions of civil society. 'Notably missing from these formulations – yet urgently needed – is attention to the multiply inflected capitalisms that have gone into the making of globalization' (Hart 2001, 651).

The concept shed light on the 2008 financial meltdown, offering a path beyond prevalent debates at the time as to 'whether we now find ourselves in a postneoliberal era, and if so how to characterize it' (Hart 2009, 118). Moving the debate beyond 'an ideal-type (or, for that matter, yet another iteration of post-ist critique),' Hart argues, 'the imperative is for analyses that can illuminate the shifting relations of force in the present conjuncture – precisely because, as Gramsci points out … political dynamics can't be read off economic crises' (118–119). With this Gramscian understanding of political economy in mind, the notion of D/development as always formed together through the interconnection of political-economic processes with policy interventions provides a framework to think through the 'relations of force at various levels' (Gramsci 1971, 184–185). The result is a conjunctural analysis of key turning points since the 1940s that sheds light on the post-2008 global financial crisis, in particular by making explicit the connections of shifts in Development policy to the development of capitalism.

Hart attributes Gramsci's attention to the 'relations of force' as informing the concept of D/development. The concept brings together a Gramscian analysis with Karl Polanyi's conception of capitalism's double-movement (Polanyi [1944] 2001) 'within an explicitly spatialized frame of understanding that owes a great deal to [Henri] Lefebvre's (1991 [1974]) relational conceptions of the production of space' (Hart 2009, 120). Polanyi's influence is important here, as it distinguishes Hart's D/development from Michael Cowen and Robert Shenton's writings on development as an immanent process and as intentional practice. 'Little d' is not synonymous with Cowen and Shenton's contention that development was an immanent process, distinct from intervention, 'invented to deal with the problem of social disorder in nineteenth-century Europe through trusteeship' (Cowen and Shenton 1996, 60). Rather, channelling Polanyi's double-movement, intervention is a process internal to capitalism. Tensions contained within capitalism have shaped the need to constantly redefine official discourses and practices of 'big D' Development. In contrast to Cowen and Shenton's emphasis on continuity of trusteeship over time, Hart emphasises instability and redefinition.

Geography – or, more accurately, attention to situated spatial practices – is also fundamental to the concept of D/development. Hart (2002) continues to establish this concept in relation to the interplay of political economy, culture and power. The concept of D/development turns on 'conceptions of culture as *practices* of meaning-making that are inextricably linked with situated material practices, the constitution of identities and relations of power in multiple, interconnected arenas of everyday life' (Hart 2002, 818; emphasis in original). If culture, power and political economy are made through situated practices, then critical ethnography becomes the requisite methodology to produce concepts that adequately contain the tensions and contradictions of practice. Hart advances critical ethnography as a project of ' "advancing from the abstract to the concrete" in the sense of building concrete concepts that are adequate to the historical and geographical complexity with which they are seeking to grapple' (Hart 2004, 97; see also Hall 1974; Marx [1857] 1973). Building concrete concepts out of critical ethnography is an explicitly spatial project in Hart's formulation, employing Doreen Massey's (1994) sense of place as 'nodal points of connection in socially produced space' (Hart 2004, 98).

In Hart's undergraduate lecture course, 'Global Developments: Theory, History, Geography', which must be considered part of her intellectual contribution, she periodises D/development: the 1950s and 1960s are defined by development economics, structuralism and import substitution industrialisation (ISI); the 1970s by basic needs; the 1980s by the neo-liberal counter-revolution and structural adjustment; and the 1990s by the rise and decline of the 'Washington Consensus'. Furthermore, D/development is highly geographical; different moments in this periodisation are defined by different geographies – for example, Latin America's centrality to ISI. Individual but interconnected countries and regions reflect specific trajectories of 'big D' Development that depart from, yet also produce, the global geography of Development. Recent iterations of Hart's course include a section on the 'challenges of the present moment in a global conjunctural frame', which begins by locating the US in a global conjunctural frame and examining militarism before and after 9/11. Hart identifies militarism as central to the challenges of the current conjuncture, framed here as Gramsci's attention to 'the relations of military forces, both technical and "politico-military" ' that are linked with economic and political relations (Hart 2009, 134). It is the current conjuncture of US militarism in relation to D/development to which I now turn.

The intertwined rise of militarised D/development and for-profit D/development contracting

On 26 October 2001, six weeks after the 9/11 attacks on the World Trade Center, the US secretary of state and former chairman of the joint chiefs of staff, Colin Powell, spoke at the National Foreign Policy Conference for Leaders of Nongovernmental Organisations (NGOs). Praising NGOs' work and committing to a supportive partnership with them, Powell remarked: 'Just as surely as our diplomats and military, American NGOs are out there serving and sacrificing on the front lines of freedom … I am serious about making sure we have the best relationship with the NGOs who are such a force multiplier for us, such an important part of our combat team' (Powell 2001). Powell's reference to NGOs as 'force multipliers' indicates the broader conscription of Development into the military's arsenal, exemplified in military efforts to build schools, infrastructure and microenterprises in the so-called battle for hearts and minds in the Iraq and Afghanistan counter-insurgencies. A decade later, I spoke with a US army colonel who designed training programmes for soldiers specialising in civilian interaction in both counter-insurgency and humanitarian responses. Calling attention to the military's increasing demand for troops specialising in civilian interaction, the officer commented: 'In Iraq and Afghanistan, there was a period when we were more of an NGO with guns.' These two remarks – one a civilian notion of NGOs as the military's 'force multiplier', the other a military notion of itself as 'an NGO with guns' – capture the shifting relationship between militarism and D/development in relation to the 'war on terror'.

I focus here on the role of for-profit Development companies that, since the return of counter-insurgency in military doctrine in the mid-2000s, have provided pre-deployment training in Development 'best practices' to a variety of military audiences in the US. International development companies (IDCs) are a particular articulation of the development of capitalism that grew out of neo-liberalism. Militarised D/development has intensified a pre-existing trend towards for-profit IDCs, which now outpace the NGOs prominent in the remarks of Powell and the army officer in the contracts they win from the United States Agency for International Development (USAID). Security and development were closely tied to each other at the inception of USAID in 1961. A foreign service professional commented on the decade leading up to USAID's establishment: 'The State Department and Defense Department viewed economic assistance as an arm of military and political security' (Essex 2013, 31). The Foreign Assistance Act of 1961, which established USAID, was framed as a weapon in 'the battleground of freedom' against Communist victory in the 'Third World' (36). The Act was also concerned with separating bundled economic and military assistance under the Marshall Plan. In light of the present merging of security and Development, it is possible to track from this originating moment how, administratively, military and Development assistance have been entwined, separated, then entwined again at various moments.

The neo-liberal counter-revolution of the 1970s and the associated privatisation of social services created an industry of for-profit contractors in the business of providing social services (Easterly 2001; Taylor 1997; Watts 1994). 'Between 1977 and 1997 the number of for-profit providers of individual and family services, job training, vocational rehabilitation, child day-care, and residential care in the USA increased by 202 per cent' (Frumkin 2002, 4). Some of the largest international development contractors in the US today got their start in this period providing contracted domestic social services, such as Creative Associates, or executing large public construction contracts, such as the Louis Berger Group (Frumkin 2002). Companies such as these honed their expertise at home, only to find expanded foreign markets in the years following the growth of USAID.

The end of the Cold War and neo-liberal austerity efforts to shrink state institutions at home saw the internal reform and restructuring of USAID in the 1990s. Even as USAID's programmatic envelope expanded, its staff was reduced by 40 per cent between 1990 and 2008. This meant that fewer direct-hire staff had the responsibility of overseeing more and more money (Nagaraj 2015, 592). The agency cut its global staff between 1993 and 1997, from more than 11 000 to 7 600, with a growing number of positions being contract staff and foreign nationals hired abroad (Essex 2013, 93). Already entrenched in domestic and foreign-service provision, IDCs benefited greatly from these changes, as USAID shifted the responsibility of project implementation from direct employees to contractors. IDCs even absorbed former USAID employees during this period (Nagaraj 2015, 592). To give a sense of the scale of for-profit D/development contracting today, in 2010, USAID awarded contracts worth US$5.3 billion to private contractors, while it awarded a total of US$5.1 billion to non-profits, United Nations' agencies and the World Bank (588). If Chemonics, one of the world's largest IDCs, were a country, it would have been the third-largest recipient of USAID funding in the world in 2011, behind only Afghanistan and Haiti (Nagaraj 2015).

It is in this context of firmly entrenched IDCs that a series of post-9/11 institutional and financial shifts reformulated the relationship between militarism and D/development. In 2004, the State Department established the Office of the Coordinator for Reconstruction and Stabilisation (now called the Bureau of Conflict and Stabilisation Operations). In 2005, USAID established a new Office of Military Affairs (now called the Office of Civilian–Military Cooperation) in order to coordinate the agency's relationship to the Department of Defense. This new institution responded to the National Security Strategy's demand that 'development be a strong and equal partner with diplomacy and defense' (USAID 2015). The new USAID office hosted military liaisons and embedded Development personnel at the Pentagon and six of the military's geographical combatant commands. A large part of the office's work involves the sort of training for military audiences described below, as well as more recent iterations of 'Development in Vulnerable Environments' (USAID 2015).

These new USAID and State Department institutions met policy demands for a 'whole-of-government' or 'Three Ds' approach to US foreign policy. During her tenure as secretary of state, Hillary Clinton gave a speech at the Center for Global Development, in which she spoke of the need to 'elevate development and integrate it more closely with defense and diplomacy', which she called a 'Three Ds' approach (Clinton 2010, 5). In a speech at Kansas State University in 2007, Secretary of Defense Robert Gates employed similar rhetoric, reflecting that 'one of the most important lessons of the wars in Iraq and Afghanistan is that military success is not sufficient to win' and advocating for an increase in 'civilian instruments of national security' (Gates 2007).

New policy discourses and institutions emphasising the merging of Development and defence were accompanied by new financial relationships. In 2005, Congress provided the Department of Defense with the authority to transfer to the State Department up to US$100 million per fiscal year to fund small security and stabilisation activities implemented by the State Department and USAID (Serafino 2011). This blended Development/defence funding came to be known as the '1207 Fund', since it was authorised under Section 1207 of the National Defense Authorization Act from 2006 to 2010. The funding was never intended to be permanent (it expired in 2010), but rather to temporarily fund the activities of the State Department's new Office of the Coordinator for Reconstruction and Stabilization and activities coordinated with USAID. The authority fell under the Department of Defense because it was easier to obtain the funding from Congress (Perito 2008, 3). Yet the blending of Development and defence funding incited a great deal of concern at the time within Development institutions, especially among NGOs operating in the competitive contracting market. The 1207 programme meant that defence funding could essentially find its way into NGO programme budgets through opaque contracting vehicles.

A worker at one large humanitarian NGO I interviewed in 2009 described how it declined defence funding to support rural development work it was already doing in the Horn of Africa. An individual at another NGO interviewed the same year described how a long-standing rural economic development programme in West Africa had come to be funded by USAID's Trans-Sahara Counterterrorism Partnership (TSCTP), which, together with the Partnership for Regional East Africa Counterterrorism (PREACT), constitute major integrated Development and defence initiatives in Africa. The 'military-development corporations' at the heart of Vijay Kumar Nagaraj's 'market-led development-security assemblage' benefited from the 1207 programme. In Haiti, USAID contracted Dyncorps using 1207 funds for a community policing programme (Becker 2011). Although the 1207 programme is no longer active, it does represent an important moment of militarised USAID contracting to both NGOs and IDCs.

Many of the new institutions of this era designed to integrate Development and defence fed into the mode of contracting that dominated USAID's operations by the early 2000s. The established terrain of private contracting was also particularly amenable to a language of 'stabilisation' that in recent years has come to pervade Development discourse. The ways in which contract culture has already rendered aid 'a techno-administrative matter' predisposed private contractors to successfully obtain project funding for 'stabilisation' projects that became available in this period (Gulrajani 2011). A number of private contractors have thus emerged over the past decade to fill a niche market of 'stabilisation' work – Development projects that carry a security or military imperative and often directly involve military personnel. Large, established firms that have long dominated the government contracting landscape, such as Booz Allen Hamilton, have now begun to speak the language of 'stability operations' and a 'whole-of-government approach' (Sulek, Cowell and Delurey 2009). Newly established private companies have also appeared – for instance, the McKellar Corporation, established in 2006 by a retired military officer to provide translation, civilian role-players and staff for military trainings and simulations.

The firm I refer to below as 'Stability Inc.' is part of this subset of IDCs that have come to specialise in merged military/Development 'stability' operations.[1] During the period of my research, Stability Inc. was contracted by USAID to provide military audiences with training in the District Stability Framework (DSF), an instructional framework that repurposed Development 'best practices' for military operations. At that time, the DSF had become integrated into many pre-deployment trainings, particularly among the Marines, and was mandated for all US government field positions in Afghanistan. Contractors held up the Development framework as more 'sophisticated', 'academic' and 'scientific' than the initial first wave of militarised Development articulated as 'winning hearts and minds'.

'Critical ethnographies' of military D/development contractors

I shadowed Stability Inc. contractors between 2010 and 2012 as they travelled to five different military bases across the US. During one of these observations, I had accompanied the contractors to a large military base in a rural part of the Midwest, where they were to provide training in the DSF to the military component of a Provincial Reconstruction Team (PRT) as part of their larger pre-deployment training. The Navy captain in charge of the training introduced Dave, one of the contractors, as providing the trainees with a tactical toolkit that 'operationalised' the counter-insurgency theory they had learned in the class so far. Dave took over the podium from the captain and commented to the class that he had heard them that morning talking about targeting: 'Targeting isn't just about who you are seeing through the sight of your rifle. It can be a 14-year-old Afghan girl. Or a tribal shura [council]', invoking what the counter-insurgency manual refers to as a 'population-centric approach'. Dave then explained how he had worked as a civilian on a PRT in Iraq, where his team had spent large sums of money without being able to point to concrete results of their expenditure. 'How do you figure out what you should be targeting and how you are going to have an effect on that target?' he rhetorically asked the class, framing his training as a response to the failures of 'winning hearts and minds'.

Dave repeated the targeting metaphor, urging the class to think of the DSF toolkit as 'non-kinetic rounds you're sending downrange'. He began to flash a series of PowerPoint slides corresponding to each section of the DSF on two large canvas screens hovering above the podium. The first section, 'situational awareness', adopted military language, techniques and acronyms to guide the gathering of physical and cultural information in a local area. This section included a matrix organised by the acronyms PMESII (political, military, economic, social, information and infrastructure) and ASCOPE (areas, structures, capabilities, organisations, people and events). The acronyms and matrix were adopted from other military trainings, presenting trainees with familiar language.

Continuing through the four steps of the DSF, Dave used more weapons metaphors to explain how measuring the attitudes of the local population with the Tactical Conflict Survey would allow them to 'adjust fire'. The second step of the DSF, 'analysis', used a series of matrices allowing the user to prioritise the local population's grievances. This section emphasised the difference between 'needs' and 'priority grievances'. Dave warned the soldiers, 'Don't get dragged into a discussion about wants and needs. Afghans have so many needs. You'll never be able to meet all of them.' Instead, he emphasised identifying a 'priority grievance' (a need much of the population agrees on) that is also a key 'source of instability' (SOI). The second step of the DSF was supposed to help trainees make the distinction between a 'source of instability' versus 'wants and needs'.

After a short break, another trainer – Nancy – continued to instruct the class on the third and fourth steps of the DSF. She explained how the third step, 'project design', involved evaluating potential activities that address the 'systemic causes of the SOI' identified in the previous step. The potential projects are evaluated in a matrix that asks whether they meet the framework's 'stability criteria', which are defined according to a series of questions about whether the proposed activity increases support for a legitimate government, decreases support for 'malign actors' and increases 'societal capacity and capability'. Another matrix evaluates potential activities according to USAID's Development 'best practices' design principles. The final step, 'monitoring and evaluation', combines donor-centric language with counter-insurgency principles in order to evaluate how the chosen activity has improved 'stability'.

Initially, in the classroom portion of the course, many students appeared bored, their eyes glazing over or scrolling down smartphone screens while countless PowerPoint slides clicked by. Others expressed confusion at the difference between their previous training to, in the words of one security officer, 'do x, y, and z. Then it's done', whereas in this training, 'they're saying sometimes do x, but other times do y'. In addition to the PRT training discussed here, I also observed Marine and army civil affairs qualification courses on two different US military bases. Here, too, the shift in emphasis was troubling for some of the participants. In the course operated by the Marine Corps, an officer explained that his prior training in bomb disposal was 'there's an IED [improvised explosive device]. We have to dispose of it.' But now he was being asked to think: 'There's an IED. I wonder what caused him to stop farming and dig that hole.' In the Marine Corps, which had its own distinct training structure, apart from both the PRTs and the larger army, a number of personnel had been involuntarily reassigned from 'kinetic' (violent) specialisations, such as infantry and artillery, to 'non-kinetic' specialisations, such as civil affairs – a specialisation focusing on military interaction with the civilian populace.

The *Stability Operations Field Manual* emphasises the importance of civil affairs personnel, particularly in their capacity to 'provide unique area and linguistic orientation, cultural astuteness, advisory capabilities, and civilian professional skills' (United States Army 2009, 78). The trainees cited above, who commented on the multiple and conflicting roles they were now expected to play, also reflected the broader reclassification of personnel from infantry and artillery to civil affairs. The rise of this civilian-centric specialisation took place in relation to the release of military doctrine on counter-insurgency and stabilisation. Until civil affairs became part of special operations in 1987, the specialisation was considered, in the words of one defence analyst, a 'dead end career field', 'backwater' or 'dumping ground' (Sisk 2009, 48). The specialisation gained favour through its association with special operations, yet had no active duty branch until 2006, the same year the *Counterinsurgency Field Manual* was publicly released (United States Army and Marine Corps 2007).

As part of my research on how the army learned the DSF, I arranged to meet with an officer who administered the army's civil affairs qualification course. To get to a group of modular buildings housing his office, I drove through an on-base residential development of brick houses, many decorated for Halloween or sporting the flag of a favourite football team, each with a modest suburban yard. At his office on another section of the base, we sat at a table with a glass top covering at least 100 'challenge coins' bearing the insignia of different military organisations, services and branches.[2] The colonel shared his insight that, more broadly than the particular training he was involved in, 'COIN [counter-insurgency] brought a human dimension back into the conduct of military operations'. In contrast to the Marine Corps training I had observed earlier that year, which lasted five weeks and contained a number of alienated, angry Marines who had been involuntarily assigned to the classification course, the army training ran for 17 weeks, included an intensive screening process and drew from higher-ranking enlisted soldiers, albeit with infantry (the largest branch of the army) still heavily represented. Having recently interacted with a number of Marines who emphasised the contradictions of performing civil affairs, I was struck not so much by army officers' emphasis on screening out students whose 'kinetic' tendencies might interfere with their ability to interact with civilians (although this was also a concern), but rather their emphasis on eliminating soldiers who think 'this is the great American giveaway'. In other words, this particular branch of the army sought to find soldiers who understood, in the words of one officer, 'the national security imperative' for Development activities. In this most intensive, professionalised iteration of civil affairs training, the notion of weaponising Development as precisely as possible, in order to fulfil a specific military objective, came across most clearly. The army officer's comment quoted at the beginning of this section – 'in Iraq and Afghanistan, there was a period when we were more of an NGO with guns' – was made in the context of explaining how his training programme had evolved into a more precise targeting of 'stabilisation' objectives, as distinct from the work of an NGO.

Soldiers and Marines reclassified to civil affairs commented on their ambiguous impressions of training exercises that were intended to identify a village's 'source of instability' very precisely. Some of this ambiguity arose from questions the DSF required soldiers to ask villagers, which could elicit responses that the military could do nothing about. For instance, the security officer for a PRT who talked about 'doing x and y' compared the survey to asking someone if they were thirsty, then saying, 'That's nice, but I'm not going to do anything about it myself. Who do you think could solve your thirst?' He feared alienating local populations by raising their grievances without being able to resolve them.

Other trainees were concerned that the DSF was similar enough to 'human intelligence' tools that they could be mistaken for intelligence collectors. At the PRT training, a team discussed how the teams in Afghanistan they were about to replace were using a different framework to collect information about the local area. In between filling out parts of the SOI analysis matrix during one of the vignette activities, one team described how they had just been briefed on a number of projects they would inherit as soon as they arrived in Afghanistan, including building an orphanage, a courthouse and a bridge. They would not have time to fill in all the charts from this training.

One of the most striking responses to the DSF material was that it conflicted with other aspects of how soldiers understood their mission. Trainees often expressed this conflict through anger and alienation. Such expressions were most extreme in the Marine training I observed, but also erupted from time to time in army and PRT training. For instance, in a PRT training, when Nancy handed out the SOI analysis matrix and told the class they would have 40 minutes to fill it in, several soldiers sighed and muttered under their breath, while another held up the case study and exclaimed: 'This paper. I would be pissed [angry] to walk into a situation with this information.' In a different Marine training focused on humanitarian response, in the middle of filling out a matrix for a simulated flood response, one trainee burst out, 'I *hate* this fucking shit. I'd rather get shot at any fucking day.' To which his neighbour replied: 'I'd much rather be kicking in doors, blowin' up something', evoking laughter from another member of the team, who remarked that 'the good days are gone'.

Such frustrated, alienated responses to training came from many places.[3] Friction also arose through the different training and mission of the security force of a PRT versus the staff component, which brought diplomatic, agricultural, medical and engineering expertise to the 'stabilisation' aspect of their mission. Each specific branch and military team had its own distinct set of reasons as to why trainees reacted in the way they did to the material, pointing to the necessity of deconstructing 'the military' into its varied parts. Although this variation cannot be collapsed into a singular reasoning, the lived experience of training does point to the disjuncture between the policy and practice of militarised Development. It also points to the contradictions of 'stabilisation', both as a concept that is sold by private contractors and as a lived practice of military learning.

Concluding analysis

The ethnography of D/development contractors shows how the incorporation of Development 'best practices' into military training introduced tensions and contradictions into military settings. The short ethnographic vignette in this chapter shows how soldiers found that the material conflicted with other dimensions of their training. I have shown elsewhere the multidimensionality of this soldier resistance to becoming 'armed social workers' (Greenburg 2017a, 2017b, 2018, forthcoming). For our purposes, critical ethnography sheds light on how D/development is produced through situated practices that are both material and meaningful (Hart 2002, 818). Military training is a site at which military meanings of culture and power are being produced. In particular, the sorts of training explored here have sparked conflicts within military learning environments: between military personnel over whether Development would help or hinder their efforts in the field; and between contractors who believed in the material despite its shortcomings and military personnel who were often quietly dubious of training material and sometimes angry and alienated by it. In other contexts, militarised D/development has changed gendered meanings of military labour, highlighting what I have called a 'military femininity' that upholds gender essentialisms such as domesticity and motherhood at the same time as promoting women's role in combat (Greenburg 2017a).

The concept of D/development insists on the mutual production of Development policies and practices through the development of capitalism. I have focused in this chapter on for-profit IDCs as a particular articulation of the development of capitalism within the Development industry. Hart's concept of D/development provides a framework for understanding how for-profit IDCs came to dominate the terrain of Development contracting in the years leading up to a pervasive language of 'stabilisation' in military and Development discourses and practices.

The 'techno-administrative' character of aid under contract is reflected in the technical language of the DSF (Gulrajani 2011). Articulations of 'stabilisation' such as the DSF flowed easily into the steady stream of USAID contracts to IDCs, intensifying further the political-economic dominance of private Development contracting.

Following Trump-era budget cuts to US foreign aid and diplomacy alongside the Heritage Foundation-backed increase to the Pentagon's budget, the terrain of militarised D/development is today changing again. A common critique of the proposed increase in US military spending has been to uphold the value of Development for security objectives. A 2017 *Politico* article penned by retired Navy Admiral Mike Mullen and retired Marine General James Jones laments cuts to USAID and State Department budgets, proclaiming, 'Our experience has also taught us that not all foreign crises are solved on the battlefield; in the 21st century, weapons and war fighters alone are insufficient to keep America secure. That's why we support a robust development budget to advance our national security objectives' (Mullen and Jones 2017). Inserting militarism into a periodisation of D/development provides a sobering antidote to promotions of securitised Development that are likely to become even more amplified under President Joe Biden. The framework of D/development serves as a useful reminder to keep the development of capitalism tied to analyses of Development projects as we grapple with the challenges of the present conjuncture. Likewise, the concept reminds us, calling on Gramsci, that 'political dynamics can't be read off economic crises', offering critical ethnography as a way to create concepts adequate to concrete political circumstances (Hart 2009, 119).

NOTES

This article contains a substantially revised section of my article 'Selling Stabilization: Anxious Practices of Militarized Development Contracting' (Greenburg 2017b).

1 'Stability Inc.' and the names of individual contractors in this chapter are pseudonyms.

2 A 'challenge coin' is a small coin or medallion bearing the insignia of a military organisation. They are often given to service members by high-ranking officers to commemorate an accomplishment. Historically, they acted as evidence of one's allegiance; however, they are today more frequently exchanged among members of the military and collected as memorabilia.

3 For a fuller analysis of where this expletive-laden humour, alienation and masculinised violence comes from, and what it produces, see Greenburg (forthcoming).

REFERENCES

Becker, David C. 2011. 'Gangs, Netwar, and "Community Counterinsurgency" in Haiti'. *Prism* 2: 137–154.

Clinton, Hillary. 2010. 'On Development in the 21st Century'. Remarks for the Center for Global Development, Washington, DC, 6 January. https://www.cgdev.org/doc/2009/Clinton%20Transcript2.pdf (accessed 31 July 2010).

Cowen, Michael and Robert W. Shenton. 1996. *Doctrines of Development.* New York: Routledge.

Easterly, William. 2001. 'The Lost Decades: Developing Countries' Stagnation in Spite of Policy Reform 1980–1998'. *Journal of Economic Growth* 6: 135–157.

Essex, James. 2013. *Development, Security, and Aid.* Athens: University of Georgia Press.

Frumkin, Peter. 2002. 'Service Contracting with Nonprofit and For-Profit Providers: On Preserving a Mixed Organizational Ecology'. Cambridge, MA: Ash Institute for Democratic Governance and Innovation, Harvard University. https://ash.harvard.edu/files/service_contracting.pdf (accessed 13 January 2022).

Gates, Robert M. 2007. 'Remarks Delivered by Secretary of Defense Robert M. Gates'. Kansas State University, 26 November. https://www.k-state.edu/media/newsreleases/landonlect/gatestext1107.html (accessed 13 January 2022).

Gramsci, Antonio. 1971. *Selections from the Prison Notebooks.* Edited by Quintin Hoare and Geoffrey Nowell Smith. New York: International Publishers.

Greenburg, Jennifer. 2017a. 'New Military Femininities: Humanitarian Violence and the Gendered Work of War among US Servicewomen'. *Gender, Place, and Culture* 24, no. 8: 1107–1126.

Greenburg, Jennifer. 2017b. 'Selling Stabilization: Anxious Practices of Militarized Development Contracting'. *Development and Change* 48, no. 6: 1262–1286.

Greenburg, Jennifer. 2018. '"Going Back to History": Haiti and US Military Humanitarian Knowledge Production'. In *Spaces at the Intersection of Militarism and Humanitarianism*, edited by Emily Gilbert and Killian McCormick, special issue, *Critical Military Studies* 4, no. 2: 121–139.

Greenburg, Jennifer. Forthcoming. *At War with Women: Military Humanitarianism and Imperial Feminism in an Era of Permanent War*. Ithaca: Cornell University Press.

Gulrajani, Nilima. 2011. 'Transcending the Great Foreign Aid Debate: Managerialism, Radicalism and the Search for Aid Effectiveness'. *Third World Quarterly* 32, no. 2: 199–216.

Hall, Stuart. 1974. 'Marx's Notes on Method: A Reading of the 1857 "Introduction"'. Working Paper No. 6. Centre for Contemporary Cultural Studies, Birmingham.

Hart, Gillian. 2001. 'Development Critiques in the 1990s: *Culs de Sac* and Promising Paths'. *Progress in Human Geography* 25, no. 4: 649–658.

Hart, Gillian. 2002. 'Geography and Development: Development/s beyond Neoliberalism? Power, Culture, Political Economy'. *Progress in Human Geography* 26, no. 6: 812–822.

Hart, Gillian. 2004. 'Geography and Development: Critical Ethnographies'. *Progress in Human Geography* 28, no. 1: 91–100.

Hart, Gillian. 2009. 'D/developments after the Meltdown'. *Antipode* 41, S1: 117–141.

Lal, Deepak. 1985. 'The Misconceptions of "Development Economics"'. *Finance and Development* 22, no. 2: 10–13.

Lefebvre, Henri. (1974) 1991. *The Production of Space*. Oxford: Blackwell.

Marx, Karl. (1857) 1973. 'Introduction'. In *Grundrisse: Foundations of the Critique of Political Economy*, 17–44. New York: Penguin.

Massey, Doreen. 1994. *Space, Place, and Gender*. Minneapolis: University of Minnesota Press.

Mullen, Mike (Adm., Ret.) and James Jones (Gen., Ret.). 2017. 'Why Foreign Aid Is Critical to U.S. National Security'. *Politico*, 12 June. http://www.politico.com/agenda/story/2017/06/12/budget-foreign-aid-cuts-national-security-000456 (accessed 10 August 2017).

Nagaraj, Vijay Kumar. 2015. '"Beltway Bandits" and "Poverty Barons": For-Profit International Development Contracting and the Military-Development Assemblage'. *Development and Change* 46, no. 4: 585–617.

Perito, Robert M. 2008. 'Integrated Security Assistance: The 1207 Program'. Special report. Washington, DC: US Institute of Peace.

Polanyi, Karl. (1944) 2001. *The Great Transformation*. Boston: Beacon Press.

Powell, Colin. 2001. 'September 11, 2001: Attack on America'. Remarks to the National Foreign Policy Conference for Leaders of Nongovernmental Organizations, Washington, DC, 26 October. https://avalon.law.yale.edu/sept11/powell_brief31.asp (accessed 17 May 2016).

Sachs, Wolfgang, ed. 1992. *The Development Dictionary: A Guide to Knowledge as Power*. London: Zed Books.

Serafino, Nina M. 2011. 'Department of Defense "Section 1207" Security and Stabilization Assistance: Background and Congressional Concerns, FY2006– 2010'. Washington, DC: Congressional Research Services.

Sisk, Kurt. 2009. 'House Divided: The Splitting of Active Duty Civil Affairs Forces'. Master's thesis, Naval Postgraduate School, Monterey, California.

Sulek, D., R. Cowell and M. Delurey. 2009. 'Mission Integration: A Whole-of-Government Strategy for a New Century'. White Paper No. 10.183.09. Herndon, VA: Booz Allen Hamilton.

Taylor, Lance. 1997. 'The Revival of the Liberal Creed: The IMF and the World Bank in a Globalized Economy'. *World Development* 25, no. 2: 145–152.

United States Army. 2009. *The US Army Stability Operations Field Manual*. Ann Arbor: University of Michigan Press.

United States Army and Marine Corps. 2007. *Counterinsurgency Field Manual*. Chicago: University of Chicago Press.

USAID (United States Agency for International Development). 2015. 'Office of Civilian–Military Cooperation'. https://www.usaid.gov/military (accessed 17 December 2015).

Watts, Michael. 1994. 'Development II: The Privatization of Everything?' *Progress in Human Geography* 18, no. 3: 371–384.

7 | Articulation, Translation, Populism: Gillian Hart's Engagements with Antonio Gramsci

Michael Ekers, Stefan Kipfer and Alex Loftus

Gillian Hart's discussions of articulation, translation and populism consistently challenge the schisms between political economy and cultural studies, and Marxism and post-Marxism(s) that have shaped so many debates in social theory since the dying days of the Cold War.[1] In this chapter, we argue that this challenge has been enacted in part through Hart's engagements with Antonio Gramsci's writings. In the first instance, Hart's work has accepted the challenges brought forward against colour- and gender-blind conceptions of Marxism *on the terrain* of Marxism itself (broadly and globally conceived) and *through historical materialist methods* (in their most promising, open-ended and dialectical form). In the second instance, Hart has contributed to what one might call an ongoing political turn in critical geography. She has insisted on the importance of politics as an active and transformative force in the production of time–space without elevating politics to an ontology unfazed by inherited, limit-setting forces of history and geography. In both cases, Hart's strategy to critically engage, recast and develop Gramsci has been an important avenue through which to forge – and put into practice – what she calls 'Marxist postcolonial geographies' (Hart 2018).

We write this chapter as co-conspirators, comprising what Hart occasionally refers to as the 'Gruppo Gramsci'. Naming in this way foregrounds the collective and collaborative process in our shared discussions and editorial work that resulted in the edited collection *Gramsci: Space, Nature, Politics* (Ekers et al. 2013). Such co-production is particularly evident when it comes to the reconceptualisation of translation, which was partly undertaken through working with Stefan Kipfer. The absence of Hart in authoring this piece means we cannot be entirely faithful to the process that has informed our work together. However, we hope that the collaborative spirit of the Gruppo Gramsci still animates this chapter as we discuss the strong Gramscian influences in Hart's work and the significance of these influences for broader debates in geography and beyond.

Throughout this chapter, we contemplate Hart's philological engagement with the Gramscian conceptions of articulation, translation and populism, demonstrating how such an engagement provides a window on the coming together of two shared concerns: the development of a nuanced relational method and the excavation of Gramsci's philosophy of praxis. After developing Hart's understanding of articulation, we analyse how she mobilises understandings of translation and populism through grappling with the politics of South Africa. Drawing on these concepts, we conclude by discussing how Hart is furthering and translating her Gramscian approach to understand the virulent forms of right-wing populism in the global North today.

Articulation

Although Hart refers to articulation in her earlier writings, *Disabling Globalization* (Hart 2002a) deploys the concept prominently to analyse the shifting relations of 'race', class and, to a lesser degree, gender, that temporarily coalesce, or splinter, around particular political economic processes and struggles for hegemony. Articulation, as we discuss in this section, demonstrates most clearly Hart's Gramscian mode of analysis.

It is Stuart Hall's work that Hart engages with most directly in her development of articulation (Hart 2002a, 2002b, 2007, 2013a):

she credits her attention to both materiality and meaning to Hall's writings, particularly his 'Race Articulation and Societies Structured in Dominance' (1980) and 'On Postmodernism and Articulation' ([1986] 1996b). In doing so, she follows Hall (1980), who established an intellectual pathway for avoiding the pitfalls of previous readings of articulation, in particular Louis Althusser's (1977) structuralist understanding and Ernesto Laclau and Chantal Mouffe's (1985) 'post-Marxist' iteration. The concept of articulation was first deployed by Althusser in *For Marx* (1977) and, in his writings with Étienne Balibar, in *Reading Capital*. Althusser et al. (1970) theorise that the articulation of different modes of production, superstructures, understood as political-legal institutions and relations, and forms of knowledge produce particular conjunctures and social formations. Articulation, in their work, refers to the joining together of different structures, but each structure (mode of production, superstructure) is relatively autonomous from others, meaning they cannot be collapsed into one another. However, as Hall (1980) suggests, processes of articulation are not arbitrary: certain structures are 'dominant' and play more of a determining role than others – Althusser's 'determination in the last instance by the (economic) mode of production' (1977, 111). Althusser et al. (1970) were not alone in deploying a structuralist reading of articulation. A number of people in the 1970s and 1980s sought to understand the coexistence and relationship of multiple modes of production (see, for example, De Janvry 1981; Goodman and Redclift 1981; Hindess and Hirst 1975). For Hart, South African debates, and Harold Wolpe's contribution to these debates, are of great relevance. Wolpe (1975, 1980) argues that in the context of South Africa, the capitalist mode of production was conjoined to a mode of production based on subsistence agriculture. The persistence of subsistence production was not a pre-colonial hangover that would be slowly eroded by the spread of capitalist social relations. Rather, self-provisioning and petty commodity production had the effect of producing an artificially cheap labour force, as capital was not responsible for the costs of reproducing workers. Apartheid rule actively maintained the articulation of non-capitalist and capitalist modes of production through deeply racialised policies, practices and forms of legitimation.

In the late 1970s and early 1980s Laclau (1977) and Hall (1980) would take this work forward by developing an understanding of articulation that departed from the structuralism of Althusser and the discursive rendering of the concept that would later come from Laclau and Mouffe (1985), emphasising indeterminacy and the production of subjects through discourses. In contrast to his later work, Laclau (1977) stresses that while the class content of nationalist and populist sentiments and movements is not uniform and can vary, this content needs to be specified in any analysis of such sentiments. For this purpose, he suggests that nationalism and populism are best understood as being contingently articulated with class relations through hegemonic projects in particular historical contexts. Hall (1980) further develops the concept of articulation to steer a path between an economistic and a sociological/voluntarist understanding of the relationship between race and class. Hall leans heavily on Althusser and Gramsci, arguing the articulation involves 'both "joining up" (as in the limbs of the body, or an anatomical structure) and "giving expression to"' (1980, 328: see also [1986] 1996a). Hall builds on this approach, and departs from Althusser, to argue that 'one must start, then, from the concrete historical "work" which racism accomplishes under specific historical condition – as a set of economic, political and ideological practices, of a distinctive kind, concretely articulated with other practices in a social formation' (1980, 338).

Hart's grounding in Gramsci is very much connected to a series of pieces written by Hall (1978, 1980, 1988, [1986] 1996a, [1986] 1996b) between the late 1970s and mid-1980s. In these texts he was working on a Gramscian terrain, but was also crucially engaging with debates on race and class in South Africa, most specifically in his well-known 1980 essay 'Race Articulation and Societies Structured in Dominance'. While still working with Althusser, Hall mobilised Gramsci to offer critiques of the French thinker in order to develop a Gramscian understanding of racialised capitalism and apartheid rule, which is precisely why Hall is so important for Hart.

For Hart, articulation is a concept that allows her to account for how different relations of class, race, nationalism and populism become linked to different political economic and hegemonic projects. For instance, on a number of occasions she has discussed the changing articulation of race within the African National Congress (ANC) (as an institutionalised historic bloc) as the party tries to maintain its hegemony in the light of the racialised inequalities defining South Africa (Hart 2002a, 2007, 2013b). For instance, she discusses how Nelson Mandela relied on an ideology of the post-racial Rainbow Nation to secure the support of a multiracial coalition in the post-apartheid years. From there, she tracks how Thabo Mbeki re-articulated the relationship of race and accumulation in the 1990s by championing the African Renaissance, which resonated with many black South Africans' experiences of struggle against apartheid rule and racism. More specifically, Hart argues that 'Mbeki's pro-African, anti-poverty stance in international forums reinscrib[ed] national strategies to align "the people" with the power bloc' (2002a, 32), even as the ANC globalised the economy and pushed through neo-liberal reforms. As we will see in our discussion of populism, such work begins to foreground Hart's more recent work in *Rethinking the South African Crisis* (2013b) on the simultaneous process of de- and re-nationalisation.

Hart's attention to the changing articulation of political economic processes with relations of race, class and nationalism stems from a continual insistence that an analysis of hegemony in post-apartheid South Africa must be, in Gramsci's words, 'earthly' (1971, 465) and rooted in concrete and spatial histories and experiences (Hart 2013b). The appeal of articulation as a mode of analysis for Hart is precisely in the historicist impulse behind the concept. The ways in which material and meaningful relations cohere, or unravel, is always a historical question rooted in political struggles and political economic transformation.

While Hart (2002a, 2007) is critical of Althusser's argument that the economy plays a determining role in the last instance, some of which remains latent in Wolpe, she is also deeply critical of the evisceration of any type of determination in Laclau and Mouffe's work. Building again on Gramsci (1971), Hart highlights how different articulations are *historically determined*. She writes: 'Rejecting economism emphatically does *not* mean neglecting the powerful role of economic forces and relations, but rather recognizing that economic practices and struggles over material resources and labor are always and inseparably bound up with culturally constructed meanings, definitions and identities, and with the exercise of power, all as part of historical processes' (Hart 2002a, 27; emphasis in original).

Processes of determination require our attention, Hart argues (how else would we know how hegemony is constructed, maintained and contested?) but determining processes must be seen as distributed throughout the entire fabric of historical and geographical conjunctures. Here, Hart echoes Gramsci's 'new concept of immanence' (Gramsci 1971, 400), which the latter uses to understand how political movements, the economy and culture represent preparatory and determining moments for one another.

We now want to highlight two ways in which Hart develops understandings of articulation. The first key contribution is her attention to the contradictions created as various relations are historically and geographically conjoined. Insofar as historically determined articulations bring together particular relations and processes that remain relatively autonomous from one another, there is always the potential, if not the likelihood, for what is articulated – the 'differentiated unity' that both Marx ([1858] 1973) and Hall (1977) discuss – to unravel or for certain processes to come into conflict with one another. For instance, in 'Changing Concepts of Articulation', an article accounting for the popular appeal of Jacob Zuma, Hart reflects on the 'double-edged character of articulations of nationalism as liberation' (2007, 97). She stresses 'how they are key elements of the post-colonial hegemonic project, while at the same time deeply vulnerable to charges of betrayal' (97). Hart argues that fostering nationalist sentiments alongside advancing regressive neo-liberal policies created the space for the emergence of Zuma and forms of populism that we discuss in more detail below. In making this argument, she enrols Gramsci, specifically his argument that hegemony is never complete or seamless, but rather is defined by contradictions and struggle. However, Hart's attention to the 'double-edged character' of articulation, worked through the politics of South Africa, represents one of the key ways in which she advances this concept from earlier uses.

The second key contribution made by Hart to debates on articulation is the importance of language. In *Rethinking the South African Crisis*, she picks up on a growing interest in the role of language within Gramsci's writing and analysis (Hart 2013b). Insofar as articulation as a concept is bound up with meaning and expression, engaging with Gramsci's understanding of language allows for greater theoretical and analytical precision in terms of processes of meaning making and subject formation. Language, for Gramsci, is crucial in the struggle over hegemony: language is the bearer of various ideologies and spatial histories (consider linguistic differences between the city and country, as Gramsci does) and thus is one of the vehicles through which meaning is established through processes of articulation. Hart points to the role of language in linking together popular forms of nationalism with the rise of Zuma in South Africa. She explains that Zuma's 'signature song and dance "Awuleth' Umshini Wami" (Bring Me My Machine Gun) … evoked the pain and euphoria of the struggle years, constituting "a discursive site enabling publics to participate in national debates" (Gunner 2009, 28)' (Hart 2013b, 316). Hart's attention to cultural politics, language and articulation is crucial as there is a risk of leaving this terrain to those such as Laclau and Mouffe, who miss the importance of language in Gramsci's writings, all the while charging him with economism. Despite her indebtedness to Hall, Hart stresses how he also overlooks Gramsci's linguistic engagements: in his turn to Michel Foucault and post-structuralist approaches, it seems curious that Hall was not more attentive to the language question in Gramsci and in his own understandings of articulation. Hart's contribution to these debates is focused on the role of language in processes of articulation. She suggests that this results in a more subtle understanding of subject formation that occurs not only through processes of interpellation, which entails the making of subjects through ideologies that result in an identification with those same ideas, pieces of language, messages and philosophies. While not discounting these, Hart points to the importance of lived experiences that ground subject formation, which are always understood and narrated through the social character and meaning of languages.

It is evident that Hart takes forward the concept of articulation in a double sense: first, through using the concept to dissect particular political conjunctures from Mandela through to Zuma and the historical blocs they represent and, second, by asking how the analysis of particular political moments compels a refinement and translation of articulation itself as a concept. Such a refinement informs her analysis of the contradictory, double-edged and linguistic dimensions of articulation. As we will now show, Hart's development of the concept of articulation is of direct consequence for her engagement with the question of translation.

Situating 'translation'

Rooted in her ongoing investigations of how different social relations cohere or become fractured in particular conjunctures, translation (as a concept and practice) has been at the core of Hart's work for many years, particularly since 2013. As developed by Hart, translation focuses attention on how concrete political analysis, tied to social theory, might be rethought and challenged, based on the emergence of distinct historical and geographical conjunctures. As with articulation, Hart's engagements with Gramsci are emblematic of such an approach. Thus, the Sardinian's writings cannot simply be invoked to understand the turbulent politics of South Africa without simultaneously asking what his work enables and forecloses within this very different context. Texts and theories become a material and political force precisely when they are brought to bear and challenged by the earthly world they are supposed to account for.

If intimations of a practice of translation can be found in a number of Hart's essays, her most explicit engagements with a specifically Gramscian conception appear in her work on the languages of populism in South Africa in *Rethinking the South African Crisis* (Hart 2013b) and in 'Translating Gramsci in the Current Conjuncture' (Kipfer and Hart 2013). Both texts need to be read alongside the growing body of scholarship that now stresses the importance of linguistics to Gramsci's writings (see, for example, Ives 2004; Ives and Lacorte 2010). Pushed to its extreme, some, such as Franco Lo Piparo ([1979] 2010), claim that the roots to Gramsci's key concepts are found not in Marxism, but in his linguistic studies in Turin, hence Lo Piparo's provocative – and problematic – claim that the distinctiveness of Gramsci's conception of hegemony is to be found within 'the linguistic roots of Gramsci's non-Marxism', the title of his piece. Such a binary choice between a Marxist Gramsci or a linguistic Gramsci is clearly a false one and Hart instead deploys translation as a concept that can be understood linguistically while simultaneously drawing on and deepening Gramsci's specific reading of Marx and Marxism.

Quoting Peter Ives (2004), Kipfer and Hart (2013) stress that the etymological roots of translation imply *both* transmission *and* betrayal. Thus, 'for Gramsci translation is not just a matter of transmission but of transformation that may well be "traitorous" to the original (con)text' (Kipfer and Hart 2013, 327). Building on this practice of transmission/transformation, they first develop their own distinctive reading of Gramsci's writings on translation by emphasising the active role of politics in transforming a range of social relations, in particular through the moment of hegemony in which a range of different social forces come to be articulated. By developing a careful reading of the relations of force, Gramsci moves against economistic interpretations of social change: translation enables an analysis that simultaneously works across multiple temporalities and spatialities. Having established this claim, Kipfer and Hart then make the suggestion that translation might be allied to relational comparison, an approach in which comparisons utilise a relational and not bounded understanding of space (see chapter 3 in this volume). Translation might then be viewed as a framework for better understanding the de- and re-contextualisation of theory as it travels.

Building on this jointly political and linguistic reading of translation, Kipfer and Hart put the concept to work as part of a larger critique of the speculative left's (Bosteels 2011) abstract declarative readings of 'the political', or 'proper', 'real' politics (Kipfer and Hart 2013, 324). Contrasting Gramsci's conception of 'politics as translation' (323) to such speculative leftism enables Kipfer and Hart to put Gramsci's philosophy of praxis to work in the current conjuncture. 'Philosophy of praxis' refers to Gramsci's critical reconstruction of theory and philosophy on the basis of a critique rooted in, and emerging from, everyday working-class practice and conceptions of the world. A crucial reference point for Kipfer and Hart's development of Gramsci's concept of translation is Peter Thomas's wide-ranging analysis of the philosophy of praxis in *The Gramscian Moment* (2009b). More specifically, in an article titled 'Gramsci and the Political', Thomas (2009a) counters metaphysical and transcendental readings of politics through the twin concepts of translation and translatability. Gramsci's development of these twin concepts can be viewed as a response to Lenin's call for a translation of the Bolshevik Revolution into the languages of the West, a task that relates to Hart's own method of relational comparison, as we argue later. Of course, as Thomas is acutely aware, translation and translatability are also adapted from Gramsci's linguistic studies and his patient attention to 'the always unfinished and therefore transformable nature of relations of communication between social practices' (Thomas 2009a, 29).

While noting Thomas's careful attention to the question of translation in relation to questions of the political, Kipfer and Hart (2013) nevertheless note his failure to pay sufficient attention to the broad range of relations of force (in particular, processes relating to gender, sexuality, race and nationalism) and, instead, they seek to conceptualise translation as a decidedly spatio-historical concept, working across different geographical contexts. At one level, the concept of translation provides analytical and political leverage for understanding broad conjunctures – in Hart's own work, an analysis of populism and nationalism in South Africa and beyond. At another (connected) level, translation can be used within an analysis of *la persona* (the person) and can thereby provide a useful way into deepening Gramsci's distinctive approach to the question of human subjectivity. Applying translation in this manner implies a denaturalising move, whereby a concept of translation can be used to open up the multiple relations of force out of which different classed, raced and gendered persons are produced. In Hart's words, 'what Gramsci – and in related ways Vološinov and Bakhtin – contribute to this conception of the person is a theory of language as productive of meaning, as well as inseparable from practice and from the constitution of the self in relation to others' (2013a, 313). This shaping of the person can simultaneously be understood as a socio-ecological process in which the person is shaped out of a multiplicity of internal relations with human and non-human others (Ekers and Loftus 2013; Loftus 2013).

If such a reading of translation can be found explicitly and implicitly within Gramsci's writings, it also pushes him up against the limits of his own approach and thereby requires moving with and beyond him. Translation here is necessarily an act of interpretation as well as a traitorous act that transforms the original text: it is both an actualisation and a redirection of Gramsci – a translation – 'in a properly postcolonial, explicitly feminist, theoretically spatialised, and antiproductivist fashion' (Kipfer and Hart 2013, 331). Indeed, deploying Gramsci alongside the work of Frantz Fanon, Henri Lefebvre and Himani Bannerji, as

Kipfer and Hart (2013) seek to do, has implications for political practice: rethinking translation in this manner therefore enables one to better make sense of the possibilities for concrete political mobilisation in comparatively very distinct contexts. In so doing, an open-ended dialogue between a Gramscian conception of translation (as articulated by Kipfer and Hart 2013) and Hart's own method of relational comparison becomes possible. In this regard, it is perhaps no surprise that Kipfer and Hart's chapter sits between Hart's first development of relational comparison in 'Changing Concepts of Articulation' (2007) – based as it was on her more detailed analysis of relationally understood South African conditions in *Disabling Globalization* (2002a) – and her more recent revisiting of relational comparison in 'Relational Comparison Revisited' (2018). One of the characteristic features of the latter work is a much deeper engagement with dialectical method. Although Gramsci plays a relatively small role in the open-ended and non-teleological understanding of dialectics that Hart deploys, it is clear how her reading of Gramsci animates the relational understanding within this article. Relational comparison and translation need to be rethought in relation to one another as well as in relation to dialectical method.

For Hart, translation and articulation emerge as concepts that express the spatio-historical character of her work and allow her to navigate a careful path that avoids post-Marxist, economistic and speculative approaches, all of which treat the relationship between socio-economic, cultural and political forces in reductive or one-sided ways. As we discuss in the following section, the conjoined political and linguistic aspects of translation as a practice and concept help to further expand understandings of populism.

Populism

Populism is one of the most notoriously ambiguous terms in political analysis. This ambiguity is constitutive of the concept itself, which, in various formulations, alerts us to political claims that muddy the waters, parading vague notions of the people and their enemies while also blurring class lines in political programmes and policy strategies. Debates on the matter have raised a number of key questions: Is populism an ideology, a form or technique of political intervention, or a particular regime of state action? Can one identify different types of populism – top-down and bottom-up forms, right-wing and left-wing versions? Are claims to the people expressive of the social forces invoked, or do they rather constitute those social forces in the first place? Is populism a sign of socio-economic underdevelopment and an indication of political immaturity or is it, instead, a vital element in socialist strategy, in peripheralised or imperial zones, or both?

In her engagement with the topic in *Rethinking the South African Crisis*, Hart warns against two extreme views on populism: the view of those on the left who spontaneously allow their 'distaste ... towards nationalism and populism' to 'authorize neglect and dismissal' of these phenomena (2013a, 317) and the perspective of those, most famously Laclau and Mouffe, who elevate populism to a veritable political ontology, thus emancipating the political form of populism from its complexly articulated but real social content. To develop her point, Hart offers twin theoretical manoeuvres that build upon her previous engagements with the problematic of articulation and, in turn, develop the problematic of translation as a practice of recasting theoretical insights in and through analyses and engagements situated in novel contexts. In the first, she mobilises the younger historical-materialist Laclau (1977) against his more recent post-Marxist self (2005) to insist on the importance of placing the populisms of both dominant and subaltern forces in their multiply determined historical–geographical contexts. In the second, she draws on Gramsci, Fanon, Hall and South African sociologist Ari Sitas to nudge the residually Althusserian emphasis on populism as interpellation-from-above (in Laclau 1977) towards a properly dialectical conception of populism as a relation between dominant strategies and popular traditions, or, with Gramsci, between normative and spontaneous forms of grammar (Hart 2013a, 310–312).

The initial point of these theoretical moves was to illuminate political developments in South Africa since 2000: attempts by Thabo Mbeki, Jacob Zuma and Julius Malema (who was expelled from the ANC and formed the Economic Freedom Fighters party) to recast the post-apartheid conception of the South African nation consolidated by the ANC regime under Mandela. After having properly adjusted Laclau's approach, Hart lets the Argentinian disembark in South Africa to help us to understand the populist moves by Zuma and Malema. As she puts it: 'I draw on a revised version of Laclau's theory of bourgeois populism to argue that Mbeki sought to neutralise the revolutionary potential of popular antagonisms; Zuma sought to develop them but contain them within limits – which is always a dangerous experiment, as Laclau pointed out; and that Malema sought to capture and amplify the revolutionary potential of popular antagonisms, generating a dynamic that, the SACP [South African Communist Party] maintains, has tended towards fascism' (2013b, 197).

Hart's point here is to say that the danger of populism cannot be read off its constitutive addiction to establishing an antagonistic relationship between the people and the power bloc. This danger needs to be evaluated with respect to the capacity of populist forces (here: capital-sponsored factions in the ANC leadership) to grow by joining up, in particular conjunctures and in a dialectical fashion with 'popular antagonisms in the arenas of everyday life' and, in the process, blurring the distinction between 'left' and 'right' populisms (Hart 2013b, 197).

For Hart, the sequence running from Mbeki to Zuma and Malema attests to the 'unravelling of ANC hegemony' (2013b, 189). Brutally illustrated as well as intensified by the 2012 Marikana massacre of striking miners, in which Cyril Ramaphosa, the former union organiser and freedom fighter and now ANC leader, was directly implicated as a director of mining company Lonmin, this unravelling denotes a shrinking capacity of dominant fractions to recompose ruling blocs and thus manage the fault lines of post-apartheid racial capitalism. Hart spatialises our sense of these multiple fault lines, arguing that we can understand them as results of a twin process of de- and re-nationalisation (2013b). De-nationalisation describes how South African multinational capital escaped the constraints of apartheid South Africa, the strategies of state restructuring and ruling-class recomposition that made globalisation possible, as well as the harsh class and racialised polarisations that follow from both (Hart 2015, 48). Re-nationalisation captures the ways in which Nelson Mandela and Archbishop Desmond Tutu's view of South Africa as the Rainbow Nation was supplanted through a combination of 'xenophobic violence' and 'popular vigilantism' that threatens to build 'fortress South Africa' (49). In Hart's reading, populism is thus not a simple national reaction to global forces. It embodies, shapes and recasts globalising and nationalising processes in their tension-ridden relationships.

As we will see, Hart's insistence on the ongoing (if shifting) centrality of the national question highlights the limitations of all approaches to neo-liberalism and globalisation that treat nationalism as a passive force. Of course, in the (post-)colonial South, the salience of this question is of a particular kind, related as it is to the role of national liberation struggles in shaping the 'passive revolutions' that are part of many post-independence regimes. As variegated as it is, the weight of national liberation in post-colonial formations underscores the need to run Laclau and Gramsci through another stretching exercise supervised by Fanon. For Hart, Fanon's two-sided approach to the national question retains much promise in South Africa, where some on the left either ignore the national question or treat it as a formula, as a liberal-democratic stepping stone in the gradual development of socialism (Hart 2013b, 212–215). Fanon, she reminds us, not only warns of the pitfalls of national consciousness, the danger that national liberation might yield a false form of decolonisation. In what is effectively his 'answer' to Gramsci's national-popular outlook, Fanon also insists that a dynamic, internationally oriented national culture infused by ongoing popular efforts for emancipation and self-determination remains crucial in the struggle against narrow, neocolonial and bourgeois nationalisms (221–228).

The significance of Hart's contribution can be seen clearly in comparative intellectual context. Her insistence on bringing Gramsci and Laclau to South Africa, in part through Fanon, helps us see the difference between her approach and those who have analysed the African state by keeping Gramsci apart from Fanon, such as Jean-François Bayart ([1989] 2006). His work on the state in Africa represents a rich source for those interested in translating Gramsci's conception of passive revolution to the global South (Brooks and Loftus 2016). In fact, Bayart's main suggestion, that dependency be understood as an ongoing political practice, a recurrent project to fortify ruling blocs by economic, social and institutional 'extraversion', may help to specify how to study various aspects of 'de-nationalisation' also in the radicalised form of extraversion that is structural adjustment in sub-Saharan Africa ([1989] 2006, xii). However, Bayart's decision to dispatch Fanon as a simplistic proponent of a post-colonial *tabula rasa*, rather than one of the most insightful analysts of the national question in (post-)colonial situations, is costly (56). Beyond the political stakes involved – Bayart's remark sideswipes the problematic of liberation by putting analytical complexity on a pedestal sanctioned by Gramsci – this dismissal makes it difficult to grasp the links between the comparative meanings of the national question leading up to independence, post-colonial strategies of extraversion (de-nationalisation) and subsequent reformulations of the national (re-nationalisation).

Hart's research on populism and nationalism not only asserts but also demonstrates the possibility of putting a Fanon-inflected Gramsci to work for relational comparisons across the South, beyond Africa (2015). Her more recent move to relate her work on South Africa to Indian debates on passive revolution underscores the difference between a subtle historical materialism shaped by Gramsci, Laclau and Fanon and what one might call the civilisational turn in subaltern studies (and, perhaps more broadly speaking, post- and decolonial theory). One Indian exponent of this turn discussed by Hart (2015), Partha Chatterjee (2004), has delinked seemingly Gramscian terms (civil and political society) from Gramsci's conception of the state while reinventing a dated view of Gramsci as a Western Marxist preoccupied with supposedly just Euro-American problems: hegemony, civil society and consent. In partial contrast to his earlier work on passive revolution (Chatterjee 1986), as well as other historical materialist analyses of the Indian situation (Ahmad 1996, 2016; Bannerji 2010; Vanaik 2017), Chatterjee's more recent work (2004) is not only silent on the empirical comparability of Italy and India, as well as other places like Turkey and Pakistan (Mallick 2017; Riley and Desai 2007; Tuğal 2009, 2016). Supplanting Gramsci's (and Fanon's) relational method with dualist categories and a culturalist penchant, it also hides what is essential to Hart: the manifold relationships between far right populism (in this case, the Bharatiya Janata Party [BJP] and Hindu fundamentalism), the national question, social struggle and the multi-scalar contradictions of real-existing capitalism.

Conclusion: Hart in the imperial core

What lessons does Hart's work hold for those of us working in and on the imperial North? Her efforts to develop a relational approach to comparative and international political economy do, of course, speak to politically engaged debates in the global South (in and beyond her native South Africa), as well as ongoing intellectual controversies in development studies. However, many of Hart's analyses also intervene in debates that are situated within and centrally deal with developments in the global North. Shaped increasingly by a Fanon-inflected Marxian and Gramscian method, Hart has made it difficult for thoughtful researchers to, for example, treat neo-liberalism without attending to nationalism (2008), study accumulation (by dispossession or otherwise) without reference to racial capitalism (2006), and pursue urban questions while forgetting (the) land question(s) (2018). Clearly, Hart's contributions do more than put Euro-American research in place; they redirect it in part on the basis of insights from the global South.

As we have shown, she does this always by paying close attention to the complex articulation of multiple economic, social, cultural and political forces that shape particular conjunctures and that thus provide the dynamic, contradictory and living historical material that practices of translation must confront and transform.

To understand how Hart brings the South to bear on the North, her recent take on President Donald Trump's populism in 'Why Did it Take so Long?' is instructive (2020), particularly when compared to Nancy Fraser's parallel analysis in 'From Progressive Neoliberalism to Trump – and Beyond' (2017). Fraser sees Trump as a symptom of the crisis of 'progressive neoliberalism', that fusion of neo-liberal distribution and meritocratic recognition embodied by the Clinton–Obama lineage, which, according to Fraser, defeated the 'reactionary neoliberalism' of Ronald Reagan and the Bushes. For her, the 2016 election campaign, which was dominated by 'reactionary populism' (Trump) and 'progressive populism' (Bernie Sanders), showed that progressive neo-liberalism has exhausted itself. In this context, the alternative to Trump (who, in Fraser's view, has already jettisoned populism to return to an increasingly morbid form of reactionary neo-liberalism) can only come from a different political project. Her preference: a new alliance that manages to detach popular constituencies from their conservative commitments or elite leadership strata in order to challenge finance capital. How? Fraser proposes a 'progressive populism', capable of linking an anti-neo-liberal politics of redistribution to a material, class-inflected politics of gender, sexuality and anti-racism.

Broadly speaking, Hart's work shares Fraser's interest in a Gramscian analysis of Trump as well as Fraser's refusal to separate class from race and gender in counter-strategies. However, Hart's approach allows us to distinguish the weaknesses in Fraser's approach. Recasting her earlier critique of 'impact models' of globalisation (2002a) and mobilising her analysis of bourgeois populism in South Africa and India, Hart underscores that the phenomenon of Trump (and his one-time ally Steve Bannon) makes it impossible to uphold the idea that globalism and nationalism are external to each other. As in South Africa and India, the tensions between de- and re-nationalisation run straight through Trump and the broader universe of the (far) right in the United States, in an open-ended and unpredictable way, through a dizzying dance of factional conflicts, tactical shifts and interpersonal transformations that barely registers in Fraser's more schematic discussion. Hart's fine-grained analysis allows us to see not only how Trump defeated 'progressive neo-liberalism'. It also highlights the complex ways in which Trump and Bannon have taken up, redirected and challenged their reactionary *populist* predecessors (notably Reagan, Bush and Buchanan), who, rather than defeated for good by the Clinton–Obama lineage, had alternated with the latter to shape politics in the United States since the 1980s, and this similar to the ways in which Thatcherism and the BJP have historically interacted with New Labour and Congress in the United Kingdom and India (see Hall 2011; Vanaik 2017).

While Fraser (2017) opens her article with the claim that Trump is part of a global political crisis of hegemony but never develops this claim through her otherwise nationally focused analysis, Hart's rendering of Trump is consistently preoccupied with the national–global relation. She is clear about the qualitative specificities of de- and re-nationalisation in the United States. While the range of re-nationalisations suggested or promoted by Trump (and Bannon) is part of a sequence of (typically, but not exclusively neo-liberal) authoritarian populist projects, de-nationalisation has been very distinct from what is associated with the unravelling of both Nehruvian development – economic planning, secularism, non-alignment with the United States or the Soviet Union – and apartheid (Hart 2020). Why? Because, following Peter Gowan's (1999) analysis, the 'Dollar Wall Street regime' that emerged in response to the crisis of the Bretton Woods system was built on the backs of the Southern debt crisis of the 1980s while also extending working-class consumerism through subsequent rounds of credit expansion, at least until the collapse of mortgage-backed debt in 2008. The long-muted contradictions Trump and Bannon inherit, express and intensify are thus significantly imperial in scope and character.

Hart's emphasis on the imperial dimensions of American politics helps to answer her main question: Why did it take so long for a pair like Trump and Bannon to break through in Washington? Her answer raises an additional question for Fraser: How will 'progressive populism' deal with empire? Certainly, this second question concerns anyone who is interested in strategies against the far right that take the national question seriously, even those who do not share Fraser's easy embrace of the language of populism. In the imperial core, responses to right-populism or neo-fascism cannot appropriate the national the same way as they might in the (post-)colonial periphery, semi-peripheral or sub-imperial contexts, or re-peripheralised edges of the core like Greece. In the core, national political and economic projects are never just national; they build upon imperial or settler colonial divisions of labour unless these are questioned. And even where the national question can be articulated without catering to ethnicised nationalism (which is not always possible), it cannot draw at will from the most promising strands in the history of national *liberation* against imperial rule, colonial or otherwise. This is another reason why in the metropole in particular, 'national popular' left strategies inspired by Gramsci and Fanon must proceed with special care, in organic relationship with internationalist horizons and practices (Sotiris 2017).

NOTE

1   Parts of this chapter are adapted from Michael Ekers, Stefan Kipfer and Alex Loftus, 'On Articulation, Translation, and Populism: Gillian Hart's Postcolonial Marxism', *Annals of the American Association of Geographers* 110, no. 5 (2020): 1577–1593.

REFERENCES

Ahmad, Ajaz. 1996. *Lineages of the Present*. New Delhi: Tulika.

Ahmad, Ajaz. 2016. 'Liberal Democracy and the Extreme Right'. *Socialist Register* 52: 170–192.

Althusser, Louis. 1977. *For Marx*. London: New Left Books.

Althusser, Louis, Étienne Balibar, Roger Establet, Pierre Macherey and Jacques Rancière. 1970. *Reading Capital*. Translated by Ben Brewster. London: New Left Books.

Bannerji, Himani. 2010. *Demography and Democracy: Essays on Nationalism, Gender and Ideology*. Toronto: Canadian Scholars Press.

Bayart, Jean-François. (1989) 2006. *L'Etat en Afrique: La politique du ventre*. Paris: Fayard.

Bosteels, Bruno. 2011. *The Actuality of Communism*. London: Verso.

Brooks, Andrew and Alex Loftus. 2016. 'Africa's Passive Revolution: Crisis in Malawi'. *Transactions of the British Institute of Geography* 41: 258–272.

Chatterjee, Partha. 1986. *Nationalist Thought and the Colonial World: A Derivative Discourse*. London: Zed Books.

Chatterjee, Partha. 2004. *The Politics of the Governed: Reflections on Popular Politics in Most of the World*. New York: Columbia University Press.

De Janvry, Alain. 1981. *The Agrarian Question and Reformism in Latin America*. Baltimore: Johns Hopkins University Press.

Ekers, Michael and Alex Loftus. 2013. 'Revitalizing the Production of Nature Thesis: A Gramscian Turn'. *Progress in Human Geography* 37: 234–252.

Ekers, Michael, Gillian Hart, Stefan Kipfer and Alex Loftus, eds. 2013. *Gramsci: Space, Nature, Politics*. Oxford: Wiley-Blackwell.

Ekers, Michael, Stefan Kipfer and Alex Loftus. 2020. 'On Articulation, Translation, and Populism: Gillian Hart's Postcolonial Marxism'. *Annals of the American Association of Geographers* 110, no. 5: 1577–1593.

Fraser, Nancy. 2017. 'From Progressive Neoliberalism to Trump – and Beyond'. *American Affairs Journal* 1, no. 4: 46–64.

Goodman, Michael and Michael Redclift. 1981. *From Peasant to Proletarian: Capitalist Development and Agrarian Transitions*. Oxford: Basil Blackwell.

Gowan, Peter. 1999. *The Global Gamble: Washington's Faustian Bid for World Dominance*. London: Verso.

Gramsci, Antonio. 1971. *Selections from the Prison Notebooks*. New York: International Publishers.

Gunner, Liz. 2009. 'Jacob Zuma, the Social Body and the Unruly Power of Song'. *African Affairs* 108, no. 430: 27–48.

Hall, Stuart. 1977. 'Pluralism, Race and Class in Caribbean Society'. In *Race and Class in Post-Colonial Society: A Study of Ethnic Group Relations in the English-Speaking Caribbean, Bolivia, Chile and Mexico*, edited by UNESCO, 150–182. Paris: UNESCO.

Hall, Stuart. 1978. *Policing the Crisis: Mugging, the State, and Law and Order*. London: Holmes and Meier.

Hall, Stuart. 1980. 'Race Articulation and Societies Structured in Dominance'. In *Sociological Theories: Race and Colonialism*, edited by UNESCO, 305–345. Paris: UNESCO.

Hall, Stuart. 1988. *The Hard Road to Renewal: Thatcherism and the Crisis of the Left*. London: Verso.

Hall, Stuart. (1986) 1996a. 'Gramsci's Relevance for the Study of Race and Ethnicity'. In *Stuart Hall: Critical Dialogues in Cultural Studies*, edited by David Morley and Kuan Hsing Chen, 411–446. London: Routledge.

Hall, Stuart. (1986) 1996b. 'On Postmodernism and Articulation: An interview with Stuart Hall'. In *Stuart Hall: Critical Dialogues in Cultural Studies*, edited by David Morley and Kuan Hsing Chen, 131–151. London: Routledge.

Hall, Stuart. 2011. 'The Neoliberal Revolution'. *Cultural Studies* 25: 705–728.

Hart, Gillian. 2002a. *Disabling Globalization: Places of Power in Post-Apartheid South Africa*. Berkeley: University of California Press.

Hart, Gillian. 2002b. 'Geography and Development: Development/s beyond Neoliberalism? Power, Culture, Political Economy'. *Progress in Human Geography* 26: 812–822.

Hart, Gillian. 2006. 'Denaturalizing Dispossession: Critical Ethnography in the Age of Resurgent Imperialism'. *Antipode* 38: 977–1004.

Hart, Gillian. 2007. 'Changing Concepts of Articulation: Political Stakes in South Africa Today'. *Review of African Political Economy* 34: 85–101.

Hart, Gillian. 2008. 'The Provocations of Neoliberalism: Contesting the Nation and Liberation'. *Antipode* 40: 678–705.

Hart, Gillian. 2013a. 'Gramsci, Geography and the Languages of Populism'. In *Gramsci: Space, Nature, Politics*, edited by Michael Ekers, Gillian Hart, Stefan Kipfer and Alex Loftus, 301–320. Oxford: Wiley-Blackwell.

Hart, Gillian. 2013b. *Rethinking the South African Crisis: Nationalism, Populism, Hegemony*. Pietermaritzburg: University of KwaZulu-Natal Press.

Hart, Gillian. 2015. 'Political Society and Its Discontents: Translating Passive Revolution in India and South Africa Today'. *Economic and Political Weekly* 50, no. 43: 43–51.

Hart, Gillian. 2018. 'Relational Comparison Revisited: Marxist Postcolonial Geographies in Practice'. *Progress in Human Geography* 42: 371–394.

Hart, Gillian. 2020. 'Why Did it Take so Long? Trump-Bannonism in a Global Conjuncture'. *Geografiska Annaler*, Series B, Human Geography: 102: 239–266.

Hindess, Barry and Paul Hirst. 1975. *Pre-Capitalist Modes of Production*. London: Routledge and Kegan Paul.

Ives, Peter. 2004. *Language and Hegemony in Gramsci*. London: Pluto Press.

Ives, Peter and Rocco Lacorte. 2010. *Gramsci, Language and Translation*. Lanham, MA: Rowman and Littlefield.

Kipfer, Stefan and Gillian Hart. 2013. 'Translating Gramsci in the Current Conjuncture'. In *Gramsci: Space, Nature, Politics*, edited by Michael Ekers, Gillian Hart, Stefan Kipfer and Alex Loftus, 323–343. Oxford: Wiley-Blackwell.

Laclau, Ernesto. 1977. *Politics and Ideology in Marxist Theory: Capitalism, Fascism, Populism*. London: Verso.

Laclau, Ernesto. 2005. *On Populist Reason*. London: Verso.

Laclau, Ernesto and Chantal Mouffe. 1985. *Hegemony & Socialist Strategy: Towards a Radical Democratic Politics*. London: Verso.

Loftus, Alex. 2013. 'Gramsci, Nature and the Philosophy of Praxis'. In *Gramsci: Space, Nature, Politics*, edited by Michael Ekers, Gillian Hart, Stefan Kipfer and Alex Loftus, 301–320. Oxford: Wiley-Blackwell.

Lo Piparo, Franco. (1979) 2010. 'The Linguistic Roots of Gramsci's Non-Marxism'. In *Gramsci, Language and Translation*, edited by Peter Ives and Rocco Lacorte, 19–28. Lanham, MA: Rowman and Littlefield.

Mallick, Ayyaz. 2017. 'Beyond "Domination without Hegemony": Passive Revolution(s) in Pakistan'. *Studies in Political Economy* 98: 239–262.

Marx, Karl. (1858) 1973. *Grundrisse: Foundations of the Critique of Political Economy (Rough Draft)*. Harmondsworth: Penguin.

Riley, Dylan and Manali Desai. 2007. 'The Passive Revolutionary Route to the Modern World: Italy and India in Comparative Perspective'. *Comparative Studies in Society and History* 49: 815–847.

Sotiris, Panagiotis. 2017. 'From the Nation to the People of a Potential New Historical Bloc: Rethinking Popular Sovereignty through Gramsci'. *International Gramsci Journal* 2: 52–88.

Thomas, Peter. 2009a. 'Gramsci and the Political: From the State as "Metaphysical Event" to Hegemony as "Philosophical Fact"'. *Radical Philosophy* 153: 27–36.

Thomas, Peter. 2009b. *The Gramscian Moment: Philosophy, Hegemony and Marxism*. Leiden: Brill.

Tuğal, Cihan. 2009. *Passive Revolution: Absorbing the Islamic Challenge to Capitalism*. Stanford: Stanford University Press.

Tuğal, Cihan. 2016. *The Fall of the Turkish Model: How the Arab Uprisings Brought Down Islamic Liberalism*. London: Verso.

Vanaik, Achin. 2017. *The Rise of Hindu Authoritarianism: Secular Claims, Communal Realities*. London: Verso.

Wolpe, Harold. 1975. 'The Theory of Internal Colonialism: The South African Case'. In *Beyond the Sociology of Development*, edited by Ivar Oxhaal, Tony Barnett and David Booth, 229–252. London: Routledge & Kegan Paul.

Wolpe, Harold. 1980. 'Introduction'. In *The Articulation of Modes of Production: Essays from Economy and Society*, edited by Harold Wolpe, 1–43. London: Routledge & Kegan Paul.

8 | Make 'Articulation' Gramscian Again

Zachary Levenson

If anyone were to undertake to make the mass strike generally, as a form of proletarian action, the object of methodological agitation, and to go house to house canvassing with this 'idea' in order to gradually win the working class to it, it would be as idle and profitless and absurd an occupation as it would be to seek to make the idea of the revolution or of the fight at the barricades the object of a special agitation.

— Rosa Luxemburg, 'The Mass Strike'

This chapter draws on Gillian Hart's development of the concept of articulation over the past two decades. It argues that she transforms an otherwise Althusserian concept into a Gramscian one. Beyond understandings of articulation as simply 'joining together', Hart builds on the work of Stuart Hall to add a second connotation to the concept: 'giving expression to'. By restoring the key role of meaning making to Marxist analysis, she breaks with deterministic models of politicisation. As an alternative, Hart argues that radicalisation occurs on the terrain of everyday life, meaning that politics are not imputed from some external vantage point, but rather cultivated from what Antonio Gramsci called 'common sense' into 'good sense'. The chapter concludes by setting the concept of articulation to work in the context of two South African land occupations. How organisers articulated each respective project of occupation shaped how residents mobilised in practice, which, in turn, affected the legal status of each: one occupation was tolerated while the other was evicted. Articulation helps us to understand why.

Making 'critical'

An upsurge in South African working-class militancy in the early 2000s initiated a wave of optimism among leftist observers of the country. After considerable anti-government protests at a pair of United Nations-initiated conferences in 2001 and 2002, the names of high-profile organisations directly confronting the ruling party began to proliferate: the Anti-Privatisation Forum, the Landless People's Movement, the Anti-Eviction Campaign, the Soweto Electricity Crisis Committee, Abahlali baseMjondolo, the Unemployed People's Movement and countless others. Academics were eager to link these struggles into a force capable of contesting what they perceived as the African National Congress' (ANC's) neo-liberal drift, and in 2006 they convened a Social Movements Indaba (SMI) at the University of KwaZulu-Natal for this purpose. While the conference ended in disaster, with two of the larger delegations walking out altogether, it still represented the moment of peak academic optimism in relation to class struggles on the ground.

Among the first of these confident academic narratives was Ashwin Desai's *We Are the Poors* (2002), an account of squatters' militancy in Durban, which he linked to the anti-government protests at the United Nations World Conference Against Racism. This, he insisted, would be a force capable of challenging the ANC. In *Fanonian Practices in South Africa*, Nigel Gibson (2011) romanticised another Durban-based shack-dwellers' movement (Abahlali baseMjondolo) as a Fanonian response to a failed liberation movement, contributing to a ballooning literature making similar arguments about the organisation. A series of widely cited edited volumes released in the years between these two texts documented the rise of countless additional social movements, considering them both ethnographically and in comparative historical perspective (Ballard, Habib and Valodia 2006; Beinart and Dawson 2010; Gibson 2006). Beyond the purview of formally constituted social movement organisations, Peter Alexander (2010) described a growing number of protests over access to services and housing as a 'rebellion of the poor', suggesting that these localised protests were likely to coalesce into a force capable of challenging the ruling party. When an alliance failed to materialise, Patrick Bond and Shauna Mottiar (2013, 291) attributed this to the 'lack of ideological and strategic coherence' among residents. John Saul (2012) concurred, blaming the lack of a viable 'counter-hegemonic movement' on a lack of structure.

Just as many sympathetic academics were dismayed after the SMI walkout, seeking to impose a 'correct' model of organising on the participants, critics of service delivery protests lectured those who burned tyres, marched in the streets and faced down rubber bullets, scolding them for pursuing inadequate organisational strategy and selecting inappropriate targets. Reading through some of these critiques at the time, I could not help but recall Fran Piven and Richard Cloward's injunction against this sort of sermonising more than a quarter century earlier. 'People experience deprivation and oppression within a concrete setting, not as the end product of large and abstract processes,' they point out. 'No small wonder, therefore, that when the poor rebel they so often rebel against the overseer of the poor, or the slumlord, or the middling merchant, and not against the banks or the governing elites to whom the overseer, the slumlord and the merchant also defer. In other words, it is the daily experience of people that shapes their grievances, establishes the measure of their demands, and points out the target of their anger' (Piven and Cloward 1979, 20–21). They are not suggesting that larger movements are not more effective than smaller ones – that much is obvious. The targets of their irritation are those who think movements are fragmented because participants lack proper understanding. These academic Prometheans bring knowledge from on high to the movements below, their thinking goes, enabling the struggles limited by their own immediacy to become truly politicised.

Piven and Cloward insist that importing knowledge from the realm of abstraction is futile; the point is to intervene at the level of everyday life. A voluminous literature in Marxist theory speaks to this question, whether Henri Lefebvre's discussion of revolutionising everyday life (2014) or Gramsci's discussion of cultivating common sense into good sense ([1971] 2016) – though neither theorist is substantively engaged in any of the South African debates cited above. Many would do well though to heed Gramsci's advice from his *Prison Notebooks*: 'It is not a question of introducing from scratch a scientific form of thought into everyone's individual life, but of renovating and making "critical" an already existing activity' (Gramsci [1971] 2016, 330–331). Rosa Luxemburg makes a similar point in the epigraph to this chapter: peddling an 'idea' (akin to Gramsci's 'scientific form of thought') to the masses is an exercise in futility. Instead, critical ideas must be developed organically through real material practices – what Gramsci calls the 'philosophy of praxis'. People are not at war with racism or neo-liberalism as abstract concepts; they are furious with the cop who frisks them every time they walk down their own block and they are annoyed by their university administrators (and maybe even their elected representatives) when their universities get defunded and student fees begin to skyrocket. There is no 'racism in general' (Hart 2002a, 30; cf. Hall 1980, 308) and people 'do not experience monopoly capitalism' (Piven and Cloward 1979, 20).

Intervening at this level of abstraction is strategically useless, as it fails to comprehend how individuals come to understand themselves as 'in struggle' in the first place. Instead, Gramsci's renovation and 'making "critical"' of common sense – of people's beliefs as 'already existing, self-evident truths' (Crehan 2016, x) – requires a rejection of abstract determination in favour of *historical* determination. And for Hart, this means understanding 'how diverse forces come together in particular ways to create a new political terrain' (2002a, 27). In other words, we cannot understand people's politics as the necessary consequence of certain economic (or even discursive) conditions. Both 'vanguardist' Marxism (Hart 2008, 2014) and 'account[s] of subject formation in which subject effects are automatically secured' (Hart 2008, 687) fail to understand how political subjectivity is actually produced at the nexus of diverse forces and relations. This is not to reject determination altogether, relegating subjectivity to the realm of the purely contingent, but to understand how historical determination proceeds, as opposed to abstract determination (Hart 2002a, 2004).

Towards a relational theory of articulation

Hart's key innovation in this respect has been to revive the concept of articulation, developed in Althusserian circles, though it was subsequently reappropriated by Louis Althusser's critics and developed in a Gramscian direction as a way to understand how political subjects are produced in practice. What is most remarkable in Hart's use is that she successfully excavates the Gramscian traces in these critiques of abstract determination – most notably in the early work of Ernesto Laclau (1977) and in Stuart Hall's (1980) engagement with South African race/class debates – and implores us to use a reconstructed Gramscian concept against Althusser himself.

In her earliest substantial engagement with the concept, her book *Disabling Globalization*, Hart (2002a) draws on Hall's use of the term in 'Race, Articulation, and Societies Structured in Dominance' (1980), arguing that it has a double meaning: both 'joining together' and 'giving expression to' (cf. Hart 2002b, 2004, 2007, 2013, 2014). In the work of Althusser and his students the term only refers to connectedness. By omitting the simultaneous production of meaning, she argues, we cannot possibly understand processes of politicisation. By recognising meaning and practice as inseparable (Hart 2002b, 818), we can trace how actually existing actors (and groups of actors) are alternatively enabled and constrained by material and discursive contexts. Just as

Gramsci's concept of hegemony elucidates how people understand their own interests in relation to a conjunctural balance of class relations and social forces, 'articulation' places actors in an open space in which meanings, constraints and interests are constantly in flux, articulated and re-articulated in a perpetual process of contestation (see chapter 7 in this volume). We have seen how political subjects do not target neo-liberalism or racism in the abstract; they challenge localised, observable agents. But the very identification of these agents as inimical to one's interests is itself shaped by a set of material constraints and narratives of self-understanding. The contest over these narratives, over the process of meaning making, is the unceasing struggle Gramsci called hegemony. Or as Hall puts it, 'In order to "think" real, concrete historical complexity, we must reconstruct in the mind the determinations which constitute it. Thus, what is multiply determined, diversely unified, in history ... appears in thought, in theory, not as "where we take off from" but *as that which must be produced*' (Hall 1974, 148–149; emphasis in original). Articulation is this process of production.

In her article 'Changing Concepts of Articulation' Hart (2007) fleshes out this formulation and demonstrates why it matters in a South African context. Why have left-wing challenges to the ANC failed to gain any traction since democratisation? The ruling party was able to represent itself as orchestrating a post-apartheid nation-building project, with any contestations to its reign articulated as threatening the nation. The task of the intellectual, Hart insists, is not to simply 'rip away the mask that obfuscates neoliberal class power' (2008, 688), exposing the true nature of the ANC. This sort of 'cynical manipulation from above' (Hart 2007, 94) treats potential political subjects as empty vessels, *tabulae rasae* upon which intellectuals can inscribe a purportedly universal roadmap to their own self-emancipation – precisely what we saw in the opening of this chapter. But these potential subjects already exist in the world. The 'tropes of traditional left activism' can never 'name [the] quotidian significations, singular practices, partially elaborated resentments, and ambivalent engagements with mainstream organisations and institutions' (Barchiesi 2011, 244) that comprise residents' social locations in the space of everyday life. Hart's account of 'articulation' gives us a vocabulary with which we as analysts, strategists and intellectuals can engage with questions of the apparent immobility of the working class, but without treating them as so many free agents in a game of communist fantasy football.

It is not solely by virtue of their location in some socio-economic space that proletarians revolt. Nor, as we have seen, is it the revelation of this location from on high that catalyses the formation of alliances, blocs and organisations. This is the problem with dismissals of particular racialised, gendered and sexed identities as obstacles to class unity: there *is* no class beyond that which actually exists in material reality and this classed existence is never experienced in its 'pure' state. In one of his most quoted statements, Hall writes, 'Race is thus, also, the modality in which class is "lived," the medium through which class relations are experienced, the form in which it is appropriated and "fought through"' (1980, 341). It is insufficient for intellectuals to reveal to workers that their racialised identification is 'false' or that it inhibits some inexorable unification of the class. Conjunctural race–class articulations, once internalised, become real, material facts.

In each specific historical context, these articulations take different forms and they may very well be articulated with additional elements: gender, sex, sexuality, nationality and/or nationalism and so forth. The trick, as Hart puts it, is 'understanding politics as *process*' (2002a, 28; emphasis in original), with meaning conceived as inseparable from practical activity. This is the standpoint of Gramsci's philosophy of praxis: it allows us to grasp 'how fragmentary common sense can become coherent through collective practices and processes of transformation, central to which are language and translation' (Hart 2013, 315). People produce meaning in their everyday lives, but they do so within the confines of existing determinations, both material and discursive. It is through these processes of politicisation that people come to understand their own activity in relation to the world.

Articulation allows us to understand people as located in these conjunctural nexuses of various forces and relations, an approach that has two merits. First, it is *non-reductionist* insofar as it rejects the notion that these determinations are eternal or can be conceived of as laws (Hart 2002a, 2002b, 2007). And second, it is *relational* in that it rejects a model in which agents instrumentally impose these determinations from above. Each articulation 'has constantly to be renewed [and] can under some circumstances disappear or be overthrown, leading to the old linkages being dissolved and new connections – re-articulations – being forged' (Hall 1985, 113–114). Articulation is not simply a way for understanding how various social formations produce political subjects, as if the gradient runs from state or economy to civil society, as in Michel Foucault or Althusser. In its Gramscian formulation, the state is relational, a site of constant contestation over articulations and re-articulations. People can reshape meanings, but not in a vacuum; re-articulations embody a certain agency, but they are simultaneously forged within the confines of historically specific forces and relations.

In the next section, I briefly summarise the Althusserian version of articulation, demonstrating the irony of Althusser's project. If he intended the concept as an alternative to 'reflectionist' Marxism, the old pipeline from base to superstructure,[1] in practice it ends up bolstering an instrumentalist theory of the capitalist state. Drawing on Laclau and Hall, Hart shows how Althusser lacks any viable theory of political subject formation – and therefore of politics. The closest he comes is his discussion of 'interpellation', but Hart reveals how he commits precisely the fallacy that was confronted by Luxemburg, Piven and Cloward, Gramsci, Hall, and now Hart; namely that people can simply impose a set of ideologies or rationalities from above onto the passive space of civil society. Rather, this space of civil society is a site of struggle, of a never-settled process of contestation over the production of meaning that is both an effect and a constitutive part of the process of subjects coming to understand themselves as political actors in the first place.

I then examine a concrete site of struggles over re-articulation, focusing on the politics of land occupations in contemporary South Africa. Hart argues that 're-articulating the land question could potentially link together diverse demands' (2014, 20). Access to land, she contends, is currently articulated in terms of individual restitution claims, whereas she suggests one viable strategy would be to 're-articulate them in broader and more collective terms to demand redistributive social change and livelihood guarantees' (20). Rather than making abstract demands for redistribution in general, or else for various actors to unite against some amorphous neo-liberal government, she insists we work through an existing common sense: the demand for access to land articulated as part of a post-apartheid nation-building project. It is a matter of 'think[ing] *with* nationalism *against* nationalism' (13; emphasis in original), grasping the popular appeal of land redistribution as a nationalist project, but dis-articulating access to land from blanket support for political parties.

The Althusserian legacy

One reason it remains so challenging to define 'articulation' straightforwardly is that its referents have shifted dramatically since its inception. Initially a phonetic term for the physical production of speech sounds, it made its way into the structuralist canon by way of Roman Jakobson and Claude Lévi-Strauss, coming to describe the way that seemingly disparate elements possessed underlying homologous structures. As such, they were articulated – joined – into a larger system, structured like a language on the model of Saussurean linguistics. Drawing on this structuralist lineage, Althusser deployed the concept to get away from the reductive theorisations of capitalism that continued to permeate the official Marxism of his contemporaries. Certainly less mechanical Marxisms proliferated from the end of the nineteenth century onwards, from Antonio Labriola through Henri Lefebvre, but these were largely formulated on the margins of the party. For Althusser, by contrast, the goal was to remake the Marxism of the French Communist Party.

For Althusser and his students, multiple economic systems could be articulated into a single social formation, allowing for more contextually nuanced research on actually existing capitalist economies (Althusser et al. [1965] 2015). In some of his other work, he used the term to bypass another variant of reductionist Marxism: an assumed channel from base to superstructure (Althusser [1965] 1969). Each mode of production was comprised of various 'levels', all articulated into a single system. These levels – political, cultural and countless others – were not to be read off an all-powerful economic base, but were, along with the economic level, to be considered as part of a complex, mutually determinative system. The relative autonomy ascribed to these levels would allow us to make sense, say, of a situation in which the proletariat is not particularly hot-blooded despite 'ripe' economic conditions. His student Nicos Poulantzas ([1970] 1974) put this model to work when he explained the rise of European fascism not as the Great Depression automatically generating its own political reactions, but as a response to a crisis in bourgeois politics at the time – an unthinkable origin story in the old reflectionist idiom.

Fast-forward a few decades and Hart is making similar claims to Althusser, setting 'articulation' to work as the central concept in developing any 'non-reductionist' Marxism (Hart 2002a, 2002b, 2007). Yet it is *against* Althusser that she develops the concept. How did an erstwhile critic of economism become its most notorious proponent in retrospect? Today, rather than remembering Althusserian accounts of articulated social formations for the challenge they posed to reductive Marxism, we tend to assimilate them to the reflectionist epistemology of the Second International. Largely, this is attributable to the insufficient attention Althusser paid to politics, relative autonomy notwithstanding.[2] If by 'politics' we mean the question of how subjects find themselves already engaged in struggle against antagonistic forces, Althusser ([1971] 2001) developed an account that inexplicably divorced the processes through which political subjects are made – what he called 'interpellation' – from any location in socio-economic space (his 'social formation'). Despite his earlier writings, this brief account of subject formation relies on the most abstract determination possible: ideology, part of a larger system of ideological state apparatuses (ISAs), hails or 'interpellates' individuals as subjects, subjecting them to capitalist domination in the process. As in the case of left intellectuals attempting to manipulate empty proletarian vessels, Althusser's ISAs subjectivate agents who previously lacked any subjectivity whatsoever.[3] These are not historically determined actors who are confronted with ideologies while located at the nexus of competing and intersecting forces and relations, but rather interchangeable individuals on the model of liberal political theory, or more aptly here, Lacanian psychoanalysis.

For Althusser, articulation remains in the base but fails to make its way into the superstructure. We are left without any idea as to how the subjectivating capacities of the state are related (or connected) to socio-economic context. Articulation in all of this means that these various levels are linked together as a complex totality, governed in the last instance by what Althusser called the dominant structure: capitalist relations of production. It was a way of eating his cake and having it too: on the one hand, contingency was not written out of the story, as levels were relatively autonomous; on the other hand, the narrative was manifestly structuralist, with an ultimate 'cause' located in the base. This is not a problem because we are enjoined to cling to 'the last instance' like some Marxist rosary; the problem is that the forging of political subjectivity is enacted – or interpellated – 'upon' abstract individuals instead of people with everyday lives in the modern world. They are conceived as if they were blank canvases.

Hart's entire project is to overthrow the residual top-down construction of the interpellation model, instead opting for an account of 'complex back-and-forth processes of contestation and acquiescence through which multiple, interconnected arenas in state and civil society have been remaking one another' (Hart 2008, 684). The point is not to understand locally specific articulations as '*products*' but instead as '*constitutive processes* through which political subjects are made'

(Hart 2002a, 298; emphasis in original). In its materialist iteration, we see these limits at work in Althusser's writings of the mid-1960s, with social formations producing their own ideologies. And at its idealist pole, we can identify limits in Althusser's slightly later model of interpellation in which an ideological apparatus tied to the state 'creates' subjects *de novo*.

We find something similar in both Foucault ([1978–1979] 2010) and his British interpreters (for example, Barry, Osborne and Rose 1996; Burchell, Gordon and Miller 1991; Rose 1999), akin to what Hart (2001, 2002a, 2004, 2006b, 2009, 2018) has consistently called the 'impact model': the superimposition of generalised forces from above onto localised sites. These forces appear monolithic, inexorable and, above all, active, whereas those who are subjected are represented as passive containers to be filled with ideological content from above. Foucauldian accounts of neo-liberalism-as-governmentality reproduce this impact model, providing an 'account of subject formation in which subject effects are automatically secured' (Hart 2008, 687). Subjects are passive, only becoming subjects insofar as they are interpellated from above – though in Foucault's case it is not by ideologies or an ideological state apparatus, but by governmental rationalities. There is no space in this formulation for interpellated subjects to contest, transform and re-articulate the content of ideologies, rationalities or discourses. But Hall's critique of Althusser could just as easily be applied to Foucault: rationalities 'remain contradictory structures, which can function both as the vehicles for the imposition of dominant ideologies, and as the elementary forms for the cultures of resistance' (Hall 1980, 342).

It is in this sense that Hart calls articulations 'double-edged' (2014, 200). The South African government may very well invoke the consolidation of post-apartheid democracy 'as a disciplinary weapon against social movements' (198), framing them as threatening this project; but these same movements can work within the confines of existing articulations, claiming that the state's hegemonic project *fails* to uphold the articulation of nationalism to liberation. Or, as Ari Sitas (1990, 263, 273) explains in his critique of interpellation in a South African context, prevailing 'social views and visions' – common sense in Gramscian terms – are not solely the end product of some interpellation 'from above'. A given identity or self-understanding – 'Zulu-ness' in Sitas' case – 'must be viewed as a negotiated identity between ordinary people's attempts to create effective and reciprocal social bonds (or functioning cultural formations) out of their social and material conditions of life and political ideologies that seek to mobilise them in non-class ways' (Hart 2014, 266). Identities are not simply imputed from on high, but are the constantly fluctuating products of complex processes of negotiation and re-articulation. To reiterate, ideologies and rationalities do not encounter individuals as empty vessels, imprinting them with some pre-given image. Rather, they encounter people who already have a well-developed common sense and they function to re-articulate existing components of articulations to new elements, often introduced from the outside. We might think here of Jacob Zuma's suturing of an empty black nationalism to limited black embourgeoisement, without substantial gains for most black South Africans; or we could think of Donald Trump's re-articulation of post-crisis popular resentment to a programme of deregulation he has reinscribed as transgressive. The point is that interpellations and governmental rationalities do not make subjects *de novo*, but form them out of existing materials, re-articulating elements of their common sense to be sure, but never hoisting pre-formed ideologies upon them ready-to-hand.

Struggles over the production of meaning

Althusser's articulations are social formations, with multiple socio-economic systems bound together into conjunctural combinations, including ideological, political and cultural 'levels'. Interpellation in his subsequent writing is a concept designed to capture how ideology (as part of a social formation) functions in relation to capitalist relations of production, as well as an attempt to explain the formation of political subjectivity in a capitalist context. Hart's critique of both

Althusser and Foucault is rooted in the way that these processes of subjectification proceed without regard to subject effects – that is, the extent to which these top-down processes encounter individuals who already have a conception of the world and their place in it. The nail in the coffin of interpellation, she insists, is its 'incapacity in relation to the philosophy of praxis': it does not deal with pre-existing common sense and how people's social views and visions only 'become coherent through collective practices' (Hart 2013, 314–315). By turning to Gramsci, Hart can conceive of the formation of political subjectivity as 'a cultural battle to transform the popular "mentality"' (Gramsci [1971] 2016, 348) in which articulation is a struggle over the production of meaning.

Yet, as Hart is quick to point out, meaning can never be divorced from material conditions, ripped from its class context. This was the error of Ernesto Laclau and Chantal Mouffe (1985), whose book *Hegemony and Socialist Strategy* is consistently in Hart's crosshairs. In that book and Laclau's later work (for example, 2005), articulation is deployed in direct contrast to the alleged determinism of Marxist accounts of classed politics. As Laclau and Mouffe argue in the first third of their book, a purportedly revolutionary proletariat never develops organically or of its own accord, as if its location in the capitalist relations of production should automatically yield a class-for-itself – let alone socialist politics. In nearly every instance, political content comes from *outside* the class and often from extra-proletarian sources. Whether we are talking about Marx and Engels, Lenin, or someone else entirely, they argue that politics is wholly contingent and has nothing to do with class position whatsoever.

We might turn Hart's critique of interpellation against Laclau and Mouffe as well. Do discursive formations have no material basis, as they argue? Do they not encounter classed subjects already inserted in given relations of production with all of the historical determinations and structural constraints that these entail? The very notion that populist strategy is about creating an appealing discourse that can be articulated to a 'people' (Laclau 2005) neglects to consider the material reality of that people – its common sense, in Gramscian terms, which is of course a markedly classed phenomenon. And do these populist discourses not always have classed effects? When, for example, they describe a post-war discursive shift, they can only account for it in relation to 'the expansion of capitalist relations of production and of the new bureaucratic-state forms' (Laclau and Mouffe 1985, 162).

It is here that Hart asks us to return to Laclau's earlier work (1977), in which he first developed the idea of populist articulations that do not simply reflect existing class arrangements. But at this point Laclau had not yet abandoned class and popular-democratic articulations are developed only in relation to existing class projects. Political actors construct a discourse around an antagonism between 'the people' and what, borrowing from Poulantzas ([1968] 1978), he called 'the power bloc'. But this antagonism is articulated to a second: class struggle. If class were irrelevant, how would populist politicians consistently resolve the popular-democratic contradiction (between 'the people' and 'the power bloc') without threatening the pockets of capital? In ignoring class in their later work, Laclau and Mouffe remove any material constraints that might govern the realm of possible articulatory practices, slipping instead into a concept of articulation in which only discourse produces political subjectivities. But as Hart points out, this is an ahistorical, abstract determinism that 'fall[s] back on a structural analysis of language that is every bit as rigid as the structural Marxism of which they are so critical' (2002a, 31). In the place of one determinism then, they give us another.

This abstract determinism is not so present in Laclau's earlier writing on populism, though Hart does take him to task for relying on 'interpellation' as a way of accounting for the pathway from articulations to the formation of political subjectivities. Any ideological discourse, Laclau tells us, coheres as such only insofar as it is capable of interpellating 'subjects' (1977, 101). But this falls back on a model of subjectification in which potential subjects are simply empty containers to be filled with content rather than really existing people who already have complex worldviews and understandings of their places in the prevailing order. In other words, Laclau absolutely advances our understanding of articulation, extending Althusser's sense of 'linking together' to include the production of meaning (Hart 2013, 308). With this move, we can see how these linkages are tied to prevailing worldviews, or in Gramsci's language, common sense. But he stops short, Hart insists, constrained by his reliance on 'interpellation', which constitutes subjects through discourse rather than re-articulating already existing configurations.

It was Hall who made this Gramscian breakthrough, confronting the Althusserian penchant for assuming that dominant classes have full control over ideologies, deploying them at will. Ideologies, Hall argues, already exist, both among rulers and ruled, and it is from these existing components that new worldviews must be re-articulated. He takes this directly from Gramsci, understanding these ideologies – each fundamental class's common sense – as 'themselves the complex result of previous moments and resolutions in the ideological class struggle [and as such] can be actively *worked upon*' (Hall 1980, 334; emphasis in original). Like Laclau, Hall targets reductive formulations that simply deduce political and ideological currents from some economic base. Instead, he insists that we need to depart from the 'historical premise' that these do not emerge ready-made from the conveyor belt of history but are forged in the process of re-articulation. But we must do so, contra Laclau and Mouffe, without abandoning the 'materialist premise'; namely, that ideological and political structures can never be fully detached from their material conditions of existence. A dialectical analysis of articulation would think these two premises in relation to one another, balancing contingency and determination.

It is on this count that Hall takes to task the great South African sociologist Harold Wolpe, who popularised the Althusserian meaning of articulation in relation to debates over capitalism and apartheid.

Wolpe (1972) used 'articulation' to mean a linkage, describing the South African social formation as articulated modes of production. Whereas the prevailing view in both Marxist and liberal circles at the time was that capitalist development would necessarily eradicate 'pre-capitalist' pockets (Friedman 2015), Wolpe showed how the apartheid state in South Africa actively preserved these non-capitalist enclaves, even fostering their expansion. He argued that because residents of these spaces had not been dispossessed, they had direct access to means of reproduction – meaning that they could sustain themselves independently of the market. It was the insidiousness of the South African state to create a migrant labour regime in which mineworkers could consistently return to these extra-capitalist 'homelands' and eat for free. In short, it was a means of subsidising their wages, allowing them to fall below what would otherwise be the physical limits imposed by necessary labour time.

In addition to the migrant labour system, Wolpe's model was among the first to think of processes of racialisation in relation to capitalist development, rather than assuming the two were necessarily in conflict, or that racism was some holdover from some pre-modern era of ascribed rather than achieved identities. But Hall admonishes Wolpe for bending the stick, theorising such a neat correspondence between base and superstructure as to be essentially functionalist: Wolpe argued that articulated modes of production 'required' racial subjugation. 'The level of economic analysis, so redefined, may not supply sufficient conditions in itself for an explanation of the emergence and operation of racism,' Hall suggested (1980, 322). This economic configuration does not automatically secrete racism; instead, racial stigmatisation was a conscious re-articulation carried out as a political project of the apartheid power bloc. It was this critique, Hart (2002a, 2007) asserts, that led Wolpe (1988, 50–54) to reformulate his own understanding of race–class articulations in his subsequent work. This is what Hart (2007, 86) calls the 'Gramscian conception of articulation': it harnesses

Althusser's articulation as 'joining together' to Hall's articulation as 'producing meaning'. In so doing, it captures how people grasp for fragments of understanding, piecing them together so as to create working, coherent worldviews. These assembled shards may remain in stable configurations for a time, or they may be constantly in flux. In either case, their stability is never eternal, but must be perpetually renewed, to paraphrase Hall (1985, 113). This project of renewal takes the form of creating new articulations and dissolving old ones, which in practice means that the forging of political consciousness is simultaneously a struggle over how people understand the meaning of their actions in the world. It also means that this 'political consciousness' is not necessarily invested with the powers of autonomy; it may very well mean being *subjected* to the rule of the capitalist state. It is for this reason that articulations are a site of unremitting struggle: they are polyvalent, as Hart teaches us, and as such, may go in many directions (Hart 2007, 98; 2014, 203, 207).

In the final section, I analyse an instance of contrasting re-articulations in a township in contemporary Cape Town. Despite comparable locations in socio-economic space, two groups of squatters articulated very different meanings of land occupation that had real, material consequences: one group was evicted, whereas the other was able to secure toleration from the municipal government. This analysis draws on Hart's Gramscian insight that re-articulations do not descend from on high, but are the evanescent moments of 'articulat[ing] multiple, often contradictory meanings into a complex unity that appeals powerfully to "common sense" across a broad spectrum' (Hart 2008, 692). While in the work of Laclau, Hall, Hart and other recent uses of articulation (for example, De Leon, Desai and Tuğal 2015), attention is devoted to how parties and states re-articulate fragments of common sense, in this closing section I want to emphasise how processes of re-articulation simultaneously occur in more informal civil society organisations, something akin to what Hart has called 'movement beyond movements' (2006a, 2007, 2013, 2014).

Re-articulating land claims

Land occupations in post-apartheid South Africa are nothing new. The abrogation of influx controls in the 1980s allowed racialised populations ejected from cities to return en masse, and without adequate housing options, informal settlements proliferated on peri-urban fringes around the country (Levenson 2019). But it was the 2001 occupation of Bredell Farm, just north of Johannesburg, that Hart argues was the opening salvo in her 'movement beyond movements' (2014, 21). This has less to do with the fact of the occupation – relatively unremarkable when placed in context – than it does with how this occupation was articulated. Seven thousand squatters 'purchased' plots from a small opposition party called the Pan Africanist Congress (PAC), which invoked the 'specter of Zimbabwe' (Hart 2002a, 305). While the PAC's involvement was surely opportunistic, it 'was simultaneously tapping into deep veins of morality, history, memory, and meaning, as well as the depth and intensity of poverty and inequality. In the process, it not only exposed deep and growing discontent. It also dramatised land issues as a key potential site of counter-hegemonic struggle singularly lacking organised social forces, yet widely available as the basis of mobilization that could move in significantly different directions' (Hart 2002a, 308).

The post-apartheid government was left deeply vulnerable to collective demands for land and housing. It had staked its legitimacy on claims to be a remedial force capable of reversing the material wrongs of racialised dispossession, but in practice its redistributive programmes were slowly implemented, underfunded and technocratic by design (Levenson 2021, 2022). This meant that those residents waiting for access to urban housing could occupy tracts of vacant land, especially those already owned by municipalities, but also plots held by absentee landlords, and they could claim to be enacting the same programme of decolonisation and national liberation that the ANC asserted as part of its national democratic revolution. And when municipalities attempted to evict them, they could invoke memories of apartheid-era state repression.

The imagery was actually quite comparable: an Anti-Land Invasion Unit would arrive, often flanked by large armed police tanks called Casspirs, widely associated with the apartheid state. Once they secured court authorisation, they would try to forcibly remove residents, repossessing their belongings. The popular re-articulation of contemporary eviction as apartheid redux clearly stung government officials. Bonginkosi Madikizela, the Western Cape's provincial housing minister, told one journalist, 'In order for them not to be evicted, they are coming up with this narrative and portraying us in government as monsters ... It's not true' (Birnbaum 2016).

Cape Town is a particularly contentious site of struggle, as until the 2016 local elections it was the only major municipality in the country governed by a party other than the ANC. Madikizela, once an ANC stalwart, joined the Democratic Alliance (DA) about a decade ago. With the ANC in opposition in Cape Town but in power nationally, residents are able to legitimise their demands by claiming to be implementing the ANC's programme when they occupy land, insisting that they are doing so against the inability of the DA to realise the post-apartheid promise. But associating with a party is not without its attendant risks. By participating in a party-orchestrated occupation, squatters remain open to allegations of opportunism, as well as politicising what might otherwise be perceived as a struggle for survival.

In 2011 a group called the Mitchells Plain Housing Association (MPHA) organised a mass land occupation in Mitchells Plain – Cape Town's second largest township. Many of the participants lived in overcrowded houses in surrounding neighbourhoods, houses that the apartheid government had provided to their parents or grandparents when they were initially removed to Mitchells Plain in the 1970s. Now, a couple of generations later, the children and grandchildren of these evictees are *gatvol* – 'fed up' in Afrikaans – of living in overcrowded houses. Many others live in shacks erected behind formal houses. If they are lucky, they may stay with relatives, but more likely, they pay rent, electricity and water. Or else they cannot access toilets and taps in the house and have to scavenge for water elsewhere. Indeed, backyarding is the most common type of informal dwelling in Cape Town, and more than one in five of its residents currently live in a shack.

The MPHA was actually a front group of sorts for the ANC. It did not openly identify as party affiliated, but its leadership were exclusively ANC members and they hoped to move ANC-sympathetic residents into a neighbourhood that historically has voted for the DA without exception. They articulated their claims to land in narrowly individualistic terms – akin to what Hart calls 'individual restitution claims' instead of collective redistributive demands (2002a, 309; 2014, 20). On the day the occupation began, residents thought they were participating in a legitimate, state-sanctioned housing programme. The land was an open field next to a commuter railway station and owned by the municipal government. They paid a small fee to the MPHA and when they arrived, along with a thousand others, people were on their hands and knees with members of the association, marking out plots of land with bits of string and wooden stakes – as if it were actually private property. Even if the homes were flimsy and the plots small, residents perceived themselves as homeowners in the making, acquiring a sense of autonomy absent to backyarders.

The confidence of MPHA members gave residents the impression that the occupation was legal. It took a few days for participants to accept that they had committed an illegal act. One participant described the revelation in her journal:

On Tuesday 17th May [2011] the sheriff of the court said over an intercom that we were there illegally and we were not allowed to be there. They gave us an interdict and gave us 5 minutes to vacate the land. Once again they removed whatever we had. People lost their IDs, their papers, their dentures … That was when we realised that this is illegal, we were not going to get anything. Nobody was going to be able to help us with this. We had been manipulated into the situation we are in now.[4]

While she felt that they had been manipulated, there is another way to understand what transpired. MPHA leaders consciously sutured moralising discourses of becoming a homeowner to a sub-proletarian politics of necessity, both of which were already present in squatters' common sense. They rendered this common sense 'critical' insofar as they began with people's existing desires and resentments and re-articulated them to a politics of exclusivity. In practice, this meant that people who had nowhere else to go were persuaded that participating in a land occupation was a viable option. This sense of viability was actively legitimised through discourses of ordered 'individual restitution', to use Hart's phrase (2002a, 309; 2014, 20). The distribution of ersatz property to hopeful residents by an ersatz government organisation mimicked the logic of the government's housing programme – obscuring the fact that it was just as illegal as a disorderly land occupation without any intermediary body governing 'distribution'. When the case finally made it to the High Court, the judge read this articulation of land politics as the opportunistic manipulation of residents for political ends – not as an attempt to align with a government housing programme. After a year and a half of appeals and delayed hearings, every one of the occupiers was evicted from the field.

The MPHA's approach was one possible re-articulation of demands for access to land and housing. But a second occupation just down the road from this one rejected a politics of exclusivity – the distribution of mutually exclusive plots to those who paid a fee, the exclusion of those who did not – in favour of an expansive politics of inclusivity. The party front groups initially involved in the project were immediately expelled by angry residents who accused them of opportunism. Residents constituted themselves not as passive recipients of plots, but as an active social movement that relied upon constant growth to sustain itself. Rather than attempting to re-articulate immediate needs to the state's logic of ordered distribution, residents sutured these needs to a discourse of fighting for decolonisation. The government was represented not as a force for redistribution, but as a potential initiator of eviction, recalling memories of the apartheid state. It was viewed as an obstacle to the realisation of the post-apartheid promise. The limited pace of housing delivery after apartheid allowed for this contentious discourse to be sutured to people's immediate demands for shelter.

On the day residents of the first occupation were evicted, one leader of the second occupation marched to the first, urging squatters to return with him to his occupation. 'We're not going anywhere unless you're going with us. Move with us!' he urged, backed by a dozen other occupiers. I could not help but think about the stark contrast in relation to the politics of petty proprietorship I had observed in the first occupation. There was no talk of manipulation in the legal proceedings, nor any sign of factional strife among the occupiers. Even when residents grew *gatvol* of their leadership, they called an occupation-wide meeting and elected a new representative committee. As the settlement grew, they divided it into four sections – A, B, C and D – each with its own representative, reporting back to an elected leadership. This is not to suggest that there were not disagreements – of course, there were. But it does demonstrate the extent to which residents' politics affected the outcome. The first occupation's persistent factionalism rendered it susceptible to being framed as opportunism. But the second occupation's coherent representative organisation, a consequence of its political constitution, shaped its acceptance by the High Court as a group of residents in need.

Conclusion

Far from overdetermined then, these contrary outcomes were both possible consequences of divergent re-articulations of land politics, ranging from individual restitution to collective redistributive demands, or what I have called a politics of exclusivity as opposed to an expansive politics of inclusivity. This preliminary effort to flesh out re-articulations 'from below' draws on Hart's reading of Laclau (1977) and Hall (1980), demonstrating that politics cannot be read off socio-economic conditions. Both groups of occupiers began with roughly comparable 'social views and visions' (Sitas 1990, 263, 273) and came from similar backgrounds as backyarders or residents of over-crowded homes in Mitchells Plain. But it was the conscious project of re-articulation, the suturing of elements of residents' common sense to divergent political projects, which shaped their politics in practice. Meaning and social practice were (and remain) inseparable – arguably the key insight of Gramsci's philosophy of praxis. Struggles over the production of meaning are both an effect and a constitutive part of processes of politicisation. Political subjectivity is not imputed from on high by organisers who simply manipulate individual pawns, nor is it projected through top-down processes of interpellation or govern-mentality. Rather, as Hart teaches us, 'fragmentary common sense can become coherent through collective practices and processes of trans-formation' (2013, 315), which are precisely the strategies she describes as re-articulation: the cobbling together of existing fragments into new meanings, which are simultaneously the nodes around which coalitions, alliances and blocs coalesce. It is around these meanings, in other words, that political interests and subjectivities are articulated. This process of articulation is what we give the proper name 'politics'.

But these politics do not occur in a vacuum. As Hart, like Hall before her, makes quite clear, articulations are not about suturing free-floating discourses to one another at random, with contingent assem-blages created from an unbounded rhetorical palette. Rather, these articulations are always historically specific processes and, as such, are constrained by material circumstances: 'One has to ask, under what cir-cumstances can a connection be forged or made' (Hall [1983] 2016, 121). In the instances of the land occupations analysed here, class position and location in a matrix of power relations are everything. Without this as a starting point, there would be nothing to which to articulate various other discourses, elements and narratives. Hart's turn towards meaning, in other words, does not signal some sort of cultural turn away from class; instead, it is her attempt to take class seriously, interrogating how processes of political subjectivation shape and are shaped by people's sense of the world, as well as their place in it. 'Classes ... are constituted not as unified social forces, but as patchworks or segments which are differentiated and divided on a variety of bases and by varied processes' (Wolpe 1988, 51). These bases and processes are precisely the articulations and re-articulations Hart describes. The unification of proletarian forces is not about imposing some external logic on an atomised class, importing knowledge or Luxemburg's 'idea' from the outside. Rather, it is about cultivating what material already exists – common sense, everyday life – and finding ways to develop these quotidian fragments into coherent worldviews. Therefore 'one might say that class unity, when it occurs, is a conjunctural phenomenon' (Wolpe 1988, 51).

NOTES

1   After Marx's death, Marxist thinking was formalised under the banner of orthodoxy. Especially during the reign of the Second International, it became commonplace to think about politics as an ideological 'reflection' of the material base. This crude economic determinism reduced the domain of subjectivity to what Andrew Feenberg (1986, 140) calls 'insubstantial thinking, pure reflection'. It was the goal of many subsequent Marxist thinkers, among them Gramsci and Althusser, to break with this static approach to understanding politics under capitalism. However, a word of caution is in order: as Daniel Gaido and Manuel Quiroga (2021) go to great lengths to emphasise, this 'mechanical interpretation' of Marxism should be associated only with the Second International's reformist wing. In subsequently reducing the entire legacy of the Second International to its reformist membership, Stalin erased the vibrant range of positions that actually flourished in the organisation at the time.

2   He claimed that a projected sequel to the fragmentary volume containing his famous interpellation essay would address class struggle, but this work never actually appeared (Althusser [1995] 2014, 1–2).

3   Though as Judith Butler (1997, 111) suggests, the relationship between interpellator and interpellated may be a bit more complicated in terms of temporal sequence: 'As a prior and essential condition of the formation of the subject, there is a certain readiness to be compelled by the authoritative interpellation, a readiness which suggests that one is, as it were, already in

relation to the voice before the response, already implicated in the terms of the animating misrecognition by an authority to which one subsequently yields.'

4   This was Faeza Meyer, who in collaboration with the historian Koni Benson, is planning to publish the full diary under the title *Writing Out Loud: Interventions in the History of a Land Occupation*. I thank both of them for allowing me to use this crucial source. Selections have been published in Benson and Meyer (2015).

REFERENCES

Alexander, Peter. 2010. 'Rebellion of the Poor: South Africa's Service Delivery Protests – A Preliminary Analysis'. *Review of African Political Economy* 37, no. 123: 25–40.

Althusser, Louis. (1965) 1969. *For Marx*. New York: Verso.

Althusser, Louis. (1971) 2001. *Lenin and Philosophy and Other Essays*. New York: Monthly Review Press.

Althusser, Louis. (1995) 2014. *On the Reproduction of Capitalism: Ideology and Ideological State Apparatuses*. New York: Verso.

Althusser, Louis, Étienne Balibar, Roger Establet, Pierre Macherey and Jacques Rancière. (1965) 2015. *Reading Capital: The Complete Edition*. New York: Verso.

Ballard, Richard, Adam Habib and Imraan Valodia, eds. 2006. *Voices of Protest: Social Movements in Post-Apartheid South Africa*. Pietermaritzburg: University of KwaZulu-Natal Press.

Barchiesi, Franco. 2011. *Precarious Liberation: Workers, the State, and Contested Social Citizenship in Post-Apartheid South Africa*. Albany: SUNY Press.

Barry, Andrew, Thomas Osborne and Nikolas Rose, eds. 1996. *Foucault and Political Reason: Liberalism, Neo-liberalism, and Rationalities of Government*. Chicago: University of Chicago Press.

Beinart, William and Marcelle C. Dawson, eds. 2010. *Popular Politics and Resistance Movements in South Africa*. Johannesburg: Wits University Press.

Benson, Koni and Faeza Meyer. 2015. 'Reluctantly Loud: Interventions in the History of a Land Occupation'. In *African Cities Reader III: Land, Property, and Value*, edited by Ntone Edjabe and Edgar Pieterse, 64–95. Cape Town: Chimurenga/African Centre for Cities.

Birnbaum, Sarah. 2016. 'Some South Africans Facing Eviction Say it Feels Like an Apartheid-Era Policy'. *Public Radio International*. https://www.pri.org/stories/2016-03-31/some-south-africans-facing-eviction-say-it-feels-apartheid-era-policy (accessed 18 January 2022).

Bond, Patrick and Shauna Mottiar. 2013. 'Movements, Protests, and a Massacre in South Africa'. *Journal of Contemporary African Studies* 31, no. 2: 283–302.

Burchell, Graham, Colin Gordon and Peter Miller. 1991. *The Foucault Effect: Studies in Governmentality*. Chicago: University of Chicago Press.

Butler, Judith. 1997. *The Psychic Life of Power: Theories in Subjection*. Stanford: Stanford University Press.

Crehan, Kate. 2016. *Gramsci's Common Sense: Inequality and Its Narratives*. Durham: Duke University Press.

De Leon, Cedric, Manali Desai and Cihan Tuğal, eds. 2015. *Building Blocs: How Parties Organize Society*. Stanford: Stanford University Press.

Desai, Ashwin. 2002. *We Are the Poors: Community Struggles in Post-Apartheid South Africa*. New York: Monthly Review Press.

Feenberg, Andrew. 1986. *Lukács, Marx and the Sources of Critical Theory*. Oxford: Oxford University Press.

Foucault, Michel. (1978–1979) 2010. *The Birth of Biopolitics: Lectures at the Collège de France, 1978–1979*. New York: Picador.

Friedman, Steven. 2015. *Race, Class, and Power: Harold Wolpe and the Radical Critique of Apartheid*. Pietermaritzburg: University of KwaZulu-Natal Press.

Gaido, Daniel and Manuel Quiroga. 2021. 'Marxism in the Age of Imperialism: The Second International'. In *Routledge Handbook of Marxism and Post-Marxism*, edited by Alex Callinicos, Stathis Kouvelakis and Lucia Pradella, 51–65. London: Routledge.

Gibson, Nigel C., ed. 2006. *Challenging Hegemony: Social Movements and the Quest for a New Humanism in Post-Apartheid South Africa*. Trenton: Africa World Press.

Gibson, Nigel C. 2011. *Fanonian Practices in South Africa: From Steve Biko to Abahlali baseMjondolo*. Pietermaritzburg: University of KwaZulu-Natal Press.

Gramsci, Antonio. (1971) 2016. *Selections from the Prison Notebooks*. Edited by Quentin Hoare and Geoffrey Nowell Smith. New York: International Publishers.

Hall, Stuart. 1974. 'Marx's Notes on Method: A Reading of the 1857 "Introduction"'. Working Paper No. 6. Centre for Contemporary Cultural Studies, Birmingham.

Hall, Stuart. 1980. 'Race, Articulation, and Societies Structured in Dominance'. In *Sociological Theories: Race and Colonialism*, 305–345. Paris: UNESCO.

Hall, Stuart. 1985. 'Signification, Representation, Ideology: Althusser and the Post-Structuralist Debates'. *Critical Studies in Mass Communication* 2, no. 2: 91–114.

Hall, Stuart. (1983) 2016. *Cultural Studies 1983*. Durham: Duke University Press.

Hart, Gillian. 2001. 'Development Critiques in the 1990s: *Culs de Sac* and Promising Paths'. *Progress in Human Geography* 25, no. 4: 649–658.

Hart, Gillian. 2002a. *Disabling Globalization: Places of Power in Post-Apartheid South Africa*. Berkeley: University of California Press.

Hart, Gillian. 2002b. 'Geography and Development: Development/s beyond Neoliberalism? Power, Culture, Political Economy'. *Progress in Human Geography* 26, no. 6: 812–822.

Hart, Gillian. 2004. 'Geography and Development: Critical Ethnographies'. *Progress in Human Geography* 28, no. 1: 91–100.

Hart, Gillian. 2006a. 'Movement beyond Movements: Challenges to Critical Scholarship in Post-Apartheid South Africa'. Paper presented to a plenary panel on African social movements, XVI International Sociological Association World Congress of Sociology.

Hart, Gillian. 2006b. 'Post-Apartheid Developments in Historical and Comparative Perspective'. In *The Development Decade? Economic and Social Change in South Africa 1994–2004*, edited by Vishnu Padayachee, 13–32. Cape Town: HSRC Press.

Hart, Gillian. 2007. 'Changing Concepts of Articulation: Political Stakes in South Africa Today'. *Review of African Political Economy* 34, no. 111: 85–101.

Hart, Gillian. 2008. 'The Provocations of Neoliberalism: Contesting the Nation and Liberation after Apartheid'. *Antipode* 40, no. 4: 678–705.

Hart, Gillian. 2009. 'D/developments after the Meltdown'. *Antipode* 41, S1: 117–141.

Hart, Gillian. 2013. 'Gramsci, Geography, and the Languages of Populism'. In *Gramsci: Space, Nature, Politics*, edited by Michael Ekers, Gillian Hart, Stefan Kipfer and Alex Loftus, 301–320. Malden: Wiley-Blackwell.

Hart, Gillian. 2014. *Rethinking the South African Crisis: Nationalism, Populism, Hegemony*. Athens: University of Georgia Press.

Hart, Gillian. 2018. 'Relational Comparison Revisited: Marxist Postcolonial Geographies in Practice'. *Progress in Human Geography* 42, no. 3: 371–394.

Laclau, Ernesto. 1977. *Politics and Ideology in Marxist Theory*. New York: Verso.

Laclau, Ernesto. 2005. *On Populist Reason*. New York: Verso.

Laclau, Ernesto and Chantal Mouffe. 1985. *Hegemony and Socialist Strategy: Towards a Radical Democratic Politics*. New York: Verso.

Lefebvre, Henri. 2014. *Critique of Everyday Life: The One-Volume Edition*. New York: Verso.

Levenson, Zachary. 2019. ' "Such Elements Do Not Belong in an Ordered Society": Managing Rural–Urban Resettlement in Democratic South Africa'. *Journal of Agrarian Change* 19, no. 3: 427–446.

Levenson, Zachary. 2021. 'Post-Apartheid Housing Delivery as a (Failed) Project of Remediation'. In *Land Issues for Urban Governance in Sub-Saharan Africa*, edited by Robert Home, 189–206. New York: Springer.

Levenson, Zachary. 2022. *Delivery as Dispossession: Land Occupation and Eviction in the Postapartheid City*. Oxford: Oxford University Press.

Luxemburg, Rosa. (1906) 2007. 'The Mass Strike'. In *The Essential Rosa Luxemburg: Reform or Revolution and the Mass Strike*, edited by Helen Scott. Chicago: Haymarket Books.

Piven, Frances Fox and Richard A. Cloward. 1979. *Poor People's Movements: Why They Succeed, How They Fail*. New York: Vintage.

Poulantzas, Nicos. (1970) 1974. *Fascism and Dictatorship: The Third International and the Problem of Fascism*. New York: Verso.

Poulantzas, Nicos. (1968) 1978. *Political Power and Social Classes*. New York: Verso.

Rose, Nikolas. 1999. *Powers of Freedom: Reframing Political Thought*. Cambridge: Cambridge University Press.

Saul, John. 2012. 'A Poisoned Chalice: Liberation, ANC-Style'. *Pambazuka News*. http://www.pambazuka.org/governance/poisoned-chalice-liberation-anc-style (accessed 18 January 2022).

Sitas, Ari. 1990. 'Class, Nation, Ethnicity in Natal's Black Working Class'. *Collected Seminar Papers, Institute of Commonwealth Studies* 38: 257–278.

Wolpe, Harold. 1972. 'Capitalism and Cheap Labor Power in South Africa: From Segregation to Apartheid'. *Economy and Society* 1, no 1: 425–456.

Wolpe, Harold. 1988. *Race, Class, and the Apartheid State*. Trenton: Africa World Press.

9 | Grappling with 'Nationalism': Thinking alongside Gillian Hart at a South African Landfill

Melanie Samson

Nationalism is central to Gillian Hart's current work and so I was surprised to discover that the words 'nation' and 'nationalism' do not appear in the index to her 2002 book *Disabling Globalization*. When I asked Hart why and when she started thinking about nationalism, she paused and then, unsurprisingly, told me a story that involved a friend from Ladysmith. In December 2003, Hart and her friend went to a meeting where Jacob Zuma, then deputy president of the country and of the African National Congress (ANC), was received by an adoring crowd. When Zuma sang his trademark 'Awuleth' Umshini Wami' (Bring Me My Machine [Gun]), she realised his surging popularity was bound up with the ways he invoked the liberation struggle and connected with deeply held popular nationalism. While others on the left were disdainful and dismissive of both popular support for Zuma and the rise of nationalism, Hart realised something was going on that was important to understand. So began more than a decade of provocative research on nationalism, research that is ongoing to this day.

This story of Zuma encapsulates how Hart's long-term ethnographic work in Ladysmith and Newcastle grounds her research and how her quest to understand the current moment and its many prior determinations allows her to interrogate theoretically and politically important processes obscured by existing conceptual frameworks. Hart's interest in nationalism is not only or even primarily theoretical. Her political interest in understanding nationalism drives her theoretical work. As new political issues emerge (or more typically erupt), she engages with activists across the political spectrum, tests out her ideas in public lectures and newspaper articles, and stretches her thinking about nationalism as she seeks to develop concepts adequate for understanding the contemporary conjuncture.

In this chapter I present the development of Hart's thinking on nationalism, locating this in relation to the political transformations in South Africa she was responding to, as well as her engagements with political developments and ideas from elsewhere (India and the United States, in particular). I cluster Hart's writing on nationalism into three broad thematic phases that emerge chronologically but inform and interweave with one another as ideas are carried forward, articulated with new ones and at times quietly abandoned. I then discuss how my own research on the everyday nationalism of reclaimers of reusable and recyclable materials at a Soweto landfill engages with, complements and presses beyond Hart's work on nationalism.

Phase one: Nationalism, populism and the rise of Jacob Zuma

Hart first began to grapple with nationalism in her article 'Changing Concepts of Articulation' (2007) and her 2007 Antipode Lecture – 'The Provocations of Neoliberalism' – subsequently published in 2008 (Hart 2008). Her insights after the December 2003 meeting mentioned above were prescient. In the subsequent years, President Thabo Mbeki came under increasing attack by the ANC's Alliance partners – the Congress of South African Trade Unions (COSATU) and the South African Communist Party (SACP) – for his elitist approach and neo-liberal policies. Support for Zuma continued to increase. Even though he had been tried for rape and had numerous charges of fraud, corruption, racketeering and money-laundering against him, in 2005 the ANC's National General Council forced Mbeki to retain Zuma as the deputy president of the ANC after Mbeki dismissed him from the same position in government over the corruption charges. Subsequently, at the 2007 ANC national congress, Zuma ousted Mbeki as the president of the ANC and in 2008 (after the completion of Hart's articles) this was repeated in parliament as Zuma ascended to the presidency of the country.

The fact that Hart came to nationalism through her interest in struggles for hegemony within the Alliance had important implications for how she approached the subject. In this first phase of her work on nationalism, Hart focused on what she refers to as two 'keywords of the ANC alliance' (Hart 2015b, 49) – the national democratic revolution (NDR) as the first stage of the SACP's two-stage theory of revolution (establishment of non-racial bourgeois liberal democracy first, socialism second) and the 'national question'. In addition, she increasingly engaged with debates related to populism in order to interrogate the relationship between popular support for Zuma and nationalism (see chapter 7 in this volume for a discussion of Hart's work on populism).

Drawing on Neville Alexander (2002), Hart notes that the NDR and the two-stage theory had long been the subject of withering critique by the left outside of the Alliance (Hart 2007, 85).[1] However, she argues:

> Precisely because the NDR remains a live and influential social category, it is insufficient simply to point to its analytical inconsistencies and political shortcomings, and then set it aside. What needs to be grasped more fully is *how* meanings of the NDR have been redefined and articulated as part of the hegemonic project of the ruling bloc within the ANC, along with how and why these meanings have become an increasingly vociferous site of struggle and contestation within the ANC Alliance and in grassroots politics. (Hart 2007, 86; emphasis in original)

Debates on the NDR were, indeed, alive within the Alliance. However, although Hart referenced grassroots politics, this was not the subject of her analysis and she did not interrogate whether the NDR resonated with or animated understandings and struggles on the ground and, if so, how. Instead, Hart's analysis of the NDR focused on contestations within the Alliance that took the relevance of the NDR (or at least invocations of it) in the forging of the post-apartheid nation as given, and she analysed it on these terms.

Hart focused on two related ways that the Alliance considered the NDR central to the forging of the post-apartheid nation. First is that, for the SACP, South Africans could only become a single nation (that is, within their understanding, the national question could only be resolved) in the context of the NDR (Slovo 1988, 25, cited in Hart 2013b, 57).[2] Second, within the logic of the SACP, the NDR would establish the basis for a struggle for socialism. Within the two-stage theory, the NDR *required* the creation of a non-racial, liberal, bourgeois democracy that not only left capitalism and capitalist exploitation intact, but promoted their further development, including the development of a black bourgeoisie. As Hart's work on nationalism developed, she increasingly drew on Frantz Fanon's analysis (1963) of the betrayals by the national bourgeoisie in what the SACP referred to as the first stage, the tremendous potential dangers of their self-interested nationalism, and the possibilities of an alternative national consciousness rooted in a new humanism (Hart 2013b, 2015a).

For Hart, this discussion made clear that, far from purely 'political', the conceptualisation of the nation in the NDR could only be understood and debated in relation to capitalism and class struggle. Hart emphasises this point when she argues that post-1994, each new ANC policy needs to be framed as a reformulation of the NDR, as the NDR 'makes the case for accommodation to the inequalities of post-apartheid capitalism as a transitory phenomenon, to be superseded by an ever-receding second, socialist phase' (Hart 2015b, 49). Hart argues that each redefinition of the NDR was also a 're-articulation of race, class and nationalism' that advanced specific racialised class interests within the Alliance, as well as more generally (see chapters 7 and 8 in this volume for a discussion of Hart's work on 'articulation'). The shift from the Reconstruction and Development Programme (RDP) to the more thoroughly and overtly neo-liberal Growth, Employment and Redistribution (GEAR) macro-economic strategy in 1996 was therefore a 'consolidation of conservative forces bent on working in alliance with white corporate capital to create a black bourgeoisie nominally more responsive to "development" ' (Hart 2007, 93). Simultaneously, and of necessity, 'this redefinition of the NDR embodied a powerful drive to contain working-class pressures, along with a sharp disciplining of the left within the ANC Alliance' (Hart 2013b, 184).

On the basis of this analysis, Hart was able to return to her initial question regarding support for Zuma within the Alliance. She argues that as COSATU and the SACP increasingly opposed Mbeki's neo-liberal economic and social policies, 'the NDR [became] a site of increasingly vociferous contestation' (Hart 2015b, 49). According to Hart, COSATU and the SACP rallied around Zuma because he expressed support for their vision of the NDR and the post-apartheid nation, which encompassed their framing of the economy and class struggle. While not specifically articulated by Hart in this way, support for Zuma was also bolstered as he cultivated the impression that under his presidency, COSATU and the SACP would regain status and power in the Alliance lost during Mbeki's presidency (Hart 2007, 2008).

Turning her attention to the surging popular support for Zuma, Hart shifted from a focus on the forging and meaning of the nation in terms of the NDR to analyse how Zuma 'tapped into' popular nationalisms. To do so, over the course of several publications, she developed a particular understanding of the relationship between populism, nationalism, class, race and gender (Hart 2007, 2008, 2013a, 2013b). From Ernesto Laclau's early work on populism (1977), Hart took the crucial argument that rather than reaching beyond class, populism is always articulated with it (although not to any specific class, hence its relevance to myriad political projects). Laclau's argument that appeal to the masses via populism is crucial when a new fraction of the 'dominant block' seeks hegemony was profoundly relevant to analysis of Zuma's populist strategy (Hart 2007, 92–93; 2013b).

However, rejecting Laclau's Althusserian position that within populism people are constituted as subjects and hailed from above, Hart drew on Ari Sitas' argument that '"Zulu-ness" must be viewed as a negotiated identity between ordinary people's attempts to create effective and reciprocal bonds (or functioning cultural formations) out of their social and material conditions of life and political ideologies that seek to mobilise them in non-class ways' (Sitas [1990] 2010, 266). Her former student (and co-editor) Mark Hunter's arguments, rooted in long-term ethnographic analysis, provided important insights into how Zuma was able to present himself as a respectable patriarch to a wide range of poor, black South Africans, including women, even in the context of his rape trial (Hunter 2007, 2011; Hart 2008, 2013a, 2013b).

Hart argues that the national question played a central role in enabling Zuma to connect with his emerging constituency's understanding of their daily lives and the state of their liberation and the nation. While her discussion of the national question and the NDR focuses on how the Alliance answered the question, here Hart focuses on how the national question 'conjures up struggles against colonialism and imperialism, the indignities and violence of racial injustice and dispossession, the sacrifices and suffering embodied in movements for national liberation, and the visions of social and economic justice for which many fought and died' (Hart 2013b, 156–157).

Hart observes that these issues had been submerged during the transition, but were revitalised by Zuma who 'positioned himself as a hero of national liberation' and as the 'rightful heir' of the struggle (Hart 2008, 692). Informed by Liz Gunner's insightful work (2008), Hart argues that when Zuma launched into struggle songs (and in particular his signature song 'Awuleth' Umshini Wami'), he was seen as championing a struggle that was ongoing. She highlights that Zuma presented and represented a vision of the nation starkly different to that of Mbeki. Zuma's nation was not the domain of intellectuals. It included people who, like him, were not formally educated and were 'by implication extremely smart'; celebrated and promoted 'traditional' Zulu values and practices; and was rooted in a powerful, militant masculinity (Hart 2008, 692). In 'Exposing the Nation', Hart (2013a) draws on moving and deeply insightful media articles by Amukelani Chauke (2012), Justice Malala (2012) and S'thembiso Msomi (2012) to grapple with the profound social divisions that were revealed and exacerbated by Brett Murray's depiction of Zuma's exposed genitals in his painting *The Spear*. Hart argues that the painting reopened the wounds of crucial, unresolved aspects of the national question and generated tremendous popular support for Zuma, contrary to the artist's intended critique.

However, emphasising that hegemony is always contested, Hart is quick to remind her readers that tapping into popular understandings also threatened both Mbeki's and then Zuma's hegemony, as 'service delivery' protests and 'escalating struggles over the material conditions of life and livelihood are simultaneously struggles over the meaning of the nation and liberation, as well as expressions of profound betrayal' (Hart 2008, 678).

Phase two: De-nationalisation, re-nationalisation and the South African transition

The publication of *Rethinking the South African Crisis* (Hart 2013b) heralded the second phase of Hart's work on nationalism. As the title suggests, she continued working through many of the key issues and concepts from the first phase. However, the focus of her analysis shifted and broadened. In her earlier work, Hart studied nationalism and conceptions of the nation in order to better understand struggles for hegemony by and within the ANC and the Alliance. In the second phase, she engaged with the nation and nationalism as part of her efforts to gain deeper insight into the post-apartheid transition. This required Hart to interrogate and theorise the nation and nationalism in new ways.

Perhaps because of her focus on the meaning of the nation for the Alliance, in the first phase Hart had not fully elaborated her own understanding of the nation and nationalism. In *Rethinking the South African Crisis*, she introduces and draws on Manu Goswami's relational, spacio-historical understanding of nationalisms that focuses 'on the processes, practices and meanings entailed in the production of specific – but always interconnected – national spaces in relation to wider global conjunctures' (Hart 2013b, 17). Resonating with Hart's approach in the first phase, Goswami argues that analysis of specific nationalisms requires 'sustained elaboration of the dialectical relationship between material, social, and cultural fields and the experiential contradictions and lived practices of individuals and social groups' (Goswami 2004, 6). For Hart, understanding the nation and nationalism in the context of the South African transition therefore required analysis of South Africa's specific history of colonialism and apartheid, 'the lived interdisciplinarity of everyday life' (Goswami 2004, 6) and the globally interconnected historical geographies of South African capital.

Arising out of this approach, Hart then developed the dialectically related concepts 'de-nationalisation' and 're-nationalisation' through which she analysed the transition. In 'Political Society and Its Discontents', Hart explains that de-nationalisation 'includes the extremely conservative package of neo-liberal economic policies set in place in 1996 but also precedes and extends beyond it', as it 'highlights South African corporate capital's post-1994 efforts to resolve its accumulation crisis by restructuring and de-nationalising its operations' (Hart 2015b, 48). This strategy was tailored to address the specific form of capital's crisis, which was rooted in what Ben Fine and Zavareh Rustomjee (1996) refer to as the 'Minerals-Energy Complex' (MEC). Forged in the late nineteenth century around large-scale minerals extraction and related industries, the MEC is deeply dependent on cheap coal-based energy and underpins white monopoly capital's domination of the South African economy (Hart 2013b, 159–160). As the MEC is predicated on the gross exploitation of migrant, black, male labour, both the MEC and the crisis were shaped by the 'historical and geographical specificities of southern African racial capitalism and settler colonialism' (Hart 2013b, 7). De-nationalisation emerged out of and deepened racialised dispossession, humiliation and exploitation, giving them new form in the present (Hart 2015b). This is why Hart argues that de-nationalisation signals 'the simultaneously economic, political and cultural practices and processes that are generating ongoing inequality and "surplus" populations, and the conflicts that surround them' (Hart 2013b, 7).

Hart argues that while de-nationalisation re-established secure conditions for accumulation by white South African corporate capital (2013b, 165), it was insufficient on its own, as capital also needed the ANC to contain the fallout from the resulting dispossession and deepening immiseration (2014b). De-nationalisation was therefore accompanied by re-nationalisation, which encompassed efforts 'to produce a new nation, and how these play out in multiple arenas of everyday life' (Hart 2013a, 65). Re-nationalisation incorporated and further developed Hart's earlier analysis of the roles of the NDR and the national question in the forging of the nation. In addition, it also included: 1) the early 1990s non-racial 'rainbowism' of Nelson Mandela and Archbishop Desmond Tutu's Truth and Reconciliation Commission (TRC), and 2) 'Fortress South Africa' – a concept borrowed from Jonathan Crush (1999) that captures the state's anti-immigrant legislation, policies and practices, as well as vigilantism, police abuse, detention of non-South Africans and xenophobia (Hart 2013b, 8).

According to Hart, rainbowism and Fortress South Africa represented an effort to forge the nation by creating a common identity among all South Africans within the context of bourgeois hegemony, and othering and rejecting those from elsewhere (other parts of Africa, in particular). However, just as Hart notes that invoking the national question and NDR could lead to a deep sense of betrayal and opposition, she draws on Sitas' analysis of the TRC to argue that while rainbowism and the TRC facilitated the transition (in the specific form that it assumed), they also fostered deep opposition (Sitas [1990] 2010). Hart observes that they ignored and could not address the historical and ongoing dispossessions, indignities, painful memories and exploitation with which the majority of the population continue to live (2013b, 168–171; 2014b). Indeed, rejection of rainbowism and the TRC exploded in the 2015 and 2016 #RhodesMustFall and #FeesMustFall student uprisings. Hart therefore argues that dialectical analysis of de- and re-nationalisation illuminated both the form that the transition took, as well as the sources of its instabilities.

Phase three: Conjunctural nationalisms

More recently, Hart is focusing on nationalism itself as she works to develop a relational analysis of the contemporaneous resurgence and intensification of ethnic/religious nationalism and populist politics in South Africa, India and the United States. In keeping with her understanding of the inseparability of theory, politics and methodology, this extension of her work on nationalism is rooted in developments in each of these three interrelated spheres.

After the publication of *Rethinking the South African Crisis*, Hart increasingly turned to Indian scholars interrogating the rise of Hindutva (Hindu nationalism). Aijaz Ahmad's work on the emergence of Hindutva (2000, 2015) and Himani Bannerji's attention to masculinity in the making of Hindutva (2006) were particularly influential (Hart 2014a, 2015b). Hart took note of India and South Africa's common roots in British imperialism, as well as their contemporaneous moves in 1990 to neo-liberal capitalism, increasing inequalities and surplus populations, expansion of democracy in terms of race and caste, and intensifying expressions of nationalism. She concluded that a comparative analysis of nationalisms in the two countries could illuminate the specific forms of nationalism in each, as well as the broader forces that underpin them (Hart 2014a, 2015b). Narendra Modi's election as the Indian prime minister in 2014 sharpened parallels with nationalism and populism in South Africa, as well as the political stakes and potentialities of a relational study (Hart 2016, 375–376).

Hart soon expanded her comparative analysis to include the United States. She had long written and spoken (including in her DS100 first-year development studies course) of how Bobby Kennedy's 1966 speech at the University of Cape Town illuminated parallels between South Africa and the United States rooted in their shared histories of settler colonialism, slavery and racialised dispossession. In 'The Provocations of Neoliberalism' (Hart 2008, 679), she also highlights how Kennedy's analysis played an important role in her development of the method of relational comparison (see chapter 3 in this volume for a deeper discussion of relational comparison). Donald Trump's election in 2016, and the ways Trumpism resonated with the national exceptionalism, juxtapositions of race and class, and nationalist populism that were so central to South African politics, established the importance for Hart of including the United States in her comparative study of nationalism and its relation to populism (Hart 2018).

Conducting this analysis required Hart to deepen her method of relational comparison to become a more thoroughly conjunctural comparison (2016).[3] This methodological innovation speaks precisely to the requirement that Hart's Marxist method places on her to develop methods of inquiry and concepts adequate for the specific task at hand. Hart first proposed the method of conjunctural comparison at a 2014 public talk at the University of the Witwatersrand's Centre for Indian Studies in Africa (2014a). Drawing on a range of Indian and South African authors, she argued against the dominant approach of comparing the two countries through Partha Chatterjee's ideal type concepts of 'political' and 'civil' society (2004). Instead, she deepened her engagement with Goswami's relational theory of nationalism, and in her 2016 Progress in Human Geography Lecture at the Association of American Geographers annual meeting (published in the journal later that year) clarified that conjunctural comparison entails 'bringing key forces at play in South Africa and other regions of the world into the same frame of analysis, as connected yet distinctively different nodes in globally interconnected historical geographies – and as sites in the production of global processes in specific spatio-historical conjunctures, rather than as just recipients of them' (Hart 2016, 373).

Everyday nationalism at a Soweto landfill

I began thinking about nationalism in South Africa soon after Hart, but for quite different reasons. My PhD dissertation explored how the 2008 global economic crisis was produced and contested at the Marie Louise landfill in Soweto. Given my training in feminist political economy, when I arrived at the landfill I expected to focus on articulations of race, gender and class. These were important, but I soon realised that nationality was the key power-laden social relation (with which the others were articulated) at Marie Louise, and that a very specific understanding of the nation and a very specific form of nationalism were central to the production of the crisis at the landfill.

Marie Louise lies on the boundary between the black township of Soweto and the historically white municipality of Roodepoort, both of which are now part of the Johannesburg Metropolitan Municipality. Marie Louise is one of four functioning landfills owned by the City's Pikitup Waste Management Utility. It was opened in 1993, on the cusp of democracy. Despite legal prohibitions, high fences and security guards, reclaimers fought their way into the landfill and began working there soon after it opened.

Contrary to the assumption in almost all literature that the global economic crisis impacted on reclaimers (and other informal workers) as an outside force, Marie Louise was already deeply integrated into global circuits of capital. Global commodity markets governed the prices for the recyclables salvaged there and some recyclables from the landfill were sold as far afield as China and India. The global economy was an integral part of how Marie Louise was constituted as a site for the production of value (rather than the commodity cemetery it was designed to be). What was required, therefore, was a dialectical analysis of how the crisis and reclaimers' value struggles transformed each other.

It is here that the centrality of national identity and nationalism came into sharp relief. Although the original reclaimers at Marie Louise were South African, by the time of the crisis 41 per cent were Zimbabwean. Global prices for recyclables crashed with global commodity prices in late 2008. Buyers at all levels of the value chain were forced to sell their materials for a fraction of what they paid for them. In order to insure itself against future price drops, when the largest purchaser of scrap metal salvaged at Marie Louise reopened, it reduced the prices that it paid by a larger proportion than the decrease in the price that it received. The small buyers at Marie Louise did the same – not just for scrap, but for all materials. Reclaimers therefore experienced a disproportionate fall in income. They had significant potential bargaining power, as many of the small buyers were completely dependent on them. However, instead of uniting to fight for higher prices, South African reclaimers evicted the Zimbabweans so that they could maintain their income by salvaging more recyclables.

As Hart was one of my supervisors, my engagements with her facilitated my ability to 'see' the nation and nationalism at the dump. Her work and our conversations as we both grappled with nationalism made me conscious of the crucial importance of denaturalising the facts that the reclaimers identified and mobilised on the basis of nationality (which is key to my understanding of nationalism) and that South African reclaimers wielded power over Zimbabweans at a landfill where they had no formal authority. Hart's method of critical ethnography provided a route through which I was able to follow Goswami's injunction to 'reconstruct the "historical labour of dehistoricization" that had enshrined the nation form as natural' at the landfill (Goswami 2004, 20), and to be attentive to intertwined social, political, cultural and economic determinations as I did so.

My reconstruction tracked back to the specific history of how and when the original South Africans first began to reclaim at the landfill. As noted above, the South African reclaimers had fought their way into the landfill and transformed it into a resource mine at the very moment that South Africa was formed as a democratic nation, and they understood themselves and their own actions within the context of this conjuncture. Rather than passive recipients of freedom, the reclaimers frequently cast themselves as freedom fighters who had been actively involved in the struggle for their own liberation and that of the country. This identity was bolstered when advocate George Bizos (who had represented Mandela and many other struggle luminaries) successfully represented them in a court case against Pikitup and the City. One reclaimer explained how their association with Bizos affected their status, saying: 'It made a huge difference. A huge difference! I mean, Mr Bizos used to represent prominent leaders here and activists. So, we felt very honoured and people were respecting us.' In the eyes of many of their fellow residents, the reclaimers were transformed from 'scavengers' worthy only of revulsion and contempt to valiant militants in the lineage of Mandela who were fighting for socio-economic transformation and liberation.

The court victory prevented Pikitup from implementing its plans to remove reclaimers from the landfill and grant a private company the exclusive right to extract recyclables at Marie Louise. This was widely interpreted to mean that the original reclaimers 'owned the dump'. This understanding was quickly adopted by the large number of Zimbabweans who began arriving at Marie Louise in 2005–2006 after fleeing the economic and political crisis in Zimbabwe. One newcomer explained, as if it were fact, 'They do own it because they fought for the dump and they won the case in court.'

The arrival of so many new reclaimers began to affect the original reclaimers' access to recyclables and income. Building on the landfill's foundational myth, the South African reclaimers deployed their claim to a place within the nation to claim control over both the space of the landfill and the non-South Africans who worked there. Explaining why they should have greater rights to materials at Marie Louise than Zimbabweans, one South African reclaimer stated: 'We fought for this garbage ... so we are the ones who should be working here, not the people who are coming from outside, because we are the ones who are voting.'

As at that time the South Africans could not create a physical border to prevent new people from entering the landfill, they entrenched a shift system that established a spatio-temporal border inside Marie Louise – the 'South African shift' worked from 9 a.m. until 2 p.m., while the much larger 'Zimbabwean shift' could only work from 2 p.m. until 5 p.m. The shift system was so effective that a central part of being Zimbabwean at the landfill meant being temporally, as well as spatially, confined. The extent of control over one's time therefore became a key component of citizenship at Marie Louise.

A significant number of newly arrived South Africans were placed in the 'Zimbabwean shift' and were aggrieved that they were caught on the wrong side of the border. Reaffirming the relationship between nationality and rights at Marie Louise, one exclaimed: 'The time they were fighting cops here, I was not here; I was still at school. They were fighting, I do understand, they were fighting. But my question was that, okay, we understand that you were fighting, but even our Mandela, he did fight, not for only his family, but for everyone in South Africa, more especially those who were oppressed. So were we supposed to leave school to come for a fight?'

Despite being in the 'Zimbabwean shift', these South African reclaimers retained privileges rooted in nationality. Unlike Zimbabweans, when spots opened up in the 'South African shift', they were able to move there and by the time of the eviction most had received cards from the morning shift committee that enabled them to stay.

The South African reclaimers' actions were shaped by national government policy that limited the rights of Zimbabweans in the country and cast them as a threat to economic security. They also took place in the context of attacks on non-South Africans that occur with impunity throughout the country on an ongoing basis, and which reached a peak in 2008. However, rather than simply enacting identities forged elsewhere and being interpellated into a pre-given nation, the reclaimers infused national identities and the nation with new meanings at the landfill by creating very locally specific rights to trash associated with citizenship.

Zimbabwean reclaimers also were not just interpellated into the nation at Marie Louise. They resented the ways they were framed and treated, as well as the limitations on their working time and income. Many articulated a more pan-Africanist view and thought that all Africans should be treated equally. However, they did not challenge the national boundaries at the landfill or the differentiated rights based on citizenship for a range of reasons. Virtually none of them had been political activists in Zimbabwe. As the majority intended to return home when the political and economic context changed, they did not see it as a permanent workplace. Instead, they viewed Marie Louise as a place to earn money in the meantime and did not want to jeopardise their access. One explained: 'We do not have any say because we only came here as we are poor, we need to work. So, when you are in a person's house you have to behave, because you came needing help.' In addition, the 2008 attacks loomed large in their minds.

My study of everyday nationalism at one landfill provides a number of insights into how we understand articulations of nationalism and political economy, the economic and the political, and the social and the cultural. Reclaimers are often framed as the epitome of so-called human waste, assumed to be cast outside the economy and the polity, and as emblematic of the surplus populations that Chatterjee (2004) confines to political society. The reclaimers' use of the court and creative reinterpretation and deployment of its ruling belies the distinction between civil and political society. In addition, my study revealed that reclaimers were deeply linked into global circuits of capital and that nationalism and claiming a place within the nation were central to their daily praxis. This challenges both Mbeki's two economies thesis (Mbeki 1998) – discussed in chapter 5 of this volume – and the assumption that 'surplus populations' are relegated to and governed within a distinct political society where the state makes economic interventions to counter the effects of primitive accumulation (Chatterjee 2004; Sanyal [2007] 2014).

Although Hart included xenophobia as a key component of re-nationalisation, she relied on secondary sources and did not interrogate whether what she was referring to was best understood as xenophobia. My analysis of the multiple determinations of what could easily be categorised as xenophobia reveals that the South African reclaimers' actions were informed and shaped by how the global crisis refracted through pre-existing locally specific national identities, power relations and the institutions forged to enforce them. Rather than hatred towards cross-border reclaimers, the reclaimers' actions were animated primarily by the daily praxis of nation building and the establishment of specific rights and powers within the nation at the dump that were deeply articulated with reclaimers' material interests.

In keeping with other critiques of the de- and re-nationalisation framework that Hart herself has since moved away from, this analysis of everyday nationalism at the landfill demonstrates that the cluster of economic activities that Hart includes as part of de-nationalisation do not just call forth efforts to bind people to the nation. Instead, they are an integral part of forging the nation, as reclaimers worked to form the nation in particular ways as they laboured to shape the form of the global crisis and globalised economic processes at the landfill. In addition, the opening of the economy to global capital and the associated abandonment of the Freedom Charter's commitments to nationalising the economy are key characteristics of the post-apartheid nation in and of themselves.

Just as Hart notes that invocation of the struggle for national liberation by the ANC is 'not just a cynical manipulation from above' (Hart 2007, 94), it is crucial to note that claiming a space within the nation is more than a tactic to make economic claims. This is because 'wageless life'

(Denning 2010) is not just about economic marginalisation and poverty, but also entails political and social marginalisation. My research demonstrates that in addition to mobilising to improve their economic situation, reclaimers also mobilised to forge a sense of belonging in the economy, polity and society. Like all of us, reclaimers are complex, multifaceted human beings who seek belonging to and forge their identities within interconnected social, political, economic, cultural and environmental terrains. In different moments different terrains are more prominent, but they are never detached from the others.

Drawing on another key concept from Hart, in addition to looking at the articulation of race, class and gender (Hall 1980; Hart 2007), I argue that we need to interrogate the articulation of the social, political, cultural and economic aspects of our beings, and how as a sense of belonging in one sphere is strengthened or weakened this shapes our pursuit of belonging in the others. Locating this interrogation within an extroverted sense of place will also facilitate exploration of the fact that even as South African reclaimers can deploy their claim to a space within a nation to gain hegemony at the landfill, this does not erase the discrimination they face as people who work with waste in gaining recognition and acceptance as members of the polity at the scales of the city and the nation. Reclaimers must, therefore, continue to struggle at multiple scales and in multiple spheres, starting, perhaps, within the landfill to redress the power-laden social relations they forge between themselves that limit their ability to undertake united struggles at other scales.

Conclusion

In a sense, Hart and I focused on the political work of nationalism at opposite (but interconnected) ends of the political landscape. While Hart analysed the role of nationalism and different conceptions of the nation in hegemonic struggles by and within the ruling ANC Alliance, I interrogated their role in struggles over the production of value between reclaimers at a landfill. The 'concrete' that Hart sought to understand led her to populism as a way to analyse how the Mbeki and Zuma factions sought to control and tap into popular nationalism, while my ethnographic fieldwork at the landfill led me to focus on how reclaimers' everyday nationalism led them to forge the nation at the landfill in ways that were shaped but not determined by official nationalism.

Although Hart and I began our studies of nationalism at different scales and employed different methods, her interrogation of nationalism in contemporary South Africa, method of critical ethnography, focus on how power-laden social relations are produced and articulated, insistence on rising from the abstract to the concrete, and mentorship were crucial in enabling me to conduct my study and develop my analysis of everyday nationalism. Moreover, our work has been complementary, fleshing out different aspects of the complex whole.

In Hart's more recent work, she is focusing more directly on developing an approach to conduct such holistic analysis. When she gave the prestigious 2018 Vega Lecture at the Swedish Academy of Sciences, she developed a powerful 'three-level framework' that 'incorporates spatio-historical *global conjunctures* and praxis in the arenas of *everyday life*, with national level projects and processes of *bourgeois hegemony* mediating between global forces and everyday life' (Hart 2018, 4; emphasis in original). She further refined her 'global conjunctural' approach in the revised version of the talk published in 2020 (Hart 2020) and is continuing to do so in a forthcoming book. At the current Covid-19 conjuncture, in which advanced capitalist countries' responses to a global pandemic are characterised by vaccine nationalism, Hart's nuanced approach to analysing nationalism is more crucial than ever.

NOTES

1   Hart also notes powerful critique from within the Alliance by Ruth First (Hart 2013b, 177–178).
2   See Edward Webster and Karin Pampallis (2017) for discussion of the range of left positions in South Africa on the national question.

3   At this point, Hart employed the concepts of de- and re-nationalisation as
     a way to understand how politics were playing out at a local level in both
     countries. However, by her 2018 Vega talk (Hart 2018), these twin concepts
     no longer formed part of her theoretical framework for the conjunctural
     comparative analysis of nationalisms.

REFERENCES

Ahmad, Aijaz. 2000. *Lineages of the Present: Ideology and Politics in Contemporary South Asia*. London: Verso.

Ahmad, Aijaz. 2015. 'India: Liberal Democracy and the Far Right'. In *The Politics of the Right: Socialist Register*, edited by Leo Panitch and Greg Albo, 170–192. London: Merlin Press.

Alexander, Neville. 2002. *An Ordinary Country*. Pietermaritzburg: University of KwaZulu-Natal Press.

Bannerji, Himani. 2006. 'Making India Hindu and Male: Cultural Nationalism and the Emergence of the Ethnic Citizen in Contemporary India'. *Ethnicities* 6, no. 3: 362–390.

Chatterjee, Partha. 2004. *The Politics of the Governed: Reflections on Popular Politics in Most of the World*. New York: Columbia University Press.

Chauke, Amukelani. 2012. 'Memories Evoke Tears'. *The Times*, 25 May.

Crush, Jonathan. 1999. 'Fortress South Africa and the Deconstruction of the Apartheid Migration Regime'. *Geoforum* 30: 1–11.

Denning, Michael. 2010. 'Wageless Life'. *New Left Review* 66 (December): 79–97.

Fanon, Frantz. 1963. *The Wretched of the Earth*. New York: Grove Press.

Fine, Ben and Zavareh Rustomjee. 1996. *The Political Economy of South Africa: From Minerals-Energy Complex to Industrialisation*. Boulder: Westview Press.

Goswami, Manu. 2004. *Producing India: From Colonial Economy to National Space*. Chicago: University of Chicago Press.

Gunner, Liz. 2008. 'Jacob Zuma, the Social Body and the Unruly Power of Song'. *African Affairs* 108, no. 430: 27–48.

Hall, Stuart. 1980. 'Race, Articulation, and Societies Structured in Dominance'. In *Sociological Theories: Race and Colonialism*, 305–345. Paris: UNESCO.

Hart, Gillian. 2002. *Disabling Globalization: Places of Power in Post-Apartheid South Africa*. Berkeley: University of California Press.

Hart, Gillian. 2007. 'Changing Concepts of Articulation: Analytical and Political Stakes in South Africa Today'. *Review of African Political Economy* 34, no. 111: 85–104.

Hart, Gillian. 2008. 'The Provocations of Neoliberalism: Contesting the Nation and Liberation after Apartheid'. *Antipode* 40, no. 4: 678–705.

Hart, Gillian. 2013a. 'Exposing the Nation: Entanglements of Race, Sexuality & Gender in Post-Apartheid Nationalisms'. In *Geographies of Power: Recognizing the Present Moment of Danger*, edited by Heather Merrill and Lisa Hoffman, 53–76. Athens, GA: University of Georgia Press.

Hart, Gillian. 2013b. *Rethinking the South African Crisis: Nationalism, Populism, Hegemony*. Pietermaritzburg: University of KwaZulu-Natal Press.

Hart, Gillian. 2014a. 'Political Society and Its Discontents, towards a Conjunctural Comparison of South Africa and India'. Public lecture presented at the University of the Witwatersrand Centre for Indian Studies in Africa, Johannesburg, 6 October.

Hart, Gillian. 2014b. 'Response to Vishwas Satgar's review of *Rethinking the South African Crisis: Nationalism, Populism, Hegemony*'. *Antipode*, 5 April. http://defendingpopulardemocracy.blogspot.com/2014/04/satgar-and-hart-debating-neoliberalism.html (accessed 19 January 2022).

Hart, Gillian. 2015a. 'Confronting Resurgent Nationalisms: Fanon Meets Subaltern Studies'. Public lecture presented at the University of the Witwatersrand Humanities Graduate Centre, Johannesburg, 3 August.

Hart, Gillian. 2015b. 'Political Society and Its Discontents: Translating Passive Revolution in India and South Africa Today'. *Economic & Political Weekly* 50, no. 43: 43–51.

Hart, Gillian. 2016. 'Relational Comparison Revisited: Marxist Post-Colonial Geographies in Practice'. *Progress in Human Geography* 42, no. 3: 371–394.

Hart, Gillian. 2018. 'Resurgent Nationalisms & Populist Politics in the Era of Neoliberal Capitalism: A Conjunctural Framework'. Lecture delivered at the Vega Symposium on Resurgent Nationalisms & Populist Politics, Stockholm, 18 April.

Hart, Gillian 2020. 'Why Did it Take so Long? Trump-Bannonism in a Global Conjunctural Frame'. *Geografiska Annaler: Series B, Human Geography* 102, no. 3: 239–266.

Hunter, Mark. 2007. 'Left behind in a KwaZulu-Natal Township: Thinking about State, Gender and Class after the Zuma Rape Trial'. Paper presented at the Development Dilemmas workshop, University of KwaZulu-Natal, Durban, 16–18 November.

Hunter, Mark. 2011. 'Beneath the "Zunami": Jacob Zuma and the Gendered Politics of Social Reproduction in South Africa'. *Antipode* 43, no. 4: 1102–1126.

Laclau, Ernesto. 1977. *Politics and Ideology in Marxist Theory*. New York: Verso.

Malala, Justice. 2012. 'Why Malini Cried'. *Sunday Times*, 27 May.

Mbeki, Thabo. 1998. 'Statement of Deputy President Thabo Mbeki at the Opening of the Debate in the National Assembly on "Reconciliation and Nation Building"'. 29 May. http://www.dirco.gov.za/docs/speeches/1998/mbek0529.htm (accessed 13 January 2022).

Msomi, S'thembiso. 2012. 'Zuma Has Become the 21st Century Saartjie Baartman'. *The Times*, 23 May.

Sanyal, Kalyan. (2007) 2014. *Rethinking Capitalist Development: Primitive Accumulation, Governmentality and Post-Colonial Capitalism*. New Delhi: Routledge.

Sitas, Ari. (1990) 2010. *The Mandela Decade 1990–2000: Labour, Culture and Society in Post-Apartheid South Africa*. Pretoria: UNISA Press.

Slovo, Joe. 1988. *The South African Working Class and the National Democratic Revolution*. Johannesburg: South African Communist Party.

Webster, Edward and Karin Pampallis, eds. 2017. *The Unresolved National Question in South Africa: Left Thought under Apartheid*. Johannesburg: Wits University Press.

Contributors

Sharad Chari is an associate professor in the Department of Geography at the University of California, Berkeley, in the United States, and affiliated to the Wits Institute for Social and Economic Research (WISER) at the University of the Witwatersrand in Johannesburg, South Africa. He is the author of *Fraternal Capital* and *Apartheid Remains* (forthcoming), and is working on queer struggle at apartheid's end and oceanic capitalism in the southern African Indian Ocean. He is on the editorial team at the journal *Critical Times*.

Jennifer A. Devine is an associate professor in the Department of Geography and Environmental Studies at Texas State University in San Marcos in the United States. Her research examines the environmental impacts of the war on drugs, sustainable development, environmental justice movements, tourism and cultural heritage conservation. She has published articles on these topics in journals such as *Global Environmental Change*, *World Development*, *Journal of Peasant Studies*, *Land Use Policy*, *Antipode* and *Journal of Latin American Geography*. Popular press outlets worldwide, such as NPR and BBC Science Focus, have reported on her research team's findings.

Michael Ekers is an associate professor in the Department of Human Geography at the University of Toronto, Scarborough, in Canada. He is a co-editor of *Gramsci: Space, Nature, Politics* and a number of journal collections on Gramsci, political ecology and environment readings of the 'spatial fix'. His current work looks at the endurance of colonial enclosures, and specifically private forest lands, in British Columbia, Canada.

Jennifer Greenburg is a lecturer (assistant professor) in international relations in the Department of Politics and International Relations at the University of Sheffield in the United Kingdom. She holds a PhD in Geography from the University of California, Berkeley. She is the author of *At War with Women: Military Humanitarianism and Imperial Feminism in an Era of Permanent War* (forthcoming) and numerous articles, including publications in *Antipode, Critical Military Studies, Gender, Place, and Culture* and *Development and Change*.

Mark Hunter is a professor of human geography at the University of Toronto, Scarborough, in Canada. He is the author of *Love in the Time of AIDS: Inequality, Gender, and Rights in South Africa* and *Race for Education: Gender, White Tone, and Schooling in South Africa*. He is currently researching drug use in South Africa.

Bridget Kenny is a professor of sociology at the University of the Witwatersrand, Johannesburg, South Africa. Her work concerns political subjectivity, gender and race in service work and precarious employment. Her books include *Retail Worker Politics, Race and Consumption in South Africa: Shelved in the Service Economy* and *Wal-Mart in the Global South*, co-edited with Carolina Bank Muñoz and Antonio Stecher.

Stefan Kipfer teaches urbanisation, planning and politics in the Faculty of Environmental and Urban Change at York University, Toronto, Canada. He has published widely on urban politics and social theory, articulating Marxist and anti-colonial currents of theory and practice. He is also author of 'Urban Revolutions: Urbanization and (Neo-)Colonialism in Transatlantic Context' (forthcoming) and co-editor of *Space, Difference, Everyday Life: Reading Henri Lefebvre* and *Gramsci: Space, Nature, Politics*.

Zachary Levenson is an assistant professor of sociology at the University of North Carolina, Greensboro, in the United States, and a senior research associate in sociology at the University of Johannesburg in South Africa. He is the author of *Delivery as Dispossession: Land Occupation and Eviction in the Post-Apartheid City* and a founding editor of the journal *Spectre.*

Alex Loftus is a reader in political ecology in the Department of Geography at King's College London in the United Kingdom. He is the author of *Everyday Environmentalism: Creating an Urban Political Ecology* and is co-editor of *Gramsci: Space, Nature, Politics* as well as two other collections on the right to water. He is currently part of the *Antipode* editorial collective.

Melanie Samson is an associate professor of sociology at the University of Johannesburg in South Africa. Her current research arises out of and contributes to her political work with reclaimer (waste-picker) movements. Her writing on dispossession, non-wage labour, organising and political ecology has appeared in journals such as *Historical Materialism, International Labour and Working Class History* and *Capitalism, Nature, Socialism.* She is completing a book titled 'Revitalizing Recyclables: Forging the Economy, Polity and Nation on a Soweto Garbage Dump'.

Ahmed Veriava is a researcher and writer who lives and works in Johannesburg. He also makes a living by teaching political studies at the University of the Witwatersrand, Johannesburg, in South Africa. He has published in journals such as *Social Dynamics, African Studies, South Atlantic Quarterly* and *Comparative Studies of South Asia, Africa and the Middle East.*

Index

Printed and bound by CPI Group (UK) Ltd, Croydon, CR0 4YY